Done With the Crying

HELP AND HEALING FOR
MOTHERS OF ESTRANGED ADULT CHILDREN

Sheri McGregor

Sowing Creek Press

San Marcos, California

Sowing Creek Press
711 Center Drive, Ste. 105, Box 129
San Marcos, CA 92069
Email: info@sowingcreekpress.com
www.sowingcreekpress.com

Done With The Crying: Help And Healing For Mothers Of Estranged Adult Children/
Sheri McGregor. —1st ed.
ISBN: 978-0-9973522-0-7 (print)
ISBN: 978-0-9973522-1-4 (ebook)

Library of Congress Control Number: 2016906492

DISCLAIMER:
Although care was taken to ensure the research and information in this book was correct at the time it went to press, the author and publisher do not assume and hereby disclaim any liability to any party for loss, damage, or disruption due to any errors or omissions— whether the result of negligence, accident, or any other cause. This book does not substitute for medical, spiritual, or psychological advice. Content is based on the author's personal experience, as well as studies and research, but is the author's opinion. Readers should contact a licensed physician, psychiatrist, psychologist, or other licensed practitioner for diagnosis and care.

Book cover design by Cathi Stevenson

Recommendations

The book is a must read for parents of estranged adult children and mental health professionals working with these families. Sheri McGregor's work is a breath of fresh air offering a new perspective and providing support, encouragement, resources, and compassion to good parents who have found themselves in an unimaginable situation.

—Maritza Parks, LMHC, *Inspired Journeys Counseling*

While Mothers are mentioned on the cover, dads, this is for you too! *Done With The Crying* is for any (and all) family member who wants to heal and move forward. This wonderful book will help you see how you can hold your chin up high, dry your eyes, and get on with your life.

—Joi Sigers, *Self Help Dailly.com*

Done With the Crying also provides much time for reflection, for taking time to think about ones life and to read the stories of other women who are going through a similar situation. The book is easy to read, and provides much support and insight in a gentle and understanding way.

—Hennie Weiss, M.A., *Metapsychology Online Reviews*

This is my best resource to assist families whose adult children have rejected them. In my role as a family life educator, I work with those affected by a loved one's mental illness, and the sad phenomenon of estrangement is rampant. I've searched for resources and education, but there is precious little available to help rejected parents move forward. It did not take me many pages in to see the value for my work, and often recommend this compassionately written book to parents and families who are in so much pain.

—Mara J. Briere, MA CFLE, President and Founder,
Grow a Strong Family, Inc.

Dedication

For smart mothers everywhere. *Enjoy your lives.*

Contents

Acknowledgments

Thank you to those who so generously shared your stories. You breathed life into this book—and helped others in the process. Many of you have become virtual friends, cheering me on with kind words and emails during my long years of research and writing. I hope you will find this book worth the wait.

As always, I'm grateful for the encouragement of my wonderful family. Thank you for your patience and support.

To my writer friends with whom I laughed, shared frustrations, and sometimes argued—thank you for your honest and sometimes brutal feedback. I couldn't have completed this project without you.

Thank you to my father and mother, whose memories live on, and continue to inspire me.

And finally, thank you to God, whose nature grounds me.

Why I Wrote This Book:
The Short Answer

How could this happen? That's the million dollar question so many parents ask. I was devastated when one of my five children left our family. My search for answers turned up very few. In short, that's why I wrote this book.

The Whole Story:
How This Book Came To Be

In his twenties, one of my five children, Dan, rejected me. Lonely and shamed, I turned to what I know best: writing. With a long career as a professional writer, using words to deal with the loss, anger, disbelief, and embarrassment came naturally to me. Eventually, as I poured out my feelings, and researched the topic of estranged adult children, my education in psychology and human behavior, along with my training and work as a life coach, pushed me to reflect and share.

As I coached myself to move beyond the heartbreak and loss, I began to see truths, connect my healing to my history, and come to conclusions that empowered me. One of those connections has to do with my mother whose long-suffering nature and silent shame led her to an early grave. I knew I had to deal with my pain over my son's estrangement in a way that helped me live—and to help others. I had to speak out.

When my mother died suddenly at age 54, we went through her things. In one of her drawers, hidden beneath her nylon slips and suntan pantyhose, we found poetry, penned on a narrow notepad in her careful, slanted hand. In the lines of my mother's lyrical but biting words, she spelled out secret sorrows in a songbird's voice. She revealed glimmers of truth about her childhood the rest of us never knew.

Seeing her poems brought up memories from my childhood. I recalled my mother's soft brown eyes growing distant. Her words broke off mid-sentence as she left yet another story from her Arkansas childhood unfinished. She painted only incomplete glimpses of a long ago life. She loved the dogwood trees in bloom, and remembered a beautiful young colt—and that her father was not a good man. My mother and her siblings were boarded out as workers. Her father collected their pay. As a powerless child, she had suffered at his hands, and those of others for whom she'd worked.

My mother might have used her writing to help others who'd had similar experiences, but she wasn't one to dwell publicly. Besides, attitudes were different back then. Today, few subjects are taboo—at least that's what I thought. Then my own son disowned me, and at first, I was shamed into silence.

My quest for information revealed little help. Experts may blame parents, or make trite, useless statements. They tell us to never give up, or to do whatever it takes to reconcile. But reuniting isn't within our control. Repeated, futile efforts only set us up for more hurt. We can make our hopes known, but we can't control what our adult children do.

I found no support for moms like me. While we wallow and wait, blaming ourselves, yet not understanding why, time slips away, and our other relationships suffer. My family needed me present and fully living, not forever hoping and waiting, standing still while the world went on without me. Taking care of ourselves and our important relationships requires effort, but that's a challenge when we're preoccupied with looking back. When emotionally spent, even our physical health can suffer.

For the first time in my life, I began experiencing frightening visual disturbances and periods of partial blindness in one eye. Was I having a stroke? Later, I discovered the episodes were ocular migraines, perhaps brought on by stress. I had to take action. I'd spent too many sleepless nights, and blamed myself too often for the tiniest mistake I'd mined with a fine-toothed comb from memories of my son's childhood. I'd seize upon any tiny infraction and blow it out of proportion as I struggled to find some answer to my echoing question: *Why?*

My son was an adult, making adult choices. He had excluded me and the rest of his family. We were no longer a part of his life. It was up to me to take charge where I could, *in my own life*. I needed to stop worrying about how things would turn out with Dan and focus on the family members who stood by me. I told myself I was *done with the crying*. And I meant it.

As a caring mother who had always tried to do my best, I had a right to step forward, embrace my circumstances, and get on with my life. At that time, I remember thinking of my mother. How might her life have been different if she had shared her pain? How might she have helped others? I could learn from her silence. I could choose to speak out. That's why I've written this book.

Helping others as I helped myself began with my blog at www.RejectedParents.NET. In sharing my experience, I could bring this crisis of modern families to light. Exposing society's automatic judgment could help to remove the unfair shame and stigma. After an estrangement, loving parents who did their best should not automatically be judged as uncaring, neglectful, or abusive.

I'm a regular mom, a nice woman who is like so many I have come into contact with and interviewed for this book. We never expected the children we nurtured and loved would wash their hands of us. When the unthinkable happens, moms like us need kindness, and support.

Writing this book is a natural progression of my work that began at the blogsite, opening a support forum, and launching a survey. Emails from parents began pouring in, saying my articles were helping them move beyond pain and get on with their lives. Within a few weeks, hundreds of hurting moms had completed my survey. As of this writing, more than 9,000 parents have completed it. That number is growing, and many more have shared their stories as blog comments, and in the support forum. Our voices shed light on the growing trend of children who disown their parents. Together, we help others get through the pain of this humiliating experience, and reclaim our lives.

Revealing my real name and sharing my experience honors my mother's memory as well as helps provide a voice for parents of estranged adult children. I think my mother would be happy to know that I learned from her, and chose to speak about my pain rather than let the trauma fester and burden me.

In the pages ahead, I hope that you can learn from my experiences and those of other parents who have dealt with the trauma of estrangement. You'll also find the most up-to-date research, questions posed to help you move forward, and the life-coaching exercises I used and have shared here to help you. Most of all, I hope my words are kind and supportive as you journey from a path of unexpected pain toward healing.

Who This Book Is For

I'm a loving parent like you. A mother who knows the pain of an adult child's estrangement—the horrible shock that wrings you dry, triggers denial, blame, and even shame. I'm a mother of five to whom the unthinkable happened. One of my sons, Dan, walked away from our family. His departure sent me reeling into despair over a situation I never expected, and found very little help for.

The experience can be so isolating. At a time when you need help and support more than ever before, embarrassment can keep you silent and suffering alone. I know about all of these feelings and more. But I've managed to beat the pain of estrangement, and am living a full, rewarding life. I believe you can too—and this book can help.

Ahead, you'll find experiences pulled from thousands of mothers who shared with me, as well as the latest research to help you navigate beyond the sadness and pain. You'll find some answers, and recognize that you are not alone.

Some of your children were easy-going, and sailed through the teen years without any trouble. Then, in young adulthood they acted out, sometimes with a vengeance. Estranged moms talk of troubles including addiction, risky behavior, and even crimes. Other children were negatively influenced by friends. A love interest or a trusted relative might have driven a wedge between you. Your child may have left for illogical reasons, made accusations that weren't true, or turned his back at a time when you were sick or otherwise at your most vulnerable. An absentee parent may have unfairly stepped in, perhaps with money and gifts, and then took over. There are even some mothers who reached a sort of breaking point and had to step back from an adult child who had become abusive. And finally, some of us can see that our children drifted off, while we stood by and watched, assuming the angst of youth would right itself and our children would return to us. But they didn't.

We nurtured our children. We stuck by them through tough times. We suffered through phases when our kids didn't respect our feelings, our boundaries, or even our wallets. But we still loved them. Now they're grown, and making choices we can't control. Rather than remain victims to the pain their rejection brings, we can hope for the best—and nurture ourselves.

Telling people about our plight is tricky. Beliefs about how much parents influence children's development are pervasive and oversimplified. Because of ideals about unconditional love within the mother-child relationship, those who speak out about adult children who estrange themselves are often judged, or even shunned. So we tend to isolate ourselves, fearing we'll be looked at with speculation as to what we did wrong. We may even look at ourselves this way, wondering how our lifelong love for our children could ever be interpreted another way.

Before the break with my son, I remember two people telling me they had no contact with an adult child. And as I listened, I held a sliver of judgment. After all, children don't turn on *good* parents, do they? That's what I would have believed. And that's why I can forgive others' ignorance now.

Our friends can't relate. Perhaps they don't want to consider the possibility that their own children could grow up and abandon them. Telling others creates tension. Faces tighten. Arms fold. People look away. As estranged mothers, we feel misunderstood and alone. We're embarrassed to tell our neighbors, our relatives, and even clergy. Will they blame us? Will they think our family is dysfunctional, and that we're covering up? In a state of shock and confusion, we may even feel anger toward our child, and then feel guilty for it. How could this have happened? And how can anyone relate?

We search for help and find very little. Even so-called experts may judge us. They believe we must have been too strict, too lenient, too nosy, too opinionated, too.... But shaming good moms who have done their best only isolates us. Humiliated and hurt, abandoned moms face a quandary: tell and perhaps be judged (and further hurt), or suffer in silence (and cut ourselves off from any possible help).

My husband and I are fortunate to have four grown children with whom we still enjoy close relationships. Some parents don't have other children. Some single mothers work their entire lives to care for children, and are left with nothing but calloused hands and a broken heart. Others have grandchildren they have never met. Or perhaps worse, the adult child rips away the grandchildren with whom they've bonded.

Frequently, estranged adult children don't explain their reasons for the break, so moms are left with burning questions, slammed-down phones, or silence. Sometimes, a child sets off on a pursuit of character assassination, pasting accusations, and lies all over the Internet. The scenarios are endless. If these mothers are "good," why does this happen? That reasonable yet accusatory question elicits shame.

My son's decision to leave the family tore at my very core, and sent me down a lonely road of questions and sorrow. The experience threatened my family's happiness, and poisoned my relationships. Like other estranged mothers, I balanced hope with the need to move on. Ultimately, I've come away from the experience a stronger person. You can too. If that's what you seek, then this book is for you.

A Note to Fathers

You might wonder why I have chosen to direct this book to mothers. In the support forum at www.RejectedParents.NET, and among the thousands of parents who completed my survey, the vast majority are mothers. In fact, less than seven percent of my survey respondents were fathers. Of these, a great many ticked off only the basic, categorical answers, ignoring the empty boxes in which so many mothers poured out their sadness as they wrote in their stories. That's why I have chosen to title and direct the book to mothers as the main audience—but that doesn't mean this book won't help you.

Women frequently report that their husbands aren't as burdened by the estrangement as they are. It's more likely that you handle your emotions in different, and perhaps more subtle ways. The fact is that regardless of gender, no two individuals are the same. We all process emotions and handle problems differently, based on a variety of factors such as personality, upbringing, and our particular history.

While the stories in the book are from the mother's perspective, many of the examples are of couples, and include the experiences of fathers. Some passages directly highlight men's reactions by using my husband's emotions, as well as the reactions of other men. The principles presented are relevant to fathers, and the strategies for coping can be used by anyone.

Fathers, I hope you will reach out, and let me know how you used the book—and how I might better help you in the future.

Organizing Your Progress

The book is organized in a logical fashion, starting with the shock, the questions, and the feeling of being stuck, and progressing outward to scenarios that provide information and practical advice. You may find that the tone, too, goes from the soft voice of a soothing mother or friend, to one that reminds you you're strong, and motivates you ever forward for your own good.

I've included tools and exercises in each chapter. These are derived from my own healing process, and from insights gained from thousands of parents of estranged adults whom I interviewed, or who shared their stories in the survey, or by email contact via my website (www.RejectedParents.NET). The exercises, reflection prompts, and suggestions are informed by current studies and research, as well as my education and experience. I hold a bachelor's degree in psychology and a master's degree in human behavior. I am also a certified life coach, helping others move beyond dilemmas and find meaning in their lives.

I believe you will get the most benefit from this book by reading the chapters in succession, and doing the exercises along the way. Pausing to complete the exercises as you progress can help you fully explore your thoughts, apply the topics and scenarios to your own life, and better interact with the material. How do you feel about what's presented? How do the situations and discussions apply to your own life?

In doing the exercises, the print version of the book provides space to write down your answers and thoughts. A dedicated notebook can help the healing process, and is a must for e-book readers. Take time to fully explore your responses to the provided prompts and question sets.

The exercises and reflection questions follow a logical healing progression, but it's possible some will not resonate with you or your situation. Don't feel pressured by any of the questions, or feel a need to come up with the "right" answers. Don't worry that your answers might be "wrong," or stress over them in any way. Don't get hung up on perfection or completeness. Each of us is unique. Our situations are individual to us. There are no "correct" answers. There are only your honest reflections, decisions, insights, goals, and intentions. Any reflective prompts, questions, or exercises are intended to help you get in touch with your feelings, work through your situation, and foster your well-being.

Preparing For Success

While it is acceptable to skip what doesn't resonate with you, please examine why you feel the need. With regard to the exercises, perhaps you're fearful someone else might read what you've written. Would you be embarrassed or even feel judged? If so, take care to keep the book somewhere private. The reflection questions and exercises are for your personal use and growth. They may be too personal for you to comfortably share with others.

As much as you can, examine your emotional responses to exercises you're inclined to dismiss or are reluctant to do. They may, in fact, be helpful. Perhaps they aren't relevant to your situation. However, those sections may hold clues to areas that bother you the most. Avoiding stressors rather than learning to deal with them may hinder or postpone your ability to successfully move beyond the hurt.

Some of you will have a tendency to want to read through and think about the exercises without actually writing anything. Be aware that the act of writing stimulates several areas of the brain at once. Writing things down generates more focus than simply thinking. Because of the brain's engagement, writing triggers the close attention your thoughts deserve. Also, when you express yourself freely through writing, you may discover that your breathing slows as the ink flows. The act of writing then becomes a form of meditation, and a powerful way to de-stress.

Here are a few more tips to get the most from the material:

Make some room to grow. Give yourself some quiet space to read, reflect, and do the exercises. Maybe you can do your best thinking in a natural setting. Perhaps you sit in your car on your lunch break, away from the stress of your workplace. The library, a coffee shop, or some other location in which you feel safe and productive are good options.

Don't rush. While some of the material may spark instantaneous decisions, don't force yourself to hurry. Reading through a section or exercise in the morning, and then going on about your day, may provide unpressured space to reflect. Sometimes, letting the mind ponder something even when we're not purposefully concentrating on the topic, makes coming to conclusions seem like less of a struggle. There's no hurry. Each chapter is packed with information, so use the sections within them as stopping points to pause and reflect. Don't hurry.

Share if you can. If you are working with a counselor, the exploration you do using your copy of *Done With The Crying* may provide useful discussion points for your therapeutic talks. Increasingly, I hear from therapists who are grateful for my work in helping parents at my website, because it helps them help clients who are grappling with this issue. The book is an extension of the website. You could also bring up the topics in self-development, well-being, coaching, or parents-of-estranged-adults community groups. In doing so, you may discover that you're not as alone in your thoughts and feelings as you might believe.

Reflect. If you find that you repeatedly resist the tools provided in each chapter, you'll need to consider whether you're ready to move beyond the devastating loss and pain. The first step toward healing requires that you make a decision to take action for your own well-being. Picking up this book is a good start.

Identity Protection

Revealing my real name as a mother who has suffered this heartache is part of my healing. I believe that my doing so has also helped other parents to feel comfortable opening up their lives to me. However, to protect others' privacy, I have used a pseudonym for my son, and I have changed or omitted all other identifying details such as appearance, background, profession, and place of residence. I have done the same for the parents and adult children who agreed to share their stories in this book. To further protect identities, many additional details have been changed, the stories have been altered, and some of the people described in this book are composites based on several different families. Any similarity between the fictitious names and identifying characteristics I have used here, and any real people, is purely coincidental.

Additionally, although I have shared a great deal of my own story, you won't find every detail here. The book is not intended as a tell-all. Nor is my intention to lay blame, antagonize, or cause anyone hurt. Rather, sharing my story among the others is meant to help parents move beyond pain, and enjoy rich, rewarding lives. I have shared as much of my story as I'm comfortable sharing in this public way. As mothers of estranged children who have likely devoured every bit of material you can find on the subject, I trust you to read this book in an empathetic manner. In fact, as you read any of the family stories shared here, remain loving and kind. We each have unique circumstances, but share a bond in our sorrow.

Turning a New Page

Done With The Crying: Help And Healing for Mothers of Estranged Adult Children is the most comprehensive book on the subject to date. In the chapters that follow, we'll explore the shock, the grief, the questions, and the pain. You'll learn more about me and my story, some of the pitfalls parents commonly encounter, and how estrangement can affect physical and emotional health, confidence, and relationships. By reporting on current research and the shared experiences of thousands of other moms, I provide some answers to common questions, practical suggestions, smart coping strategies, and a trusted shoulder on which to lean as you embark on your healing journey.

As one wise mother who is moving on despite a traumatic estrangement recently told me, "We can learn from each other. And this is all so much easier with support."

You will get through this. You will perhaps even learn more about yourself, come to accept the situation, and grow stronger. You can forgive, even forgive yourself, and heal. Throughout the book, you'll find the inspiration of many to help you go from disbelief and bewilderment, to a place of strength and confidence.

In time, you may come to accept the wisdom of one of my sons, who is a parent himself. One day, early into his brother's estrangement, we discussed the many influences on a child's life. Mothers don't provide the only nurturing that interacts with a child's nature. There are teachers, neighbors, media, and a host of other influences. Even acknowledging this, I expressed self-blame. "This is my greatest failure," I told him.

My son quickly replied. "You're not responsible for this. Maybe nature meets nurture, but people make their own choices. They add to the tapestry of the world."

I've accepted that now. Hopefully, you can too. Turn the page—and move confidently forward on a new and even better path.

CHAPTER ONE

The Early Daze

To remain close to her grandchildren, widowed Evelyn spent years going along with what she calls a "relationship charade." Her son and his wife would ignore her for months. Then they'd show up suddenly, requesting she babysit their two young sons.

Sometimes, they would leave the boys for several days at a time. Often, they wouldn't say where they'd been or when Evelyn would get to see them next. Months would go by. Then they'd bring the kids again.

When her grandchildren reached school age, Evelyn happily agreed to pick them up each day and keep them through dinner. By then, her son and daughter-in-law had a third son, but the newborn's daycare was close to their places of work. Each night, her son honked from the curb, and Evelyn would bring her grandsons out.

When the oldest grandchild entered second grade, the teacher asked Evelyn to volunteer in the class. By then, she was known around the school. At her son's request, she was the one who attended school functions, teacher meetings, and other events. Volunteering seemed a natural progression, so when the teacher asked, Evelyn was thrilled. But her elation didn't last. "That's when my son fired me," she says.

That evening, her son didn't honk from the curb. He and his wife came inside, and sent the kids to the car. Then, in Evelyn's own living room, they told her to have a seat.

"Calmly, with their air of authority as lettered people, when I never went to college, they told me I had no right to step into their son's classroom and forge a relationship with the teacher," Evelyn explains. "Apparently, I had overstepped a line." The couple told her they had arranged for another babysitter. After what had become a pattern of her involvement at their request, Evelyn was baffled. "When I started to argue, my son put his finger to my mouth to shush me. They both stood, and my daughter-in-law headed out first. My son stepped out of the house backward, holding up his palm to make sure I didn't speak."

A few days later, Evelyn was surprised and embarrassed when the teacher phoned to ask if she was all right. She had assumed her son had informed the school she would no longer pick up the children or be able to volunteer. Evelyn apologized, saying that something had come up.

During the next several weeks, Evelyn joined the children for their school lunch a few times. Then her son got wind of her visits, and gave orders not to let her in. She received a certified letter from her son's attorney, who called her visits "harassment," and threatened a court order if she continued.

Sick with worry, Evelyn wondered what her grandsons thought about her sudden disappearance from their lives. What had they been told? She was in shock, but what could she do?

Nearly a year passed before she heard from her son again. The family had moved more than 90 miles away. They wanted to come for Christmas, and Evelyn agreed. "I let myself believe they wanted to make things right," she says. "I bought presents and cooked a ham."

While happy to see her grandchildren, Evelyn was also heartbroken. Her son and daughter-in-law didn't bring gifts, and spent most of the time on their cell phones or huddled together alone in the game room. They also made sure Evelyn knew they were watching and listening in on her interaction with her grandsons.

"At least I got to see the kids," Evelyn says. With the older boys, she picked up where she'd left off. The youngest, now two, didn't know her. "Me and the boys made a snowman together," says Evelyn. "By the end of the day, even my youngest grandson had warmed to me."

When the family left, Evelyn's son and daughter-in-law offered perfunctory hugs. They told her not to worry, and that they'd see her again sometime. "But my son was so cold," says Evelyn. "He also reminded me of his attorney's earlier letter. Then he kissed the air beside my cheeks." The older boys hugged her like crazy, but their parents hurried them into the car. "I stood there waving for so long my tears started to freeze."

Once again, Evelyn was in shock. Like so many mothers whose adult children break contact—either fully, or in fits and starts—she didn't understand the reasons why. She was devastated by anger, sadness, and even guilt that she didn't understand. How could Evelyn get past her pain, manage her uncertainty about the future, and carry on?

A State of Shock

Like Evelyn, you're probably in a state of shock. For me, that meant kicking into a sort of self- and family-preservation mode. I gathered everyone close and kept to routines. But looking back, I can see that disbelief, denial, and detachment also reigned.

When my son called up to trash plans for his wedding rehearsal dinner we had agreed to host, we were stunned. Then, a few days later, he disinvited us all to his wedding. When he used the term, "your side," to describe his own family, I was angry and confused, but also worried.

By then, I'd had a few days to stew over possible motivations for his initial call. Maybe he was caught up in some drama from his fiancée's side, I reasoned. In turning his back on the family who loved him, he was surely making a mistake. But I also wondered: *Has he lost his mind?* If he could disown us, his own family, what else might he be capable of? Dan had never given me reason to be fearful, but I was stunned and distraught. I even asked my husband to change the lock on our front gate.

Looking back, I can halfway see that maybe Dan had begun to distance himself some time earlier. But at the time, his decisive brush-off seemed sudden. He was our son. And I didn't understand. During a couple of rocky years, Dan seemed to lose direction. He dropped out of college and quit an internship we were proud he'd won. But our family had been patient. He was one of us, and we loved him.

After he began a new relationship with a young woman we believed was good for him, he had regained his footing. With her encouragement, our easygoing son who had a mind for math and computers started working again, and we let out a sigh of relief. We thought all would be well. Grateful he was back on track, my husband and I encouraged the return of his independent spirit, which we'd always admired. At a discount, we offered Dan a small rental house we owned nearby. Despite her parents' disapproval, his girlfriend soon joined him in living there.

We were happy for Dan. That's why months later, when he confided his plan to propose to her at Disneyland on his birthday, we bought them the entrance tickets. The last thing we expected was his sudden dismissal of us two weeks before his wedding.

In my agony, and in pure shock at my son's 180 toward us, my imagination spun. I became hypervigilant. I slept lightly, and dreamed of Dan, a jumble of real memories and wild imaginings. In my nightmares, the telephone was often electrified, perhaps my subconscious mind's way of telling me the calls had put me in a state of shock.

I couldn't quite believe this had happened to us. The crushing disbelief, confusion and helplessness had me waiting expectantly for another phone call. Surely he would contact us and clear things up. I leapt with hope every time the phone rang. Even so, I sighed in relief when it wasn't him. What would he say if he did call? He had been so cold.

Since those first weeks of what I now know as "estrangement," I've learned that my feelings are common. For mothers previously close to their sons or daughters but who find themselves suddenly blocked, disbelief is pervasive. In the course of writing this book, more than 9,000 parents have communicated this feeling to me. Let's look at a few examples.

Julia and her husband raised their only son in California. At 31, he still called daily to chat with his mom as he commuted to work. Then her son became estranged. In the early morning when he used to call, time suddenly gaped. As sunlight strained in around the slats of the blinds in her kitchen, Julia would hold her mobile phone in hand. The moments ticked by, void of her son's companionship that she so missed.

Kathleen, a mother of four from the Great Lakes area, received a matter-of-fact email from her oldest daughter who was away at college. "This is not a phase," her daughter said. "Respect my wishes." In shock, Kathleen read and re-read her daughter's words: "Don't contact me."

Mothers who have been subjected to harsh words, criticism, and a clear dictate their child wants nothing to do with them, feel powerless and alone.

In those early days, Julia didn't tell anyone. She is like so many mothers who find the situation isolating. Revealing the bad behavior of an adult child we have always loved feels like betrayal. We don't want to make our child look bad in others' eyes. Or we hope it's a phase that will soon resolve, and be put behind us. Those who do tell others may be struck by their discomfort, or even their judgment.

Deanne, a single mother from Rhode Island, had enjoyed a close relationship with her daughter. That is until she reached her late twenties and began dating a man from a wealthy family. Then her daughter stopped communicating, and over a period of several months, their relationship deteriorated. When Deanne reached out, her daughter responded with two-word texts. At first, Deanne phoned repeatedly, asking what was wrong, and insisting they talk it out. That's when the verbal assaults began. Still, Deanne continued to call. This was her beautiful daughter, whom she so terribly missed.

Deanne confided in friends but she says, "Nobody understood. They asked me why I allowed her to treat me that way." Deanne didn't *allow* her daughter to berate her and eventually sever ties. At 28, her daughter was an adult. Deanne had no control over her.

The Haze of Emotions

While situations are unique, the resulting feelings are often similar. In those early days and weeks, you may feel as if you're walking through a fog. You may have difficulty concentrating, or find that your mind wanders. You may feel numb, almost as if you're outside yourself. Eating may be the last thing on your mind. Or you may take extra comfort in food. Normal patterns are no longer routine.

Accepting the hurtful reality can be difficult. You may pretend the estrangement isn't happening and hide your feelings to the outside world. Distressing thoughts may crowd your mind, your child's words relentlessly looping. You may replay memories, searching for what you said or did to cause this.

In cases of estrangement, adult children may inflict pain with verbal assaults or make a sudden break, and then follow up with silence. Mothers are left ravaged and confused, but are often too embarrassed to ask for help.

✈ Give Voice to Your Experience

How we describe our pain can provide insights into its expression in our lives, thus help us move forward in productive ways. Some use visceral terms. Their hearts break, their legs grow weak, or they feel numb. Others call it a battle. They're under attack. Some focus on loss—of their child, their hope, and their identity. Many express fears or anxiety. Let's look at a few examples, and discover insights.

- *"I'm always on edge. Just one step away from falling."*

Imagine being always "on edge." Anxiety rules this woman's life. Taken literally, she must guard against a compulsion to keep looking back, and moving toward the dangerous edge she describes. She may benefit from deep breathing and an ordered environment. Routines may help her take small but purposeful steps in another direction.

- *"I feel like I've been mauled by a bear."*

How might this second mother take action? Should she just lie there, defeated? She may need to assess her situation, and admit how powerless she feels. She'll need to muster the strength to seek safe support that can help her heal from the emotional mauling.

- *"He might as well have stabbed me in the heart."*

The third mother expresses a devastating blow. Maybe her words provide insight into a need to care for her physical health. She may need to be extra wary of coping in physically harmful ways, and make efforts to take good care of herself. Perhaps her focus on her heart is significant. With a doctor's approval, routines to aid cardiovascular health are wise. The heart is also symbolic of the spirit, so watching for signs of depression, and facilitating joy might be helpful.

Another woman said she felt as if her legs had been blown off, which provides a clue to her difficulty in moving forward. She may need support to get going again.

Now it's your turn. How do *you* describe the experience of estrangement? Write the first thought that comes to mind. If you feel up to it, write additional phrases to relay your pain, shock, and loss. Don't censor yourself. As you write, think of yourself as a loving friend and caring listener.

_____

_____

_____

Read back what you've written—aloud if you can. Recent studies demonstrate that as we verbalize our emotions, the areas of the brain associated with language and speech become more active, while the areas associated with pain are less active.[1, 2]

Ancient storytellers who returned from a harrowing adventure or hunt, and then shared their tales beside the campfire, may have instinctively known that putting feelings into words was good for them. Among the women I've interviewed, many expressed that they felt better by the end of the call. They echo the feelings of those who have shared their stories via the survey, in email, or in the forum. Put your feelings into words. It helps.

Read what you've written again. Just as we reflected on the how the mothers in the examples expressed anxiety, abandonment, or physical pain, contemplate your words. *What clues exist in your own words about how the experience of estrangement expresses itself in your life? What must you guard against?*

In the next set of lines, jot down thoughts about your own situation. *What can you do to help yourself?*

_____

_____

_____

_____

Don't Be Hasty

An estrangement is traumatic, so put off big life decisions. In times of grief or shock, I've seen people console themselves with big-ticket purchases, lavish vacations, or gambling. But adding debt heaps burden on already stressed lives. Money aside, beware—your judgment may not be its best right now.

A dozen years ago, shortly after my father's death, I brought home two puppies. We loved those little dogs, but my decision to get them wasn't entirely sound. In my need for comfort, I fell prey to a breeder that I later realized wasn't reputable. The tiny pups had health problems. Remembering this, I was careful not to unwittingly comfort myself after Dan's rejection. But I did make some other hasty choices.

One was defriending my son and his fiancée on Facebook. At the time, witnessing their "likes" and "shares" hurt me. They moved happily forward, while I suffered. Their smiling faces and postings about their nuptials were too much for me to bear. Some months later, though, I wished I'd have used the social site's limiting functions instead of deleting my son and his wife from my friends list. I could have chosen not to "follow" them, or to "hide" their posts. I later wondered: *What message did my hasty action convey?* Maybe anger; or perhaps that I didn't care. Maybe, with my quick act of self-preservation, I had strengthened the wedge between us.

While swift, decisive action has served me well in many stressful situations, in this case a slower, more deliberate decision might have been a better choice. Perhaps my hindsight, as well as that of Julia and Deanne, will help you make sound decisions in the midst of your shock.

Julia is a hardworking mom who prides herself on practicality and common sense. But she's the first to admit to a quick temper. Soon after her son's estrangement, she sent Christmas gifts for him and his wife. When her son returned them, she repackaged and mailed them again—this time to his mother-in-law's address. Although Julia's presents were intended to build bridges, her hasty reaction to her son returning them created more conflict. Her son was furious.

Deanne was elated when, after months of silence, her daughter called. Maybe they could work things out. Her daughter was marrying the man she'd been dating when their estrangement began. She gave Deanne her address, and said the wedding would be held at the home she was already sharing with her fiancé. They were living in an upscale neighborhood close to his well-to-do folks. She also confided to her mother that her future in-laws were controlling. Deanne asked questions, but her daughter cut short the call when her fiancé arrived home. A few hours later, Deanne received a phone call from the young man himself. He warned her not to make further contact.

Deanne wishes now she'd have let some time pass, and cooled down before reacting. But she is a strong woman whose history includes fleeing an abusive relationship while pregnant. She raised her daughter alone. Worried that her daughter might be in an abusive, controlling relationship, she drove over to the house. She needed to see her daughter face to face, and perhaps try and reason with her fiancé. But when she arrived, she walked in on a gathering of her future son-in-law's whole family.

"He denied ever speaking to me," Deanne says. "Not even my daughter would look at my call log as proof. I ended up seeming like a lunatic, the poor single mom who wanted her daughter back. In front of all of them, I think my daughter was embarrassed of me."

Like these women, when we're faced with shocking emotional upsets and unexpected events, we often fall back on behavior that comes naturally to us. For Julia it's action. For Deanne it's confrontation. For another, it may be harsh words. Be aware of how you might respond without thinking, and take time to reflect. You'll want to behave in ways that you can feel okay about later. Also, whether you like it or not, you're being watched. Some people believe parents must have done something to cause their child to turn against them. Don't let your actions fuel the belief.

You might also find yourself willing to do almost anything to return to your son or daughter's good graces.[3] When it comes to being ostracized, studies show that as a way to cope, some people who are rejected try extra hard to be included. That could mean complying, obeying, or cooperating to an unhealthy or even unsafe degree—even when doing so goes against better judgment.

In short, don't be hasty.

Pause and Reflect

- *What decisions would you be wise to put off for now, or even rethink entirely?*

- *How might others be affected by your decisions?*

Have I Lost My Mind? Not Likely

In the first few weeks after my son's shocking phone calls, I couldn't rest. A fearful sense of foreboding mixed with an oddly numb feeling, as if I were outside looking in. I couldn't stop replaying the conversations, and hearing my son's voice, so calm and cold. But I was also dazed. Even on the telephone that first night, after my initial reaction of disbelief, his comments didn't quite penetrate. It was as if the cruel words floated by, a stream of drifting language I couldn't quite absorb.

Am I crazy? The thought occurred to me during those first weeks of confusion. And I'm not alone. Many parents who suffer a sudden break with an adult child express similar feelings. Some of our children even *tell* us we're crazy. Thrust into a situation we never imagined possible, we fear our son or daughter could be right. Other times, the sheer shock and confusion trigger the worry.

When faced with emotional traumas of all sorts, people may feel numb, dazed, or detached. These feelings may be a protective reaction against fully experiencing the devastating emotional impact. These, and other symptoms such as reliving the event in memories or dreams, difficulty concentrating, and avoiding people or situations that serve as reminders of the trauma, are common. They fit an acute stress response. In fact, in the case of some other sort of trauma, Acute Stress Disorder (ASD) might be quickly diagnosed. However, mothers experiencing an adult child's rejection rarely have experts on hand, expecting the symptoms and immediately caring for them, as would occur in a more public trauma event.

The experience of ASD begins or occurs within the first few weeks after an emotionally distressing event (or other tragedy), and may last for several weeks. Continued intrusive symptoms could indicate the need to seek professional help. Even in those early days, the ability to discuss your feelings with a therapist or other trained clinician might be helpful. Don't hesitate to seek assistance if you feel the need. See Chapter Three for information on choosing help wisely.

Symptoms such as those I experienced are typical reactions, and quite common in estrangements. It was difficult to concentrate on my work, or to participate in previously enjoyable activities. I teetered between a dazed existence and hyper-awareness. At times, I walked around in a state of confusion, unable to focus on anything, as if I weren't fully alive. And at other times, my mind wouldn't rest, crowded with the memories of my son's voice. His callous words echoed through my head.

You may feel similarly. The stress of the situation mixes with intense feelings of grief and sadness that are natural after a significant loss. The symptoms of grief can be very similar to those of acute stress.

While experiencing this mix of reactive emotions, I also became hyper-sensitive to *everyone else's* feelings. As a mom, I wanted so badly to make sure my family was okay that, for a time, I set my own feelings aside and focused on theirs.

When my husband confided that, as the father who'd raised him, Dan's actions must be his fault, I didn't admit a similar thought about my own responsibility. Instead, a wave of protective anger steeled me. *How could Dan do this to his dad?*

"Don't blame yourself," I said, troubled by my husband's pain. To ease his hurt, I became uber-wife, serving my husband's favorite foods, and catering to his every need as if he were a king. For the rest of my family, I did pretty much the same.

My adult children tiptoed around me, worried. But for their sake, I dismissed their concern, insisting we go on with our lives. The local county fair with our usual season passes and multiple visits looked daunting, but my family needed normalcy. So, I not only attended but carefully planned and executed daily outings with different family members. I made healthy take-along lunches to lessen the junk food frenzy, and mapped out days for each to get the most from the fair. Some days I took my grandson in a stroller, on other days my granddaughter—and then both. I spent some days with my husband alone, others with each of my daughters, and then finally, days with our whole family.

While I did have some fun, I also longed for the agony to end. Waiting while my family rode rides, I burst into tears. While I strolled through the exhibits, the displays and people drifted past unseen. Occasionally, bouts of intense anger straightened my shoulders, and perhaps even kept me going.

In photographs from those days, I'm smiling, squished into kiddie rides with my grandchildren, but my recollections are fuzzy. I wasn't fully present in those moments. Instead, vivid memories of happier times haunted the fairgrounds. I relived the past.

In the Kids Zone, I saw Dan as a preschooler with rosy apple cheeks, his bright eyes alight. One chubby hand waved, the other honked the horn each time the miniature semi-truck rounded the clattering track. In the outfield, my happy nine-year-old with mussed hair posed for a class photo, his ribbon held high. And in the display tent, as a young teen with a hint of peach fuzz, he jogged ahead, searching through a maze of art displays to point out his colorful, second-place model, a 3-D Egyptian cartouche.

But I didn't share those memories with my family. "I'm fine," was my standard answer, brushing off my family's concern with a pasted-on smile. Then, consulting the program with my penned-in notations and highlights, I'd urge my companions to hurry on—to the Monster Trucks, the milking demonstration, or whatever else I'd scouted ahead.

I'm not unlike Kathleen, who after her daughter's devastating email asking for no more contact, insisted the family take their annual ski trip. They didn't talk about the situation, but Kathleen describes her daughter's absence like a specter, hanging over their cabin in the snow.

Looking back now, I understand that assigning my pain onto everyone else, and carrying on for their sake, helped me cope. My husband and I were hurting, but Dan's adult siblings seemed less upset. "He's been distant for years," one told me. "He wasn't all that close to us anyway," said another. For them, Dan's drifting off seemed to have started much earlier. Although angry and hurt, they weren't as surprised as my husband and I were. Or perhaps, as I later learned occurs often in families, they were minimizing their responses to protect me.

Over the months since Dan's girlfriend had moved in with him, her presence had widened the distance between Dan and his siblings. We all saw less of him, but whenever we did see him, he seemed happy. And Dan was grown. It was natural for him to become close to his own special person. Besides, he was always very independent, and we admired him for that trait. As a grownup, he made his own choices, and we encouraged him. Still, upon reflecting on our lives with him, perhaps we should have seen what we'd always viewed as natural independence as more of a warning sign (although of what I don't know).

While our children had always talked and laughed together, beginning in his high school years, Dan spent less time with his siblings. But we hadn't been concerned. He was happy and had nice friends we had become acquainted with through the years. Dan got good grades, and seemed well-adjusted. A high school teacher familiar with our family once commented to me, "Dan, and every one of your kids, is so steady." That assessment made me proud—and I agreed with him.

We never expected Dan would walk away from us. While I originally thought his girlfriend would bring him closer to our family, her presence seemed to have contributed to the distance instead. And after the adrenaline-rush roller coaster that filled the months leading up to his formal wedding that felt so foreign to our more casual family, his last-minute dismissal of us felt like falling off a cliff.

Situations are unique, and every family has its own sad story. But even when an adult child slowly drifts away over months and years, the final blow is cutting. The realization hurts: *My child doesn't want me.*

There are consequences to that realization, which we'll explore later. For now, let's address the shock and your possible reactions to such an emotional trauma.

During those first few weeks, my family's feelings took precedence. But in my emotional shock, I also became too empathetic to strangers. I assigned them the possibility of deep sorrow like mine, so found myself worried about adding to their burdens.

Telemarketers I might previously have put off with a quick, "No thank you," now waylaid me. I waited for an appropriate break in their long sales pitches to politely end the call. On the road, I became an ultra-courteous driver. At four-way stops, I let others go first, even when doing so disrupted the flow of traffic.

In retrospect—and this sounds silly now—at the grocery store, letting a shopper with fewer items go ahead created a dilemma for me. Inevitably, another person with fewer items joined the line—and then what? Let them go too? This is embarrassing to admit, but one day, a brusque cashier helped me to see myself more clearly. She commanded a customer I'd let go ahead to wait his turn.

"Ah, honey," she told me. "More people will just walk up. You'll be standing here all day."

Her words were a wake-up call. She helped me realize my sudden lack of boundaries, which I knew stemmed from my son's rejection. Under normal circumstances, I'm a strong person, with a good sense of self.

Even my decision to invite a few relatives and go through with the dinner the night before Dan's wedding, which had been planned as a "rehearsal dinner," derived from my need to put others' feelings first. Our son and the wedding party may have cancelled, but I didn't want to disappoint the small catering company we'd hired to provide food for the event. The owner was an immigrant to America, facing the tough economy a lot of us did that year. Dan's call had given us enough time to provide the caterer with two weeks' notice, so we could have backed out. But at the time, cancelling hadn't seemed reasonable or fair.

On the night of the rehearsal dinner that wasn't, our immediate family and a few close relatives gathered at tables in our yard to help us eat the gobs of Greek food that was Dan's favorite. In the end, having my family close was probably helpful, even if I did feel detached and out of sorts that evening. Later, I berated myself for not interacting enough. There was catered food and plenty of drinks. But I was not an attentive hostess. At the party, my great niece and nephew by marriage were intrigued by our chickens as they pecked and scratched around our property. For weeks afterward, I replayed regrets: *I should have taken the kids into the coop, and let them collect the eggs from the nest boxes.*

Looking back, I can laugh at the level of importance I assigned to the experience I saw myself as *denying* those kids. But I was way too hard on myself. They were happy just to be near the chickens. I'm only human. And it was a painful night for me.

Reaching Out, Or Withdrawing? Both Are Normal

Having reflected on that early time of shock and dismay, it's obvious to me that focusing on everyone else kept me from examining my own feelings too closely. I'd taken my own needs out of the picture.

My need to gather people close may also have resulted from increased levels of oxytocin, a neuropeptide that most mothers will have heard of because it's known to promote infant-mother bonding.

Animal studies have shown elevated oxytocin in the face of separation from family groups, which has sparked exploration into oxytocin's role in human beings to promote calming and social bonding after traumatic experiences. Researchers have documented elevated oxytocin in women suffering distress in their social relationships, and have associated oxytocin with what they call a "tend and befriend" response.[4] This is the opposite of the better-known "fight or flight" response. Researchers believe that in times of stress, oxytocin plays a natural role in our need to seek support.

Connecting with others is healthy and helpful for recovery. Seeking support, though, can be tricky. Well-meaning friends and family may say all the wrong things. And you'll need to choose your confidantes carefully. In Chapter Three, we'll explore this more, as well as the delicate balance between getting support and wallowing in self-pity.

If you find yourself wanting to withdraw, your feelings are also normal. Many mothers say all they want to do is hide away. Just as an injured animal separates from the pack to avoid being jostled about and further hurt, these mothers retreat.

Julia was like that. She dropped her ceramics classes, quit her bowling team, and let friends' phone calls go to voicemail. She was embarrassed, confused, and preoccupied. She avoided everybody. "And I ached all over," she says.

Like Julia and so many others, you may tend to withdraw. Emotional pain and physical pain are similar. Rejection hurts, even physically.

In a 2011 study, MRI results showed that reflecting on the emotional distress of a past rejection activated brain regions usually associated with physical pain.[5] So, just as you might crawl into bed in a quiet room to rest while suffering a migraine, isolating yourself during the excruciating agony of your child's rejection may come naturally. But don't lock the door on everyone who loves you. Recent research has shown that holding hands with a loved one, decreased women's perception of pain.[6]

Don't be surprised if your feelings fluctuate either. You may feel like a social butterfly for several days straight, and then wake up one morning wishing you could hide away. Or, after shunning all social engagements, you may suddenly crave company. Anger, hope, self-pity, and resentment may all show up. Throughout the book, and particularly in Chapter Six, we'll more thoroughly explore those feelings. For now, accept them. Work with your feelings. You're like many mothers everywhere who face this unexpected shock.

Coping Mindfully

Whether you're in shock over a recent estrangement, or are coming to terms with a long-term loss, coping mindfully will help you on your healing journey. In my work as a life coach, clients often explore the concept of mindfulness as a tool. Let's see how mindfulness can help.

In its simplest definition, mindfulness means living in the moment. That can mean letting go of thoughts about the past or worries about the future. Or releasing concern about what must be done later and how to accomplish it all. Focusing on the present allows you to fully experience the activity you're engaged in or the people you're with right now.

Mindfulness can be a part of anything. Even enjoying the way freshly laundered clothes feel as they come out of the dryer: the warmth of a soft blanket, the nubby texture of a cotton towel, or the silky feel of a blouse as you slip it onto a hanger. As you sit at a desk, creating a report at work, perhaps you're aware of soft music playing in the background or the murmur of those talking in an adjacent office. At the computer, you feel the energy in your fingers as they nimbly shift from key to key by memory, or you become aware that you're pursing your lips as you think. Being fully present as you do almost anything provides a break from the stress of an over-active mind that's forever analyzing what went wrong, how you can fix it, or what might happen next. In that way, mindfulness can help.

Staying in the present moment can also help relationships, because when we are actively engaged in the company of another person, we are fully listening and responding. That sort of presence fosters genuine connection and conveys that we really care. Who wouldn't want a friend like that? And the company of loved ones is helpful.

Coping mindfully also means paying attention to what's going on in your head and observing how those thoughts interact with your physical and emotional self. Becoming more aware of how you think about yourself and the estrangement may help you respond more purposefully and eventually steer your responses rather than react like a powerless bystander to thoughts and emotions gone awry.

For Julia, that meant becoming aware of her outlook at the start of each day. Her son used to call and chat as he commuted to work. After the estrangement, Julia still rushed to pick up her mobile phone. But her son didn't call. He might never call again. Those thoughts fed predictions of a dismal future: holidays without joy, and grandchildren she wouldn't know. . . . Then Julia looked around her dim living room with the curtains all drawn. She'd imagine sitting there with her husband in the home where they had raised their son. The two would be together, waiting, yet so alone. Her stomach would ache. Her bones would hurt. She would feel so tired that she would crawl back into bed and cry.

While these reactions were normal, Julia knew from experience that allowing them to take over her judgment wasn't healthy. Sometimes, she quelled her nerves with alcohol, or resorted to sending texts she later regretted. But in becoming more mindful, rather than allowing her thoughts to control her, she observed them, and decided to learn from them. That's when she realized that the worst time for her was the mornings, when she missed her son's calls.

Observing her thoughts and emotions from a standpoint of curiosity helped her come up with a plan to make better choices, and feel more in control. At night, she would make a short list of things she could do the next day. She began with small tasks to get going in her life again: wash her husband's work clothes, walk around the block, plan and cook a healthy meal. She stopped looking at her phone first thing in the morning. Instead, she got out her list, and purposefully kept her mind on her tasks.

When negative thoughts intruded, she forgave herself, compassionately recognizing that the task of moving on was difficult for her. That allowed her to refocus on the present.

Although she began with very small tasks, they were things she could accomplish and feel successful about. In time, she didn't think of looking at her phone most mornings. She'd beaten the habit. Her small tasks led to bigger ones. She'd clear the garden bed outside the front window, choose new shrubs that would bloom through summer, research how to make a succulent wreath, shop for everything she'd need, and then create it. Her outlook, and her view of herself, began to improve. She reconnected with friends, and began volunteering at a local assisted-living facility where she feels valued and enjoys being of service.

Staying mindful has helped Julia to fully participate in whatever she is doing. Her mind less often wanders to the future or past. She's no longer consumed with regret, sadness or worry, so she is immersed, enjoying each moment as it occurs.

Deanne also learned to cope mindfully. She often found herself replaying the evening when she had rushed out to confront her daughter's fiancé after he'd forbidden her to contact her daughter. She vividly remembered his smug expression as he'd let her inside the house. She could hear his condescending tone as he denied ever calling her. She would see the disdain in his family's eyes as they looked down on her, a socially inept single mom. Remembering that night, choking anger would rise to Deanne's throat. Her lungs would tighten, and empty of air. Her fists would clench. She got so frustrated that she banged a pan against the sink, slammed the door, or drove so fast that she put herself in danger. Once, she even got a ticket on her way to work.

Deanne learned to recognize when her thinking began to turn south. Rather than allow those thoughts to sweep her away, she observed how they affected her emotions and even her physical well-being. Deanne would take one long deep breath, and then another, refocusing her attention to the very experience of being alive. She used her breath as an anchor to the present moment.

In time, with continued practice at observing her thoughts and their related sensations, the horrible memories of the other family, and even her daughter looking down on her, loosened their grip. She had always been an underdog. But she had done well. She'd raised her daughter on her own. She had a good job in a respectable position. Whether her daughter appreciated her or not, she appreciated herself.

Staying in the present may also help you maintain healthful habits in your daily life. Recent studies provide evidence that when people are ostracized, they may be more likely to overeat or drink. This may be because thinking about and analyzing possible reasons takes up psychological space, leaving less attention and energy to regulate our behavior.[7]

We each have a unique set of memories, uncertainties about our future, or even regrets that can run loose in our minds. Observe. Don't make judgments about your thoughts and feelings. At first, don't even try to stop them. Awareness is the first step to coping mindfully. Start to listen in and become aware. Observe how one thought leads to another, triggering sorrow, shame, anger, or other emotions. Also feel how it affects your body. Then, you can begin to make better choices, and steer your thoughts, mindfully, toward better outcomes.

In the exercise below, you'll get some practice, catered to your life.

✈ Observe, and Then Make a Plan

Consider your own experience with intrusive thoughts and memories. Can you make a plan to better handle those times as Julia did? Or perhaps you're more like Deanne. Answer the questions below.

- *What times of the day, week, or year are more difficult for you?*

_____

_____

- *How can you change how you think about that time?*

_____

_____

- *How can you use that time ifferently? Can you change your routine?*

_____

_____

_____

- *When might you practice mindfulness, even aside from thoughts about the estrangement? Jot down a few ideas. Refer back and follow through.*

_____

_____

_____

Start Healing: Three Things to Remember

Acknowledge the depth of your pain. The profound wound of an adult child's betrayal cuts deep. How could a son or daughter to whom you have given so much love and energy turn his or her back on you? The foundation you thought was solid has turned to quicksand. By accepting that your adult child's betrayal will take some time to sort through, you pull yourself positively forward without the burden of pressure.

Give yourself a little breathing room. Be kind to yourself. Recent Wake Forest University research revealed that people who forgive themselves, and who treat themselves well, fare better after negative events and personal rejections.[8]

Recognize that whatever emotions you're feeling are both common and unique. Blame, guilt, mistrust, loss, anger, disappointment, fear, embarrassment, frustration, humiliation, sadness, and perhaps even relief are all normal. While one mother feels immediately angry, another suffers guilt or shame. Each situation holds years of history that is exclusively yours with your adult child. That history, coupled with your individual personality and beliefs, will influence your emotions..

Don't get ahead of yourself. It's common to worry. What if your estranged son doesn't meet his new niece until she's ten? He'll regret not knowing her sooner. And then there's the other extreme. What if a death occurs? What if your estranged daughter waits until it's too late? She'll suffer guilt.

Speculation only fuels more worry, and tows us into a riptide of defeatist feelings. But it's essential to remember, imagined scenarios that distress us haven't occurred, and we can't control them anyway. Our adult children steer their own lives.

Make a decision now not to get too far ahead in your thinking. When you catch your thoughts heading into the unknown, observe them, accept them, and bring yourself back to the present moment. You can't control your adult child's actions. Regret, guilt, or any other negative emotion your son or daughter may at some point experience will be his or hers to live with. Remain in the present. Be aware of your thoughts, and cope mindfully.

What's Next?

Amid the sudden onslaught of emotional turbulence, the question remains: Why? In Chapter Two, we'll discuss some of the reasons, speculate when there are no clear answers, and talk about living with uncertainty.

For now, don't push yourself too hard. Allow time to reflect on what you've read here. Consider your own situation. Keeping your thoughts focused on actual events rather than worrying over outcomes you can't control is a big step. Accepting that your estranged child's possible guilt or regret is their responsibility is another big step. Any consequences that come from breaking ties with you are theirs to own. Not yours. Even if the estrangement turns out to be temporary, you will benefit by accepting what is reality now.

In his book, *The Survivors Club*, author Ben Sherwood shares the stories of people who have found themselves in all sorts of harrowing experiences, and have gone on to thrive. What these people have in common is that they took action.

Don't let yourself get stuck, but do be fair and forgiving to yourself. Accept your emotions without judgment. But keep in mind that forward momentum, *action*, helps. Examining your circumstances and stepping toward a satisfying future despite the current situation takes time, energy, and courage. You're not running a race, but you are on your way.

✈ Know Your Feelings: Moving Ahead For Your Own Good

As you progress toward reclaiming your self-worth and happiness despite the estrangement, awareness can help. As you read the statements below, rate how you feel. Use a scale of one to five, with one meaning "don't agree," and five meaning "strongly agree." Write the number on the adjacent line. Wherever a pronoun was needed, I've used "he." Substitute what's appropriate in your situation.

— I have been hurting in this situation.
— My child can't mean what he says.
— It has been difficult to get over the pain.
— I have tried to make things right.
— If it wasn't for the spouse/partner/friend, my child wouldn't be doing this.
— I have done everything I can to mend the relationship.

— I can never let this go.

— It's not right for a mother to give up.

— In all honesty, I miss my child—but not the adult he became.

— After all I've done, my child shouldn't treat me like this.

— I can change how my child feels about our relationship.

— I cannot control my adult child's behavior.

— I do not miss the strife.

— My child doesn't mean to stay estranged.

— My child owes me respect and care.

— I have apologized for mistakes. I don't see what else I can do.

— My child is disrespectful, and does not honor his parents.

— I can only control myself.

— I'm tired of being angry.

— Whether I like it or not, my child has the right to keep me out of his life.

— I'm weary of self-censoring, and overthinking everything I say to try and keep the peace.

— It's difficult to accept estrangement without understanding it.

— I can sometimes control my child's behavior.

— If I'm honest, the relationship has not been satisfying.

— Despite the estrangement, I can give myself credit for my part in my adult child's success.

— I am determined to take action for my own well-being.

— I am not ready to accept this.

— My child needs to understand that this is a mistake.

— I am committed to moving forward in my life.

— I deserve to be happy.

— No matter what I have done, it has never been enough.

— I'm tired of tip-toeing around, trying not to set him off.

Now, look back and identify the statements you agree or disagree with the most. Paying close attention to those you've marked with a "5" (strongly agree) or a "1" (don't agree), a pattern may emerge. Maybe you're fed up and ready to get on with your own life. Or perhaps you believe your child is ungrateful, which prods your anger. Your beliefs about motherhood, unconditional love, and children's duty to honor parents may influence your emotions. Take note of where your feelings fall for each of the statements. Use the next set of lines to jot down a few thoughts about the exercise, your feelings about particular statements and what you've learned about your feelings.

_____

_____

_____

_____

_____

Don't judge or criticize yourself. Mindfulness isn't about judging yourself or your feelings. Knowing where you stand in your determination to get on with your life right now provides a base point for future reference, and makes you aware of possible sticking points and areas where you might need to make more effort.

Healing requires acceptance of what you cannot change, recognition of what you must change, and a decision to take action. Read through the following statements, and consider how you feel about them.

The Pain
- I have been hurting in this situation.
- It has been difficult to get over the pain.

Acceptance
- I cannot control my adult child's behavior.
- I can only control myself.

Moving Forward

- I am determined to take action for my own well-being.
- I am committed to moving forward in my life.
- I deserve to be happy.

Most parents will readily agree with the first two statements. The reality of your grown son or daughter's rejection is painful, and getting over the pain can be a challenge. What about the "acceptance" statements? Can you accept that your child is in charge of his or her life? Accepting that you can only control your own actions is important if you're to let go of the pain.

For some, committing to the "moving forward" statements will elicit sadness or even guilt. But taking steps toward your own well-being does not have to mean you don't ever want to reconcile. Many of the parents reading this book will have already tried, maybe even repeatedly. Unable to do so, at least for the present, these parents recognize that they need to find a way to move forward—even while holding out hope they can reconnect in the future.

 Notes

CHAPTER TWO

Why?

Where did I go wrong? Like many mothers, in those first months after Dan's rejection, I obsessed over the question. I pored over a mental timeline of his childhood that started with his difficult birth—so unlike those of my other children. We had been in an alternative birthing room, meant to foster bonding. Yet, once Dan was born, the nurse whisked him away. Worried, I longed to hold my newborn, and sent my husband to find him. Left alone in the dreary room with its narrow window clouded by rain, the clock ticked off the eons-long seconds.

Unwilling to wait, I struggled from the bed. Tugging my I.V. pole along, I shuffled up the hall, a trail of blood droplets staining the stark white hospital floor. From a side room, my husband emerged. He was instantly alarmed to see me there, and helped me through the door.

Inside, the nurse stood over my nearly nine-pound baby. Spreading her arms as if to block my view, she said, "He was a little cold. Go on back to your room now. We'll bring him to you."

"I'm not leaving my baby," I insisted, stepping forward.

Dan, as it turned out, was fine, only a couple of degrees below normal temperature. As I sat near the heated Isolette, the issue promptly resolved. But I couldn't help thinking that it was nothing a heated blanket and holding my baby close wouldn't have solved—*if I'd been given the chance.*

My husband, Brian, has told and retold that story, often to illustrate his belief that I'm "the best mom ever." After the estrangement, I remembered the day of Dan's birth and despised that nurse. Those first few moments of bonding loomed, all-important—*and she had stolen them.*

One morning, soon after Dan's dismissal of me and the rest of his family, I sat in my yard sipping coffee from the colorful mug my daughter, Mimi, had given me. In bold red letters, its slogan declared: "I AM A GREAT MOM!" On that morning, I wasn't at all sure the words were true.

We'd moved to this house when Dan was just three weeks old. Those early months had been tough. Dan had colic. He cried inconsolably the first 12 weeks of his life. In brief moments of reprieve, I remember saying, "Shush. Let's not wake Dan." Sometimes, in those scarce quiet moments, I closed my eyes. Quick, dream-filled sleep overtook me—always interrupted by Dan's pitiful squalls.

But Dan's colic wasn't the only challenge. Days after moving in, we lost our miniature poodle and collie. They disappeared one morning when fog shrouded the landscape, and they had somehow wandered out. It was a trying time.

Sipping my coffee from the GREAT MOM mug, I wondered if those days left alone while my husband worked long hours, struggling to turn a profit in his fledgling business, had affected my bonding with Dan. I'd been surrounded by unpacked boxes, tired, uncertain about our finances, and unable to comfort my colicky newborn. Had our trying circumstances and my sheer exhaustion somehow shaped Dan? Had those overwhelming early days sowed seeds for his later ability to reject us?

Experts now say a connection exists between post-partum depression and colic. I hadn't been depressed, but I had been drained from lack of sleep and anxious over my infant's distress. Did I play with him enough? Smile enough? Talk to him as cheerfully as I had my other babies? Experts say a mother's mood can affect her infant's development.

Horrified to think my mood had somehow caused this later fracture, I set down my coffee mug, and ran to pull out the photo albums. In a single picture, I sat, cringing, as my newborn nursed. Labor had been induced, so the painful uterine contractions stimulated by nursing were more pronounced. But in every other photo, I looked happy, as engaged and loving with Dan as with any of my babies. I don't think I was depressed. Still, in my bewilderment, I couldn't help but wonder: *Had I only been posing for the camera?*

Mothers Blame Themselves

I'm not alone in worrying whether early childhood circumstances could have spawned later estrangement. Turning over our memories in an attempt to make sense of things is natural. It proves we're human, and that we really care. We wanted to do well for our children. We thought we did.

Take Barb, a genteel southerner who paints portraits for a living. Other than a few peaceful years, she has been estranged from her daughter for more than a decade. Barb wonders if her tumultuous first marriage had an effect. But she divorced when her daughter was only nine months old. Then she married a nice man who adopted her daughter and raised her as his own. Still, Barb wonders if her own unhappiness during her daughter's first year of life left its mark.

Sondra, a physical therapist from the Pacific Northwest, also wonders if her son's estrangement had early roots. He is her second child, now nearing age 40. Sondra believes his older sister has a mild form of autism. "Maybe Asperger's," she explains. "Autism wasn't well-known or diagnosed back then. And her condition was disruptive. That may have been hard on my son." A special needs child requires a lot of attention. Sondra wonders if her son, in his sister's shadow, didn't get enough.

Mothers worry about siblings that required extra care, a job that took them away, or circumstances such as an illness, a family member's death or some other tragedy in the early months of a child's life that caused their child's later ability to break ties. Other mothers have opposite worries. They think maybe they held their babies too often, and somehow spoiled them with love. These mothers ask: *Did we bond too much?*

Soon after my son's estrangement, a memory flickered: Dan as a young toddler, his fat cheeks like shiny apples as I sat him on a store counter while I paid. He flashed the cashier a grin.

"Boy, he's easygoing," the cashier had said, pumping Dan's dimpled hand.

I remembered a moment of disconnect when I looked at my little son like a stranger might. *Dan? Easygoing?* I remembered the newborn days of ceaseless crying. He was in obvious pain, yet the doctor and books called colic normal. That moment in the store, I realized Dan's colicky months had formed my view of him. The cashier was right. My year-old boy *was* easygoing. And after the estrangement, I began to believe those colicky early days might have continued to influence me, and shaped the way I parented him.

Dan was always happy and moving; always independent. Brian and I admired that spirit, but maybe my responses to him during those first weeks of his life were what had shaped his independence. If he wasn't crying, we tiptoed by and let him be, thankful for a few moments of peace. As Dan grew older, he was the sort of child who occupied himself. He was never bored or needy. And we weren't the only ones who admired his independence. His teachers praised him for it. Rather than bow to peer pressure, Dan followed an internal compass that served him well. Still, after the estrangement, I wondered if he had needed more guidance than we'd provided. Maybe as he'd grown up roaming our semi-rural property with its neighboring open space, I had given him *too* much freedom.

The part we played in fostering Dan's independent nature is just one theory with which I tormented myself. Other memories clamored, moments frozen in time that made me question my parenting.

Like the time my nine-year-old Dan brought home a ribbon from the county fair. His seeds for the planting contest hadn't sprouted, so he and a classmate had plucked weeds from the ground and stuck them into the pots. That day, I laughed right along with Dan when he told me about the switch. I knew the teacher hadn't been fooled. Besides, every child got a ribbon for participating.

That seems simple enough, but in the shadow of my son's rejection, I incriminated myself. Maybe I should have scolded him for trying to fake her out. Maybe I should have lectured him on ethical behavior.

One day, riding in the car with my daughters, I owned up to what I'd decided was a definitive parenting fault. "We were always too easy on Dan," I declared.

My daughters were quiet then, likely weary of my endless puzzling. Hilary concentrated on her driving. In the back seat, Mimi let out a sigh.

Looking out the window, I thought of better times. Dan had once been dependable. A young man you could rely on in a pinch. There had been no reason to parent him differently, or to be stricter with him, but I was intent on blaming myself. "I should have been tougher," I insisted. "I was always on his side."

"No, Mom." Hilary shook her head. She put on her blinker and guided the car into the exit lane. "You were always on *all* our sides, and it wasn't any different with Dan."

I was glad for my daughter's words, yet I continued speaking, as if wringing myself of anguish. "I'll never understand this," I said, suddenly exhausted. "And I'll never be the same." Painfully aware of how pitiful I must sound to my daughters, tears of anger sprang to my eyes. "How could he just walk away?"

That day, Mimi had muttered from the back seat that I shouldn't be so hard on myself. Hilary had reached over to touch my arm, and I had covered her hand with mine, grateful for the girls' support. Knowing they believed the coffee mug's declaration that I *was* a great mom, I remained silent the rest of the way home. It wasn't fair to focus on Dan. In his absence, he was stealing our precious time together. Still, I was in such turmoil. Maybe I wasn't too easy on Dan. But I'd made other mistakes. I was sure of it, just as so many other mothers are.

Theresa, a mother of five from Nevada, was shocked when her only daughter disowned the family. So, Theresa blamed herself. She fixated on inconsequential incidents and magnified them. She would sit up nights, alone in the dark, and torture herself with memories.

Once, when her daughter was fourteen, Theresa required she go along with them to church. "Her brother was doing the verse reading. It was a family event," Theresa says. Her daughter had gotten up late, so didn't have time to do her hair. Theresa had handed her a hair Scrunchie and said, "Get in the car."

Logically, Theresa knows she was just making a tough call, like all moms must from time to time. But after her daughter accused Theresa of loving her four brothers more than she had ever loved her, Theresa wondered, "If I had just let her stay home that one day, maybe she wouldn't have left the family."

When we're suffering a deep loss such as that of estrangement, irrational feelings can overshadow sound thinking. In reality, Theresa was a busy mom hustling her children off to an important event. Not a horrible mother who favored her sons. Most of us have made some parenting decisions our children didn't like, but which caused no real harm. Yet, we still may blame ourselves.

At one point, I fixated on a vivid memory. The summer Dan was 11, my schedule was full. One day, while I was on a business call, Dan interrupted. "Where's lunch?" he asked. I held up my hand, signaling for him to wait as had been our custom when I was working. But Dan had walked away, muttering, "Whatever happened to lunch?"

That memory pierced me, drew a curtain of regret. *I should have stopped, hung up the telephone, and tended to my son.* In reality, it was a single incident in one busy summer; an out-of-the-ordinary flash in time among the routine of better days when we all sat down to eat together. When I confided about the incident to a supportive friend, she shrugged it off. "He was eleven," she said. "And he didn't starve." Though the memory had haunted me, my guilt was irrational. One moment in time doesn't make or break a child's character or well-being.

It's normal to look back and wonder if we contributed to or even caused the situation. That's what normal, healthy people do: reflect, try and learn from mistakes, and then evolve into better human beings. But keep your vulnerability in mind. An injured self-esteem, and grasping for *some answer* to explain what seems so unthinkable, can affect logic. When you find a reason to blame yourself, step outside the situation. Consider how a friend might view what you present as "evidence."

Think about your own childhood. Almost all of us remember things our own parents did that could be characterized as mistakes. But most of us wouldn't dream of severing the relationships. So, why today, do so many adult children cast off their parents, and even their entire families? And as many rejected parents ask: *How can doing so seem so easy for them?*

Are Cultural Shifts to Blame?

Historians say that the way we view and treat children has evolved. So, some believe that cultural shifts may contribute to the increase in estrangements. Let's explore that line of thinking.

Until the 1980s, the word "parent" was a noun that indicated biological ancestry. Then, as the role of parents and how society perceives children changed, the word was used as a verb. Mothers and fathers *parent* a child. The word became a verb.

Experts speak of reliable birth control that allowed parents to choose when to have children, and say that because of this choice, parents may be more emotionally invested in their kids.[1] Smaller average family size may also make parent-child relations more intense.[2]

In the past several decades, experts have proliferated. Five times as many parenting books were published in 1997 than in 1975.[3] Organizations including PBS and UNICEF, as well as popular child development experts, began aligning with marketers, which leads to the question of motive.[2] Parents looked to experts instead of experienced mothers and grandmothers for trusted advice. But perhaps all the products, services, and opinions caused parents more fear and doubt, thus shaped their parenting and influenced the evolution of society's view of children.

For many children, long hours spent wiling away time in nature, playing with neighborhood kids, and learning on one's own have all but disappeared. Unsupervised exploration has been replaced by arranged play dates, private tutors, sports, and enrichment programs. Adventures largely take place in the colorful flat-screen landscapes of video game worlds. Today's children are heavily monitored and closely regulated.[1]

In past eras, children matured and gained adult responsibility by learning to drive and operate farm machinery by the time they were ten.[4] Today, children are more protected, are given less responsibility, and parents invest in them emotionally to a greater degree. In past generations, children were valued, at least in part, for their expected economic contributions to the family. Perhaps to a degree, today's children have become as sociologist Viviana Zilizer notes, "economically 'worthless' but emotionally 'priceless.'"[4]

Most parents would agree with the idea that societal expectations have evolved. As a rule, today's young adults grew up hovered over and showered with things. Every team member gets a trophy, and an emphasis on feelings and fairness permeates children's environments. All of this pampering, overthinking, and risk-reducing may not provide children the freedom to make mistakes and learn from them as was common in times past. Historians speculate that this thwarts maturation and the development of empathy for others' feelings. Instead, maybe all of the attention enhances children's focus on themselves.

Parents who are hurt and puzzled by their grown child's rejection find it incomprehensible that anything as well-meaning as extra caution, care, and enrichment provide valid reason for severing ties.

In my own childhood, my siblings and I understood that we were subordinate to our parents. As in so many families, parents' feelings about children and family activities, including what children were allowed to do and where money was spent, came first—if children were consulted at all. For the most part, we knew not to argue with our parents.

Yet, as our children were growing up, my husband and I were among the majority of parents, whose lives revolved around our children's activities and feelings much more than our parents' lives did. Providing our kids with happy childhood memories was always important to us. Thousands of mothers who shared their stories with me described a similar focus. We're not just parents. We *parent*.

Could This Be Individuation?

Some parents express frustration over experts who confuse an estrangement with individuation. Sometimes called "differentiation," the process of individuating involves a person's development into an individual self that's separate and apart from others, including parents.

While it's possible the cultural hovering over children of modern society contributes to an urgent need for some young adults to rebel like teenagers in order to individuate, that's no excuse for malicious behavior. A great many estrangements are accompanied by manipulation, verbal abuse, and character assassination. And they persist for decades, or forever. I've heard from thousands of mothers whose children first cut them off when they were in their 30s, 40s, and beyond. This seems different than the process of developing an identity as a self, separate from others, to which the term "individuation," might apply.

If you believe your young adult child with whom you have limited contact is individuating, you may have a valid reason to excuse immaturity to some extent. With that understanding, patience may be necessary.

For any of us, the process of individuation is a part of life. We learn to accept others' opinions, but also respect ourselves. A toddler might say, "I can do it myself," and a parent supports the child's developing autonomy by allowing him or her to try. We can also support a young adult's efforts at autonomy. A toddler may have been angry if we tried to button a shirt when he could do it himself. A young adult may be irritated by parental input about bigger life choices. A son or daughter might even interpret a parent's concern as a lack of confidence, and express the feeling. "Do you think I'm stupid?" your son might ask. Or, "I'm not an idiot," your daughter might say.

Recall your own young adult years. You can be sensitive to a son or daughter's inexperience and feelings, while recognizing new territory as a parent, too. Express your concerns while also conveying confidence in your adult child's judgment and ability. Explain your worries while honoring your young adult's desire for autonomy.

It's also reasonable to expect adult children to treat you with the kindness and sensitivity you expect from other adults—and you can tell them that.

Suggested Reading

Managing The Millennials: Discover The Core Competencies For Managing Today's Workforce, by Chip Espinoza and Mick Ukleja, Intended for the workplace but sensible for parents. Modern society has uniquely shaped the values and communication of millennials and created a generational barrier. The book gives insights to help bridge the gap.

The Age Of Entitlement: Are Parents Doing Too Much?

When one of my children was in the fourth grade in the 1990s, a school bully cursed at the teacher, hit another child, and shoved some desks around. The boy was sent home for the rest of the day. The teacher lectured the rest of the class about his troubles at home, and explained that he'd acted out his frustrations. The teacher asked the other children to treat him with extra kindness when he returned.

How different that scenario was than in my own elementary school class nearly 30 years earlier. A boy tipped over some desks and cursed at the teacher. The principal promptly marched the boy out and suspended him for several days. His family problems were known in the neighborhood, but never mentioned by the teacher, let alone offered as a reason for his behavior. When he returned to school the next week, he received stern warnings to behave well or be separated. In reality, he was separated anyway. Most of the kids steered clear of him.

I feel for these boys. They were unsettled over events in their lives. In both cases, there may have been smarter ways to help them. Perhaps both examples are even extreme. But the contrast sets up the question: Is it any wonder that in a world where people excuse bad behavior, some children grow into adults who expect special treatment?

Kind, supportive parents who have provided their kids with love, a happy childhood, other help and material items—such as a good education, the latest fashions, electronics, cars, expensive weddings, vacations, home down payments and more—report that when they begin thinking of their own futures and tighten the purse strings, their adult child's verbal abuse or silence begins. Hundreds of mothers have shared their experiences of asking a child over 30, who has a good job, to take over paying their own cell phone bill (or something comparable), only to be met with verbal assault and rejection. These mothers feel as if their children expect them to forever pay their way. And they express the sad reality they feel: Once they were wrung out for all the help, caring, money, time, babysitting, patience, love and support of all kinds, their sons and daughters discarded them like an old rag.

Have these children learned that they are special, and count more than others do? Or, more specifically to the situation, count more than their parents do? Some mothers have come to a conclusion that boils down to this: I did too much for my kids, and now I'm paying for it.

Are mothers who wonder if they did "too much" really to blame? Perhaps no more than the teacher who excused the bully's behavior. The teacher followed school policy and prevailing thought of the times. Mothers followed societal values. In the 1980s and 1990s in particular, the advice to bolster children's self-esteem was bandied about like gospel. Often, the focus on raising children's self-esteem was devoid of any connection to achievement.

Researchers credit cultural changes for the rising numbers of self-indulgent people who hold an inflated view of themselves. They say Narcissistic Personality Disorder (NPD) and its destructive traits such as overconfidence and not caring about close relationships, are increasing.[5]

Writing about a psychological test called the Narcissistic Personality Inventory, Jean M. Twenge, Ph.D., says she and her colleagues have analyzed the responses of 49,518 college students who took the NPI between 1982 and 2009. Their analysis reveals a striking upward trend. In 2009, fifty-eight percent more students scored highly narcissistic than in 1982.[6] Perhaps the increase in adult children who reject their parents and cast off any sense of duty in favor of their own needs, wants, and desires derives from this shift.

Some of the saddest stories I have heard are those of moms who are alone and sick, facing harsh medical treatments without the support of adult children they assumed would assist them as they aged. Many times, the children rejected their mothers at the onset of illness. The sons and daughters they sacrificed so much for don't seem to care at all—let alone drive these mothers to a doctor appointment or offer a kind word, even when they live in the same town. Sudden estrangement at the time they're most vulnerable may be particularly devastating to moms whose lifelong focus on their children has left them bereft of social support.

Mothers who told their children they were special and praised them simply for being themselves followed experts' advice that said building our children's self-esteem would help them succeed. However, as researchers note, and perhaps as our society is now bearing out, good intentions can have negative consequences.[5]

Social scientists aren't suggesting we return to the bygone days of child labor and children who were seen and not heard. But with historical insight, many ponder whether the pendulum has swung too far.

Of course, exceptions exist to any trend. This helps explain how children living in the same culture, and even in the same families as their more self-absorbed counterparts, can grow into caring, loyal adults who wouldn't dream of rejecting parents or family.

There is also behavioral epigenetics, which (in part) studies the effects of influences and life exposures that can alter how people respond to similar stimuli. I'm no expert on epigenetics, and the spinoff of *behavioral* epigenetics is even newer. Perhaps you will be interested in doing some research into the topic.

Influential Adversaries

Any discussion of reasons why adult children reject their parents has to include third-party influencers. I call them, "influential adversaries" to the parent-child relationship. Most often cited as the instigator is the spouse. Sometimes, even the spouse's family plays a part, or demonstrates a disturbing pattern of "helping" others to estrange.

Earlier, we met single mother Deanne, whose daughter married into a wealthy, controlling family. The estrangement began when her daughter got engaged. The other family showered Deanne's daughter with gifts and expensive trips. "They lured her away from me with silk blouses and vacations abroad," says Deanne. "And my daughter let them."

We also met Julia, who misses her only son. Married for nearly four decades, Julia's story is similar to single mother Deanne's. As hardworking people, Julia and her husband are proud to have put their son clear through graduate school. And they're proud of their son, who now has a good career. "We've done well," says Julia. "But we're by no means rich. Our son married into a much wealthier family. And they throw their weight around."

Julia continues, "My daughter-in-law and her mother don't care about anyone's feelings. They kept changing their minds about the wedding plans, and expected everyone to jump at their every whim. At the wedding ceremony, every dress had an issue. Even the hem on the bridal gown came loose." Quietly, Julia adds, "I never knew Karma worked so fast."

It isn't always a wealthier family that draws an adult child away. Ruby, a mother of two from Oklahoma, says her oldest son met a girl from humble beginnings while away at college. Eager to get to know the young woman, Ruby and her husband were in for a letdown. "She didn't like us from the start," says Ruby. "And that has never changed."

Ruby's daughter-in-law is estranged from her parents, which is a scenario I've heard often. Ruby also blames the young woman's absence of spiritual roots—opposite to their son's church-involved upbringing—for making it easy to reject them. But Ruby has come to accept that her son is a grown man, capable of his own choices. A few years ago, she witnessed just how much her son had changed. At age 35, he called, asking Ruby to take a short road trip with him. She leapt at the chance to reconnect. "But as soon as he got in the car, he tuned the radio to Howard Stern," Ruby says. "He was disrespectful to me and everyone. He didn't care how much he trashed a hotel room either. I was embarrassed of the man my son had become."

Like Ruby, Julia also recognizes that her son is grown, and making his own choices. She even empathizes with him, because she knows her daughter-in-law is controlling. But Julia worried her parenting had caused her son to lack enough backbone to stand up to his wife. "I became like a crime scene investigator to try and figure it all out," she says. "But this isn't my fault."

Julia's son may have stumbled into a family that actively works at alienating any newcomer from their family of origin. "My daughter-in-law's family has a pattern," Julia says. "Both of her sisters have husbands who also don't see their families. When she was dating my son, she talked about how weird those families were, but I didn't think much of it. Then, at her bridal shower, none of her father's family was there. When I asked about them, her mother told me they aren't close."

Julia's son later told her that none of the husbands see their families. She now believes her daughter-in-law's family, with her mother at the helm, conspired to take her son away.

Julia's experience is not uncommon. I heard similar stories among the thousands who shared with me. Often, these sorts of families are reported to have idealist beliefs, feel they are better or of a higher class than others, and speak of the newcomer as a person they rescued in some way.

Sometimes it is family members or friends that reshape a son or daughter's views of parents. Portrait-artist, Barb, believes a long-time friend is partially to blame. At a time when Barb was busy painting a string of community leaders' portraits, a friend often took her young adult daughter to plays and to the ballet. Barb trusted her friend, and was happy her daughter was having fun. Later, she found out her friend's values had changed. "My daughter questioned my faith, my work ethic, and everything I've ever stood for," says Barb. "I felt betrayed by my so-called friend."

Sometimes a parent's ex-spouse creates issues. An absentee parent may arrive like a sort of fairytale character, and then fulfill a son or daughter's childhood fantasies, or tell a story that excuses their abandonment. All of a sudden, the dedicated parent is the offending party, blamed for the absentee parent's neglect. Or, parents who divorce later in life, often with the support of their adult children, say the ex-spouse then warped their sons' or daughters' view of them, or even bought their love.

Parental Alienation Syndrome (PAS) is a well-known phenomenon in which one partner in a divorce denigrates the other to the minor-age children. An estimated 20 million minor children are subject to PAS in the U.S.[7] The fact that this also happens to adult children is no surprise. With PAS, the cult tactics of a leader (parent) who is charismatic, demands loyalty, and uses emotional manipulation are often present. The child forms an anxious type of attachment similar to that of people in emotionally abusive relationships.[8] It's not a stretch to see that an adult child might be susceptible to a parent who uses cult tactics. This may be particularly true for younger adult children, since legal adult age doesn't necessarily equate to emotional maturity.

If your estranged child has fallen victim to PAS, or to similar alienation patterns, take heart. Perhaps there is hope. In adulthood, people sometimes come to realize they were the child subjects of PAS. This often occurs during counseling or therapy sought for some other reason. They may go in for marriage counseling, and the estrangement issue comes out. Sometimes, they then reconnect with the alienated parent.[8]

Substance Abuse

Parents who spoke of a son or daughter's substance abuse often recounted histories going back to the teen years, and sometimes spanning decades. Some described numerous interventions, and their time and money spent on counseling and recovery programs. Eventually, some parents draw the line. That's often what motivates the estrangement.

Doris, whose only son is an addict, explains: "We've been to hell and back with him several times. It's a vicious cycle. He hits rock bottom, and comes home sick, covered with sores. He promises he'll change, and we feel sorry for him. We've paid for programs, helped him get on his feet, paid for vocational training . . . but eventually, he always starts using again." Last year, Doris and her husband moved into a gated community. They also changed their phone numbers. "It seemed like the only way to escape," she says. "But if he catches up with us, and hasn't changed, we'll have to get tough. He's a grown man, and we're finished letting him ruin our lives." Doris's son is 34.

Kim described a similar revolving door. Their third daughter of four began abusing alcohol and drugs in high school. She would disappear for weeks at a time, come home and get clean, but then always return to the drugs. Years of emotional trauma took its toll on Kim and her husband. Finally, with their other daughters' encouragement, the parents attended some educational seminars, and then took a stand. They stopped giving money, and told their 27-year-old daughter she could not return home until she proved she was able to stay sober.

Their addicted child broke the front window as she left the house, ranted against them in Facebook posts that were filled with lies, and said she'd never speak to them again. A few months later, a DUI forced her into treatment. Since then, she has seemed to get her life more on track. After three years, Kim knows her daughter lives and works nearby, and even has an infant. Kim longs to get to know her grandchild, and hopes her daughter will one day have a change of heart.

"I recently sent her a letter, telling her that we still love her," says Kim. "If she stays sober, and wants to reconnect, we'll be waiting."

Like many mothers, Kim examined her parenting skills, wondering if she was to blame. The research is mixed, but most studies point to authoritarian and permissive parenting styles, rather than authoritative or democratic styles, as possibly contributing. But let's not discount peer pressure, and other influences on a child's life. An addict who blames his or her parents for their problems is no different than anyone who looks everywhere except in the mirror to find the cause of their own issues.

Kim's daughter has never told her parents they are to blame for her drug problem. Still, Kim and her husband have wondered. They hit a rough patch when she was 15. They sought marital counseling, and have been happy since. But Kim wonders if they might have neglected her during that time. "I shared those thoughts in my letter to her," Kim says. "And I apologized if that was the case." Kim adds, "Isn't that all any of us can do?"

Mental Disorders

Mothers tell of Attention Deficit Disorder (ADD), Attention Deficit Hyperactivity Disorder (ADHD), Obsessive Compulsive Disorder (OCD), Bipolar, Gender Identity Disorder, Borderline Personality Disorder (BPD), Narcissistic Personality Disorder (NPD), and other issues that started when their children were minors. Despite patience and understanding, therapy and/or medications, problems persisted, culminating in estrangement. Others only speculate about possible disorders.

Jerri, an education administrator from Kentucky, first noticed her son's tendency to slack off when he was 12. He blamed teachers when he didn't do well in school. But he was basically a good-natured, friendly kid. He'd take summer school and manage to make up a grade. Teachers and others said he'd eventually grow out of his "lazy" stage. No diagnosis was ever made.

Still, Jerri believes there's something "not quite right" in her son's makeup. "Something that's impossible to fix," she says. "He believes his life doesn't need fixing, and his troubles are bad luck or people not being fair. As in it isn't fair he was fired after three days of no-call, no-show at his latest job." Jerri wonders if medication might stabilize him, but nearly age 30, he refuses help. Jerri and her husband are now raising his son, their grandson.

Last winter, he showed up and stayed for a few days. When Jerri encouraged him to enroll in school or apply for a job, he left. "He drove off on a motorcycle wearing only shorts in near-freezing weather," says Jerri. Like many parents, she feels powerless to help. "It's like with horses," she says. "You can lead them to water, but you can't make them drink."

Faced with estrangement, many parents do seek counseling, either individually or with their sons or daughters. When parents describe their adult child's behavior, or if the therapist directly witnesses it, he or she may speculate at diagnoses. In many cases, the son or daughter storms out and never returns—if they showed up at all. Without a desire for treatment, there can be no help.

In some cases, it's a controlling spouse who has a mental disorder. Julia persuaded her son and his wife to join her and her husband at a therapist's office. "When we tried to make her understand that we still wanted to be a part of our son's life, even on a limited basis, my daughter-in-law said to give it up. And that we needed to change our way of thinking," says Julia.

The counseling attempt didn't change anything but after witnessing their daughter-in-law's cold, unbending behavior, the therapist mentioned BPD as a possible explanation. When Julia expressed confusion as to why her son didn't stand up to his wife, the therapist asked Julia a poignant question: "If you were your son," he said, "which person would you rather have mad at you: Your unreasonable wife? Or you, the mother who has always been so kind?"

Empathizing with her son in that situation, Julia replied, "Me. He knows I'll always forgive."

The Hard Truth, And Sad Speculation

Some children give explanations for cutting ties that have little or nothing to do with their parents or how they were raised. Even so, a child's choice to end the relationship is cruel, and difficult to accept.

A handful of parents said their children came out about their sexual orientation, and despite the parents' acceptance, disconnected. They also often moved far away.

Several mothers said their sons or daughters had been diagnosed with a life-threatening illness. These children told parents they needed all their energy to fight the disease, so they couldn't stay in touch. Some said seeing their parents' concern would be too stressful. These mothers feel bound, afraid to make contact that might add stress. As such, just when they feel their child needs them the most, they're deprived of the mother's supportive role: caregiver, encourager and advocate.

One mother's ex-soldier son was diagnosed with Post Traumatic Stress Disorder (PTSD). He told her he needed time away from close connections in order to heal. Years have passed with no knowledge of him. She worries that with no familial support, he'll become a statistic, one of the 22 veterans per day who commit suicide.[9]

Others said their children left them when a parent was diagnosed with a life-threatening illness, or after one parent passed away. Some mothers shared that their children went so far as to say the parent deserved the disease, and then even wished them dead. Others were offered only silence. In stressful times such as during the heartbreak and upheaval of a family member's terminal illness or death, unresolved issues can resurface. With honesty, patience, and perhaps with guidance from a helping professional trained in such matters, issues could possibly be worked through, and resolutions found. Of course, all of this takes effort—which may be difficult, if not impossible, in times of serious illness or grieving, especially when a son or daughter won't communicate.

A few parents said their children made statements about being too busy with their own families to remain in contact. Some of these mothers say their children never call them, but if they do the phoning, the child will sometimes pick up. But a call that's occasionally answered for a five-minute chat does little to make them feel connected. This may be especially true when their sons and daughters live nearby, and are seen engaging with a variety of other people for whom they're obviously *not* too busy.

Some children leave town to pursue work in the sex industry. Often, they expect to make lots of money, and tell parents they will save for an education they plan on starting later. Their mothers may receive an occasional call or text, but worry their children are being exploited and will suffer in an industry where crime is rampant.

Perhaps your child feels guilt. Pop star Justin Bieber has said that he was ashamed, and that he knew his mother was disappointed in him. That's how he explained their estrangement. Perhaps your child doesn't want to face you because of similar feelings. Maybe your child is not ready to own up to activities that caused problems and put distance between you, but that you don't know about (or perhaps suspect).

Finally, although no survey question asked about adult children's education or professions, parents often discussed those subjects. Many parents mentioned their belief that once their sons and daughters graduated and became professionals in white collar careers, they were ashamed of their families.

Perhaps it's no coincidence that several said their child became estranged during graduate training for psychology or counseling degrees. While undergoing their own therapy—a required component of these studies—they began "diagnosing" their parents, or judging their families as dysfunctional. Some suddenly remembered events that parents say never happened. Or, they alluded to non-specified hurt. One mother related that in an email her daughter sent to end their relationship, she hinted at upsetting circumstances. "You know what happened," she wrote. "You were there." Yet, this mother *doesn't* know. Perhaps the phenomenon is an outwardly directed mental health variation of what's known as "medical student syndrome." That's when medical students who learn about disease, believe they themselves have the symptoms.

For mothers in any of these sorts of situations, I offer this: Imagine an invisible thread that connects you to your son or daughter. Though they are perhaps sick, confused, upset about circumstances, or are pursuing a different lifestyle, the thread remains, unbroken. Perhaps in time, your son or daughter will take hold. And as if a life rope, reach hand-over-hand, and return to you. Until then, use the exercises in this chapter and the rest of the book to grow stronger, and step forward for your health and happiness.

Ambushed

Contrary to what so many who haven't experienced estrangement from adult children believe, only a few mothers mentioned a big disagreement or incident that led to their rejection. Many described loving relationships that suddenly soured for no logical reason. Others say that in looking back, they ignored signs of discord, hoping to keep the peace. Some of these mothers can point to a conversation, a text, or some other communication that must have lit a match that caught and burned like wildfire.

I fall into the latter category. There was some discord that I overlooked—just as many parents do. But there was also a phone conversation with my son that must have led to drama. In that call, I had asked Dan if he was sure about getting married. It was a question I had also asked another of my children before marriage. To ask that question made sense to me. My husband and I had both felt pressured by family into marrying our first spouses. Obviously those marriages didn't last. It was a relief to hear Dan tell me he was certain.

That day on the phone, I also told Dan I'd received a Facebook message from his future wife that morning. Her mother wanted our photos for the wedding memorial table a day early. I was sensitive about those photos, and told Dan we would bring them on the wedding day, as we had previously been asked to do, rather than make a special trip. We were expected several hours early for the photographer anyway. There would be plenty of time to set out the pictures. In the call, I made a joke that I shouldn't have. I asked Dan if he thought we could trust his future mother-in-law not to alter the photographs if she got them early. Dan had laughed. He understood my feelings.

Two months earlier, at the bridal shower, the bride's mother had pulled me aside. She was concerned about our plan to make a collage for the memorial table they had planned. The collage had been Dan's idea. A few weeks earlier, he had chosen a few old snapshots of himself over the years, interacting with his grandparents. His idea made sense for our family with its multiple marriages that created an abundance of grandparents, some living, some not. But at the bridal shower that day, the bride's mother didn't agree. She showed me formal wedding-day portraits of the two sets of deceased grandparents they planned to use. She said there wasn't room on the table for our collage.

I was surprised she was upset, and also a little angry. I assured her our photos wouldn't take up much space. But the next day, I told Dan about the conversation, and we agreed to change our plans. In the end, I shopped for three frames: a 5"x7" for a photo of my parents together, and smaller ones for Brian's mother and also his first stepfather, for pictures of them alone. That way, the deceased grandparents from Brian's family could take their rightful place on the memorial table separately.

We didn't want to hurt their later spouses, the living grandparents who would attend the wedding.

That day at the bridal shower, the contrast between our families was clear. There were no divorces on their side, and no extra grandparents. Dan's future in-laws were much more structured than us, more traditional, more religious, and strict.

And there had already been tensions. When Dan's fiancée had moved in with him, her parents were so upset that they took back her car. At first, she asked me for a ride home from work at night. Then Brian gave Dan an old truck, and she drove Dan's car. For a time, her and her family didn't speak. The situation had seemed extreme. That's why the intensity of the wedding plans had so surprised us. It was as if the official marriage proposal had flipped a switch. Still, we were relieved her family had come around. We remained supportive.

On the telephone with Dan that day, we finished with other small talk. I hung up thinking everything was fine. So, I can only speculate about what happened later, who was told what, and how my conversation with Dan was retold. I only know that the phone woke us at midnight, and the bomb was launched. Her family wasn't coming to the rehearsal dinner—and it was my fault. Days later, Dan made it clear we weren't welcome at the wedding either.

Lots of mothers describe similar sorts of situations that took them equally by surprise. Like me, they can only speculate as to how a conversation, an incident, or even an idea they can't identify led to a fight, to gossip, to the silent treatment, and finally estrangement.

Barb remembers the day her estrangement began. She was working with portrait clients in her home office. Her daughter, then in her early twenties, was horsing around with her 10-year-old sister. Barb asked the girls to go downstairs. When she finished with her clients, her older daughter wouldn't speak to her. She left the house and went to stay with a friend.

Similar to Barb's situation, Sondra was also taken by surprise. After a pleasant two-week visit with her 28-year-old son on the opposite coast, she called to thank him but kept getting the answering machine. When he finally picked up, he lit into her with an abusive verbal barrage. Shocked, Sondra nearly hit the floor. Though confused, she apologized. He hung up. Later, she called again, but he wouldn't speak to her. She left messages: "What did I do? Why are you angry with me?" Her son sent ranting emails and cursed her, but he never explained.

After Sondra's son married and had two children, they reconciled. Then he divorced. Sondra moved close, and babysat his kids. Several years later, again for no logical reason, her son yelled at her, and initiated another estrangement. For a second time, Sondra felt ambushed.

Barb and Sondra are like many mothers who are confused about what happened. Even when a reason is given, it often makes no sense. That's how Theresa feels. She's distraught about her daughter's claim that she loves her sons more, but the accusation came out of left field. Bewildered, Theresa remembers good times they spent together. "She is my only daughter," Theresa says. "Of course I love her."

Studies since the 1980s have demonstrated that children as young as one are intensely aware of parents' interactions with them as compared to their siblings. Feelings of sibling rivalry can sometimes persist, and carry into adulthood.

It may not be a coincidence that Theresa's daughter expressed these feelings when she did. Theresa's youngest son was soon getting married, and the family was focused on his wedding. Even for adult siblings, a birth, a parent's illness, a wedding that brings in a new family member, or other events that stress or change family dynamics can stir up old feelings. Rivalries can surface.

Georgia, a divorced mother from Canada, is estranged from her two married daughters. During a lean period, Georgia financially helped her younger daughter, who had a newborn. Her older daughter was envious. Georgia tried to smooth things over, but nothing worked. She visited one daughter, who railed about her sister. She visited the other daughter, and it was much the same. "It was like tug-o-war, with me in the middle," says Georgia. "I insisted they stop. That's when they both dumped me."

Georgia's daughters don't speak to each other either, but one lets her see her grandchildren a couple of times a year. Georgia finally gave up seeking a resolution. "My girls are grown women," she says. "I can't make rules and enforce them anymore."

Is Estrangement In The Genes?

In the early weeks of my son's estrangement, I came across Internet postings by parents who described their children's vicious deception, manipulation, and seeming joy at causing them hurt. Some of these parents believe their children are sociopaths or psychopaths.

Those parents were hurting. Some were angry. Most expressed profound sadness, but also acceptance. Their research, and reflection on their sons' and daughters' behavior, led to an explanation that allowed them to stop puzzling over where they'd gone wrong. They had done their best. This was beyond their control.

Aside from antisocial disorders, parents may wonder if estrangement is somehow inherited. When my husband mentioned his biological father, I couldn't help wondering whether a tendency for estrangement was somehow in the genes. In the 30-plus years that Brian and I have been together, he has rarely mentioned the father who left him when he was three. But one evening, in a moment of exhaustion, Brian said, "My father left me . . . and now my son."

Coming from this strong man of few words, the softly spoken declaration screamed sorrow. Feeling for my husband, I didn't press. I had embraced him, in a huddle of solidarity. But I began to wonder: *Did Dan inherit some sort of character trait that made it easy to walk away?*

Brian's mother had been pregnant with a second son when her husband ran off. For a short time, while his paternal grandmother was alive, Brian still visited that side of his family. But he never saw his father again. Maybe that man had abandoned all of his family. And maybe our Dan would also never return.

I don't believe my son is a sociopath or psychopath. His easygoing nature just doesn't fit. However, having heard thousands of complex and heartrending estrangement accounts, I can empathize with the handful of parents who make such conclusions. Both are considered antisocial disorders, and there is strong evidence that genes can play a role in antisocial behavior.[10, 11] Lack of empathy and a parasitic lifestyle that are hallmarks of antisocial disorders could include the ability to toss aside people deemed no longer useful—including parents.

Of course, we can't peer into our estranged children's brains. I'm not asserting that the act of estrangement in and of itself is antisocial—although some might say so. No science links estrangement to the structural and functional brain differences found in diagnosed psychopaths.[10]

Parents who feel that a manipulative son or daughter has toyed with them may view estrangement as one of many behaviors that fits their conclusion. If your child exhibits other antisocial behaviors, such as a lack of empathy and remorse, exploitation of others, deceit, and coercion, among others, then perhaps you will conclude the same. It's also possible that genetics influence estrangement in some way that is not yet known. In some families, perhaps estrangement is even learned.

We Did Our Best

When we worry we're at fault, an interesting phenomenon occurs. The mind searches for evidence that proves us right. In a version of the cognitive bias known as "observational selection bias," because we're focused on a particular thing, we notice it more. It's like when we buy a new car and suddenly see more of the same model on the roads. When we start wondering what we did to cause estrangement, we find examples. Memories, like the day I was too busy working to stop and make lunch, pop up and multiply. In essence, we choose a bias in our own focus, and then prove that bias is correct—even when it's wrong.

Until my son's estrangement, I considered myself a good mom, but I didn't go around reflecting on that idea. Responding to my tiny babies' practical needs, snuggling with and singing to them, came naturally. As they grew, I read about parenting, followed my intuition and examples from my childhood and mothers around me, and did my best. Most of you will agree that you did your best too. By reading this book and seeking answers, you show how much you care. In reality no one thing you did—maybe even nothing you did—led to the estrangement.

I can own up to the fact that, beyond asking Dan if he was sure about the marriage, I should have kept my mouth shut on the phone that day. What I said was honest, but for Dan's ears only. Every one of us has said something out of turn at one time or another. That conversation didn't warrant estrangement. Neither did my dreaded memory of when Dan was 11, and I didn't make lunch. On that long-ago day, I wasn't at my best, but then or ever, hurting my son was not my intent. That single meal, perhaps that whole summer, was an anomaly. For busy mothers everywhere, we did our best.

Quality time versus quantity time was a catch phrase when I was raising my children. As a mom who had the good fortune to work from home, I had plenty of time, and felt good about that. I worked at the quality time experts said was so important. I loved my kids, and enjoyed their company, so why wouldn't I spend as much quality time with them as I could?

When I began to consider my life with Dan, and all of my children, without the veil of shame that estrangement caused me, my perspective renewed itself. I was able to reclaim my self-image as a good mother. That's when other, better memories surfaced. Like the time my husband arrived home with a business associate and found me sitting with my five children gathered close, reading a story aloud. I remember the pride and pleasure on Brian's face. His associate had asked me, "How do you do that?" Then he recounted a few months when he'd been jobless and caring for his own four kids. "They drove me nuts," he said.

Those days of reading to my children, playing games, taking them swimming or to the beach were not the exception but the rule. We spent a lot of fun time over the years. I wasn't pretending for the camera in all those pictures of me with my kids. Neither was Dan. He was happy, well cared-for and loved.

Likely, your children were, too.

Pull back the veil of shame. Focus on those memories of yourself as a good and capable parent. Set your observational bias to look for good you did. Let go of mistakes. Find the evidence that you did well.

✈ Remember the Good You Did

Instead of sifting through memories for what went wrong, focus on the good you did. Did you protect your child? Feed him properly? Cheer her on? Support his interests? Entertain her friends? Show kindness?

Make a list. Write it down. Be to the point, or much more detailed. Your list is uniquely yours. Do the exercise the way it feels right for you. Some mothers won't want to look back at good memories in detail because it hurts them so much. If that's how you feel, keep this simple. Making a bulleted list of words or short phrases is fine. Others will find that giving equal time to looking back at all the good they did helps them let go of any mistakes they've been narrowing in on and blaming themselves for. *Do what's best for you.* Below are some helpful ideas.

Talk with someone supportive. A friend, your spouse, a relative, or your other children will know how involved you always were. Someone who was there as we did our best can help us remember all the good we did.

Look at old photographs or mementos. Items you've kept or photos of happy times can trigger memories of your active, positive role. For me, old photographs helped to validate my belief in myself. It was me who pointed the camera. I captured the grin on Dan's dirt-smudged face as he posed with his hand on the doorknob, ready to run back out to play. *I remember that moment.*

I was there when he posed with his siblings in the shade of a tree at a local botanical garden. It was me who photographed him monkeying around near the gorilla statues at the zoo. And I cooked the food that's arranged on our table in another photo where he sits with his fork in hand. The piles and piles of photographs provide an endless stream, proof of happy times.

I was there as he grew from boyhood innocence into an intelligent teenager, and a productive adult. I carted him and his friends to and from school events, rode along patiently as he first learned to drive, and watched with pride as he drove off alone in his very first car. Those memories are real. And no matter what, they are precious to me.

On paper, block out the stages of your child's life. You could tape several sheets of paper together, or put pages in a notebook. Use a page for each of several stages: babyhood, toddler years, elementary school ages. . . . Or focus on categories: sports, school, friends. . . . Using stages or interests may provide direction. In each section, jot down notes about the good you did. If it feels right to you, add pictures. Or use less than a full page, and write short phrases only.

Remember the point. I shed a few tears revisiting my memories, but renewed my self-image as a loving, attentive mother. From even before he was born, I cared for my son. I helped him grow. We did have fun together. Writing down the positive things you did as a mother helps reinforce them, and provides a list you can look at later.

Remember, *how* you do this exercise is up to you—make it as complex and detailed as you like. You could make a slide show, a scrapbook, or a collage of the field trips you drove for, parties you hosted, sports games you cheered at. . . . Or simply jot a short list to represent your role as a responsible, caring parent. If it's best for you, simply stroll through the years in your mind, and relive the successful moments in your memories. Remember the point: *Focus on the good you did.*

What Now?

In this chapter, we've explored the question: *Why?* Hopefully, some of the causes for estrangement presented here have helped you to better understand your own situation. We've covered the knowns and the unknowns, including substance abuse, third-party influencers, alternative lifestyles, mental illness, individuation, genetics, shame, and the effects of cultural shifts on self-esteem and self-importance.

I have received emails from adults who are either currently estranged from their parents, or who once were. Some of these have been hateful diatribes that made little sense other than to make me a target for starting a supportive website for parents. Others have knocked Baby Boomers as a selfish, hedonistic group that ruined their children. People who say this follow a semi-popular modern philosophy that blames the Baby Boomer generation for many societal ills, often connecting their failures to the millennials' problems. A few of these emails have mentioned abusive childhood situations, which doesn't apply to the intended readers here.

You may find it useful to know that some adults who cut off their families don't fully understand why they did. Some said they didn't have any specific reason, but that they knew it was about themselves—not about their parents. As difficult as it may be to accept, perhaps your child is like one of these.

In a 2014 Australian study, parents said their adult children were punishing them for what the child perceived as an offense, such as failing to give their offspring money, asking their adult child to pay back a loan, or not babysitting.[12] If you cannot point with certainty to a specific reason, you join the ranks of a great many baffled parents. Still, in order to set yourself on a positive, forward-thinking trek, try settling on an answer you can live with, at least for now. Human beings are wired to find answers, perhaps especially when bad things happen.

Among my own wonderings is whether my parenting style provided Dan with enough structure. Perhaps his independent nature required more guidance. I also figure marrying his wife with her more traditional background contributed to the break with us. Or perhaps there are factors of which I'm not aware.

I may never have an absolute answer, but I've settled on the belief that his estrangement is likely a combination of these things. I've decided that for now, and maybe even for always, that answer is good enough. Many of the moms who have effectively moved on have made a similar decision. An answer, even one that's a placeholder, provides a turning point, a spot from which they can move forward in their lives.

In order to begin moving past the heartbreak and on to reclaim your life, if you can, answer the question: *Why?* That may mean settling on a good enough reason for now, or a combination of factors as I have concluded. If you can't feel settled on a likely cause, re-assess your need to fully understand. Then, recognize that at least for now, you can see no sensible reason. Perhaps you never will. That realization *is* an answer.

We may never have absolute certainty, but there are few areas in life where we do. Accepting this, we free ourselves of the question: *Why?* We release our energy for a more important question: *What now?*

If you have trouble moving past this, don't push yourself too hard. Take some time to reflect on the exercise, *Remember The Good You Did.* Also, if you need to, please return to the exercise, *Know Your Feelings: Moving Ahead For Your Own Good,* at the end of Chapter One. You've come this far. It may be wise to pause and return to that exercise. Take a few moments to look again at the areas you struggle with. Then focus on the statements at the very end. Reaffirm your commitment to take action and reclaim the happiness you deserve.

You did your best for your children. Now do your best *for you.*

Another Perspective: *Bookmark It!*

If you find yourself continuing to question what went wrong, consider a "bookmark."

My husband and I laughed when we learned about one way a happily married couple moves past unresolved conflicts. The husband tells his wife, "Bookmark it!" The wife rolls her eyes, and asks, "Can you put a bookmark?"

Without animosity, their "bookmark" is a stopping point that acknowledges: *the issue is there, it will come up again, there's no resolution just now.* But for the moment, the idea of a bookmark provides closure. When it comes to figuring out what happened and how our children could become so alienated, we may be in similar straits.

Every relationship has conflict. All lives have events or circumstances that remain unexplained. Questions niggle. Conditions are not fully understood. Some issues are petty, and not worth our time. Others, at least for the present, have no resolution. Instead of going over the situation again and again and again, consider a bookmark.

With a child's estrangement, even if we understand the reasoning, uncertainty exists. We may wonder whether we'll ever reconcile, question what will happen if they get sick, have children of their own, get married, or move away. . . . Let the *what-if* question go. Bookmark it.

Imagine placing a strip of paper, a silky ribbon, a lovely needle-point design—whatever bookmark feels right to you—in the pages of your life. Then close the *Why?* and *What-if* chapters for now.

To get beyond the pain and uncertainty, imagine happily shelving the issue. Do so whenever you need to. Roll your eyes if it helps. Tell yourself: *Bookmark it!*

✈ Power-up a Positive Outlook: Three Steps

In Chapter One, we explored the idea of coping mindfully. Here, we build on the concept by gaining even more awareness of our thoughts and speech. Then we'll work on reshaping them. This exercise should be completed over a week or more. And it's a good technique to revisit whenever you find yourself feeling down in the dumps.

STEP ONE: Gain Awareness. If you became lost while driving, you could go in circles until you ran out of gas, and still be lost. However, if while driving you take stock of your surroundings then admit you're lost, you can stop, get directions or pull out a map, and alter your course. It's the same with the things we tell ourselves.

One day when I was feeling particularly low, and being vocal about it, my words hung in the air like a curse to predict my future: *I'll never get over this.*

What words do *you* say that form your outlook? What thoughts run through your mind to convince you you'll never be happy again? When we're hurting, we can get so caught up in our pain that negative, unhelpful thinking and speech become a habit. Let's change that now. For the next few days, make a practice of listening to yourself—your thoughts and your speech—so you can later redirect.

Write down any negative, complaining, self-pitying, hopeless words and phrases you hear coming out of your mouth or looping through your mind. Watch out for dark cloud dictates. *I'll never get over this. My heart will always be broken.* Listen for statements that set conditions on happiness, or otherwise limit you. *I just can't go on until this is resolved. I'm too old to start over now.* Recognize self-pity. *I never expected such hurt from my own child.* Maybe you convince yourself you're all alone: *Nobody understands.* Or ask yourself defeatist questions. *What's the point?*

These thoughts may represent the depth of your pain, but they're not helpful. And they can multiply. If you indulge in negative thoughts, statements, or questions, the mind easily builds upon them. *My son isn't the first person to betray me. Why ʋo people always leave me?* Or maybe your negative thinking gets more generalized: *Bad things always happen to me.*

This sort of thinking, sometimes called "ruminating," prompts more of the same. Looping thoughts that make you feel worse and worse. Soon, you're shuffling along a deepening groove, burrowing into a cavern of despair. *Nobody understands. I might as well just hole up and never make new friends or see my old ones. If I try to socialize, I'll have to pretend. If I tell them what's happened to me, I'll only be judged, shamed and hurt more. Face it. I don't fit anymore. Not anywhere. Not ever again.*

At one point after my son's estrangement, I had to admit how far I'd sunk. I was concentrating on the loss, and consumed with worry about what else would go wrong and who would leave me. Usually optimistic, I was drowning myself in sorrow. You may find yourself at that point. I had to take control, and I know you can take control, too.

Clinical studies have linked these sorts of churning thoughts, rumination, to high blood pressure and to unhealthy behaviors such as binge drinking and overeating. Steer clear. Negative thinking and its consequences will only complicate matters.

When you catch yourself thinking negatively, notice your body too.

Are you holding your breath? Clenching your jaw? Tightening your fists? Reaching for junk food or an extra glass of wine? You may be experiencing a harmful stress response. Changing your thoughts changes your body's responses too. Try focusing on anything you handled well, or imagine offering forgiveness.[13] The way we think about things can reduce physical stress responses, and more positively affect our health.

To benefit from awareness, keep writing down the negativity that runs through your head. Jot down phrases that linger, and take notes about how they lead to other negative thoughts. If you then connect that sort of thinking to the events of your day, you may clearly see how they influence you, your interaction with others, and your overall mood.

Don't try to rush past this step. For some of you, the negativity may immediately spring to mind. But spend a few days listening to your thoughts and speech to make sure you're fully identifying it.

I've provided a few lines here, but consider using a notepad for more room. It's important to take your time, to really listen in on your thoughts, and to seriously contemplate how your outlook affects you.

_____

_____

_____

_____

_____

Review your notes. Based on what you've recorded in writing, create a list of negative adjectives to describe your emotional state. In the table on page 86, leave the right-hand column blank for now. Use the left-hand column to write your descriptive words. A few from my list were: *sad, preoccupied, stuck, vulnerable,* and *pitiful.* Once you have your list, consider whether the words describe the *real* you. Is this how you were *before* the estrangement? Is the list representative of who you want to be?

Negative	Positive

Return to your notes for any repeated phrases or thoughts. *I'll never get over this. How could he do this to me? It must be my fault. Maybe everyone else will leave me too.* Think about those phrases. Are they helpful, or do they set you up for worry, fear or anger? Do they make you feel hopeless and powerless? Do they keep you stuck?

Getting a clear view of your outlook can be painful, so don't allow yourself to wallow. Don't get stuck in the mire of what you've discovered and lapse into self-pity. In the wake of such loss, it's natural to feel pitiful, touchy, angry, or whatever other emotion you experience. But do you want to feel that way forever? If you did, you wouldn't be reading this book. Make a decision to be done now. You're done with the crying, the anger, and the self-pity. You can commit to a change for the better.

STEP TWO: Commit To Positive Change. In Chapter One, you identified what you could not change, and you committed to moving forward for your own good. To accomplish that task, you'll need to recognize the importance of improving your outlook.

Right now, take a few moments to imagine some unknown, uncertain point in the future. See yourself in that future, several months or years from now. I remember wondering: *If my son ₊oes return, will he fin₊ me wallowing? Fulfilling my own hapless pre₊ictions? The woman I'₊ ₊escribe₊ on my pitiful list?* **No.** I was determined he would find me well and happy, the capable mother he left.

Even if we never reconciled, imagining myself happy and capable helped me want to reclaim my life—not only for me, but for the people around me whom I love. That tiny glimpse into my imagined future helped me find my way back, and to see myself in a positive light. Strong, resilient, determined. You can do this, too.

Return to the list of adjectives you created in the table in Step One. In the right-hand column, write their opposites. Pick your own words. Here's how part of my list looked:

Negative	Positive: The REAL ME
vulnerable	*resilient*
preoccupied	*present*
stuck	*strong*

Once you have created your second list, give that positive list a title that makes you feel good. For instance, "The Real Me." Or perhaps something like, "The Strong Woman I Am." Then, transfer your titled list of positive words onto a fancy strip of paper, a note card, or your calendar. Put it somewhere handy. On the refrigerator, in your wallet, or tacked to a bulletin board. At one point, I printed words on magnet sheets and stuck them on our exterior doors. That way, I saw the words every time I left the house. If you're into scrapbooking, make a page that features these words, and include a photograph of yourself that you really like. You could also make up a poem with your words, and then sing or say it—*often*. Aim to fulfill the meaning of those positive words.

Now that you've gained more understanding of how negativity may be keeping you down, and have come up with some words to serve as focal points for a fulfilling future, you're ready to move to the last step in powering up a positive outlook.

STEP THREE: Make The Shift. With your list of positive adjectives to aim for, let's deal with negative thinking and any unhelpful phrases you may speak. Just as it was simple to come up with opposites for the negative words, positive affirmations can spring naturally from negative ones. Take a few moments to review the negative phrases you think or speak often, and then replace them with positive versions. *I'll never get through this*, becomes: *I am moving past this.* If you fear everyone else will leave you too, change it to a more positive thought. *People who love me are in my life now.* Such a thought allows you to fully appreciate those people who are with you now, and set aside fears about what they will or won't do. You can't predict the future, but you can enjoy the present.

Now add some positive, forward-thinking statements that increase optimism. Something like: *Good things happen in my life.* Or maybe, *I get through any bad experiences, learn and grow from them. The future is bright.* Use whatever positive statement feels right to you. Just as each of our estrangement situations is unique, we are each individuals with our own set of needs, background and dreams. This is *your* exercise for a positive shift. Embrace it. Add your own spin. Make the positive affirmations your own. Here, or using extra paper, write your positive affirmations.

_____

_____

_____

_____

Once you're happy with your affirmations, use them as you did with your positive words list. Place your affirmations where you can easily access them. Be creative, or keep it simple. Here are a few ideas: Create a screensaver that scrolls the sayings across your computer screen. Make a bookmark, or post notes on your refrigerator. Create a plaque or a poster. Do what works for *you*. Then use the sayings whenever you catch yourself thinking or saying something that pulls you down. At least a few times, say them aloud, even to the mirror. And say them convincingly. Later, you can think about the affirmations, and remember how emphatically you said them to the mirror earlier.

If this feels strange or doesn't come easily, don't give up. Just like with any kind of exercise, you have to start somewhere. Telling yourself good things may feel odd at first, but commit to doing so every day. That's how habits are formed.

Practice good thinking habits now. Don't wait for negative thoughts to come up before thinking positive ones. When you get up in the morning, make a habit of telling yourself something good. *This will be a good day.* You'll be replacing a bad habit with a good one, which is always helpful. Remember how Julia stopped looking at her cell phone every morning and turned to her list of things-to-do instead? Here, you're similarly substituting a positive action for a negative one. And when you start first thing, you set the tone for your day.

Do as Julia did, and get prepared with ready ways to make your day a good one, so your prediction (*This will be a good day.*) comes true. Make a list of things you can turn to. Do an activity you enjoy. Take a walk outdoors and listen to songbirds. Feel the caress of a gentle breeze. Or notice how sunlight feels against your skin. Even a few moments of delight can break a gloomy mood, and can then be called to mind later and enjoyed again. Call an old friend. Arrange a flower bouquet and put it on your desk at work, or give it to a co-worker. Paint your fingernails to match a holiday or just for fun. Take old bread to a duck pond. Buy a cheesy light-up brooch, and wear it to a meeting or at work. Read a funny novel. Watch a silly YouTube video. Ask a co-worker to take lunch with you in a nearby park. Ride a bicycle up the block. Or bake a cake—whatever you enjoy. Doing even the tiniest activity that once brought you pleasure whets your appetite to do and notice more of what makes you happy, thus shifts your mindset to a new path. Even if you think you don't feel like it, have fun!

Just as negative thoughts of rumination can produce more negativity, positive thoughts can also multiply (and be fruitful). Besides, they feel better, and are good for our health.

- Step One: Gain Awareness.

- Step Two: Commit To Positive Change.

- Step Three: Make The Shift.

Use these three simple steps to power up your positive outlook, cope mindfully in the moment, and live a bright future today.

Notes

CHAPTER THREE

Get The Support You Need

Pam, whose oldest daughter, Martha, has been estranged for nearly a decade, says, "Seek support early." Pam didn't, and her story illustrates why many mothers become isolated after estrangement—although they really don't need to be.

Pam had never heard of a child rejecting a parent unless they'd been abused. As a loving, hardworking mom who took good care of her three children, she never expected this to happen to her. Pam supported her children's interests, participated in their activities, enjoyed their company, and paid for their education. When Martha completed graduate school and secured a job in another state, Pam even bought her a home.

"We were always so close," says Pam. "Then the phone rang one day, and everything changed." She saw Martha's number and ran to pick up. "But Martha hadn't called to chat," Pam explains. "She told me she no longer wanted a relationship."

Pam was stunned. At first, she believed the estrangement was a phase, or from some misunderstanding that in time she could fix. Confused and ashamed, Pam didn't share the problem outside her immediate family. "How can you tell people your own flesh and blood wants nothing to do with you?" she asks. "Besides, they might think badly of my daughter."

In hindsight, Pam can see that the distancing began when she divorced Martha's father. Martha was in her twenties then, and finishing graduate school. Her siblings were away at college. By that time, Pam's husband was drinking heavily. One night, after he drank himself into oblivion and created a particularly unsettling scene, Martha pulled Pam aside. She asked, "Mom, how long are you going to put up with him?"

Pam understood the comment as permission to divorce, but when Pam moved out, Martha didn't approve. Pam was shocked at her daughter's reaction. She had counted on Martha's support.

"Was I a perfect parent?" asks Pam. "No. Did anything I did or didn't do warrant Martha's alienation? No."

Every year, Pam received a Mother's Day bouquet, and sometimes Christmas or birthday cards, but there was nothing personal in them, only Martha's signature. Pam's letters, emails, phone calls and texts went unanswered. She had no choice but to accept Martha's decision. Still, she held out hope. After many years with no direct contact, she reached out during a visit to her daughter's city in another state. That's when her torch of hope was fully extinguished.

From the hotel, Pam sent a text saying that she'd like to meet. "My daughter texted back immediately," relates Pam. "She said she would be home that afternoon, and to come on by." But the text referenced names Pam didn't recognize. Believing her daughter must have mistaken her for someone else, Pam toyed with the idea of just showing up. "But that wouldn't have been fair," she says. "When I explained that it was 'Mom,' she didn't reply." Pam went home without seeing her daughter. The situation was hopeless.

After that, it was easier for Pam to talk about the estrangement. Online, she discovered forums full of rejected parents who helped her to feel better about herself. She realized she hadn't needed to suffer alone all those years. She soon began opening up to others in person as well. To her surprise, several parents in her social circles were in similar situations. "Just knowing you're not alone is a huge comfort," Pam says.

Strength in Numbers

Although it's disturbing to discover other parents whose children are estranged, it's a relief to know you're not alone. Online support groups are the quickest way to find those parents. A virtual hug, shared information, and practical advice provide a sense of camaraderie in an otherwise isolating experience.

In online forums, user names cloak identity and offer a measure of anonymity, so members share without fear of retribution. And most online groups don't *require* participation. Members can read and benefit from others' posts without commenting. According to the Norman Nielson Group, the ratio of those who "lurk" and read in online forums versus those who actively engage in discussions is an astounding 90 to 1.

To find an online group that's a good fit for you, try an Internet search for phrases such as "support for parents of estranged adults." Forums are organized under topic headings, with postings under each. Read through several topics/posts to ascertain the overall tone and content of the group. How do the postings make you feel? If you can identify with the members, and learn something that helps, the forum may be right for you.

Keep in mind that the first group you find in an Internet search is likely the busiest. If you're more comfortable in a quieter setting with fewer opinions flying, look for one farther down in the search list. In a densely populated forum, you may feel lost or burdened by the sheer number of posts. If you require a lot of support and quick answers, the slower pace of a smaller forum may not be enough for you. Some forums have an email function that provides an emailed alert when anyone replies to your postings.

If the idea appeals to you, find a gender-specific group, a Christian group, or one that in some other way shares common ground. Estranged parent forums led by a mental health professional or a peer leader might also interest you.

If you prefer the closeness of an in-person group, look for one through your community's mental health services, or at meetup.com.

Although in-person support groups for parents of estranged adult children are not numerous, a few exist. Some mothers find help in support groups for other issues—and these are often easier to locate. Parents in a divorce support group may also be facing estrangement issues. If a spouse worked to denigrate you in the eyes of your child, a group focused on Parental Alienation Syndrome might be helpful. Other specialized groups with possible crossover interest include ones for addiction, co-dependency or mental health issues.

Getting Immediate Help

If you're contemplating suicide, and particularly if you have a plan, it is imperative that you get help immediately.

- Go to an emergency room.

- Call a suicide hotline. Try: 1-800-273-8255, which is the hotline from www.suicidepreventionlifeline.org

- If you're in immediate danger, call 9-1-1.

If you are feeling unsafe, get help *now*. You matter.

Closed Door Support

For some, the private office of a mental health professional is the only environment that feels safe enough to share the intimate details of an estrangement. The undivided attention of a person who is trained in empathic listening can create an atmosphere of care that may not be present in other areas of your life. A mental health professional can help with feelings of depression or anxiety, provide coping techniques, or work on communication skills in the event of your adult child's contact.

The training, licensing, and practice of mental health professionals vary from state to state. Trained clinicians include psychiatrists (who are licensed Medical Doctors with specialty in psychiatry), psychologists, marriage & family therapists, social workers, and professional counselors.

To better understand the function and training of specific mental health professionals, see the resources listed in the box on page 119. In particular, the National Alliance on Mental Illness (NAMI) has an informative fact sheet. Here, I will use clinician titles interchangeably, except when individual mothers shared their experiences using a specific professional.

Ginny, whose oldest daughter is estranged, chose a psychologist she refers to as her therapist. Ginny says, "She has helped me feel more confident, and to look forward, whether my estranged daughter chooses to be a part of my life or not." Ginny's therapist has guided her to stay aware of her thoughts, remain focused on the present, and turn her negative thinking around. Ginny has been seeing her therapist weekly for almost two years, and plans to continue. "It's the one place I can feel completely free and unguarded," she says.

While Ginny and others laud the therapy experience, some come away with less than glowing results, or are dissatisfied. Of the more than 9,000 parents who answered my survey as of this writing, forty-two percent said they sought professional help after the estrangement. Of those people who sought professional counseling:

- 25% reported entirely positive results

- 46% reported "some" or "a little" help

- 29% said the sessions were not helpful, or made the situation and/or their feelings about it worse

Let's take a closer look at what may have gone wrong. That way, if you seek professional assistance, you can get the best help for you.

First, recognize that not all mental health professionals and their techniques are the same. To get the most benefit, shop around. Mothers who met with a trained professional who had never heard of an adult child rejecting a parent without good reason felt immediately judged. The clinician failed to create the necessary atmosphere of trust. Some parents were frustrated when their therapist focused on reconciliation even when they had already tried to reconcile, and were ready to move on for their own benefit. Others said they needed coping techniques that extended beyond the office visit, but did not receive tools or assistance of that nature.

Laura and her husband traveled from their home in the heartland to the East Coast to see a psychiatrist with their twin daughters who were attending a university there. "We were desperate to get our girls back. So we suggested therapy," says Laura. "Once there, the girls ranted on about how we'd never been there for them, but whenever *we* tried to talk, the doctor stopped us."

Laura believes she and her husband have been good parents. "Growing up, the girls did soccer and swimming and every other activity they wanted to. We volunteered at school functions, took them on vacations, and were there for them in every way. I gave up my career to be home and raise them. In the psychiatrist's office, the girls remembered the one time I had been late to pick them up, and how when my mother died I sat around crying. They were seventeen at the time, and I gave them money to buy prom dresses. They were mad I didn't go with them to help pick out dresses, and used that as an example of how I was never there for them."

At the end of the appointment, the psychiatrist scheduled weekly sessions for the twins. "My husband and I flew home. After a couple of visits, the girls stopped showing up," says Laura. "We were back to square one, and we had no homework or coping ideas to get past our grief." Laura's sadness overwhelmed her, but her husband was angry. "We were out money for plane tickets and expensive therapy appointments. Plus, we were still paying for their education," says Laura. "Deep down, I know my husband was hurting, but getting mad about the wasted money helped him cope, and maybe even stay strong for me. It was his way of separating from the sadness, and ultimately, from our girls."

A few mothers said their therapists just listened—and would have kept listening forever. While some mothers enjoyed the safe space to air emotions, and talk about estrangement's impact, others expected more.

Trudy, whose son married at 31 and then abandoned her and his father, lives in a small town where there is little privacy. She traveled to a neighboring city in order to avoid the small town rumor mill if her car was seen parked at the local counselor's office. "But I couldn't see straining my pocketbook indefinitely for a sympathetic ear," says Trudy, whose son has now been estranged for six years. "I needed to move on with my life."

Find a mental health professional with whom you feel comfortable, who has relevant experience, and who will support your goals. Does gender matter to you? Would you feel comfortable with a therapist who had no children? Look for a clinician familiar with estrangement or ambiguous loss. Some mothers found bereavement counseling helped. A few parents reported as helpful the trauma treatment, Eye Movement Desensitization & Reprocessing (EMDR), which is often used with those suffering from Post-Traumatic Stress Disorder (PTSD). When mental disorders or addiction are involved, professionals trained and experienced in those areas may be of help.

Start with clear expectations, too. Ask yourself what you intend to get out of the therapy. Then share those expectations with your clinician. That doesn't mean you can't be flexible. You might imagine your ideal outcome and then come up with an alternative you can live with.

Ginny originally thought her daughter would attend therapy with her, but her daughter would only stay for a few minutes, lay the blame on Ginny, and then leave. She soon stopped going. Ginny's therapist helped her let go of her goal to reconcile, and come up with a secondary plan. "I needed to learn to live well without my daughter," says, Ginny.

If you enter a counseling relationship, clearly communicate your expectations right away. Then, a mental health professional can better assist you. One who does not feel he or she is a good fit may recommend someone with more specialized experience, or a philosophy or method more in tune with your goals.

Let's talk for a moment about goals. Setting achievable goals requires targeting outcomes that are realistic. Some parents enter therapy expecting their lives and relationships to return to the way they were before the break. But that may not be possible. Maybe they enter therapy with reconciliation as an ideal, but haven't come to realize they can only control their own actions. That's only half the equation needed in order to reunite. Reconciliation might also include compromise a parent isn't willing to make.

There are short-term and long-term goals. A newly estranged mother may make getting through the day without crying a goal (short-term). Another may want to find meaningful use of her time, and reclaim her life (long-term).

A mother whose adult son only contacts her when he needs money may long for a more meaningful relationship. She can try to connect with him by her actions, such as phoning him, or inviting him out. But her goal to develop a more meaningful relationship with her son is dependent on his interest, and how he responds. Whether or not he reciprocates is his choice, so the mother's overall goal may not be attainable.

Setting Strong Goals

Improving the quality of our lives—our happiness, well-being, and hopes for the future—demands that we invest the time and energy to design our goals well. We can create them to fit our needs, envision their success, root them in fertile ground, and nourish them to fruition. Let's take a look at goals and how to set them.

S.M.A.R.T. is an acronym for goal-setting hat has been around since the early 1980s. Individual words represented by each of the acronym's letters vary depending on the source. Experts have added their own spin, but the general idea remains the same: Smart goals are Specific, Measurable, Attainable, Realisitic, and Timely.

While the S.M.A.R.T. acronym originated in the business arena, applying the ideas to our personal lives is a sound strategy. Let's look at an example.

New Jersey mother, Geneva, sets herself up for a setback each time she texts her daughter and receives no reply. Geneva sends texts because she wants to make sure her daughter knows she loves her and wants to reconnect. But she wonders if she comes across as obsessive, especially when her daughter doesn't reply, and Geneva finds herself sending another text within a short time. She doesn't want to nag her daughter, but finds refraining difficult. Geneva wants to set a goal to refrain from texting so often, but still let her daughter know the door is open.

Below, we'll examine the S.M.A.R.T. goal method more specifically, and see how Geneva's goal fits.

Specific. Imagine more than a fuzzy idea. A specific goal provides a target, and gives the basis for steps to take toward that target.

- Geneva defines her overall goal as follows: To keep the door open while not harassing her daughter in a cycle of texting, getting no reply, and texting again.

Measurable. If a goal is not measurable, then it's impossible to determine whether it has been achieved.

- To make her goal measurable, Geneva decides to text only once every two weeks.

Attainable. Ask yourself whether your objective is dependent on someone or something out of your control. If so, define (or re-define) your goals so they're within your control.

- Geneva's goal is attainable because she can mark her calendar and text every two weeks. She will be doing the texting herself. The goal is not dependent on another person, and is within her control.

Realistic. With your available time, knowledge, and resources, do you have the ability to achieve the specified goal?

- Geneva has the knowledge and resources to achieve her goal of keeping the door open by texting once every two weeks.

Timely. The best goals are ones that have a deadline. However, deadlines must be realistic and attainable.

- Although Geneva's particular goal does not require a deadline other than texting every two weeks, she wonders how she will feel after several months of texting—probably with no response from her daughter. Geneva decides that in three months, she will reevaluate her goal. She will either continue as is, come up with new behaviors to achieve her goal in another way, or set an alternate goal. For instance, she could decide to send a card every other month, or try making a monthly phone call and leave a voice message instead. Or maybe she will stop texting for a longer period.

Geneva's goal of texting once every two weeks to let her daughter know she cares is specific, measurable, attainable, realistic, and timely. Geneva set a sensible goal!

You may be wondering: *What if Geneva's daughter replies to a text? What then?* Geneva has thought of this too. If her daughter texts a receptive reply, she will text again, hoping the communication continues in a positive vein. However, if her daughter stops, she will end the text string on a positive note such as, "I'm so glad to hear from you." Or, "I'm glad you're well." She will then refrain from further texting, and resume the two-week interval. If a meeting or some other connection develops, she will follow through with that. Geneva's main goal of connecting while not harassing her daughter or becoming obsessive remains the objective.

While fully explored goals that use the S.M.A.R.T. method have sound objectives, they need not be binding. If, for instance, Geneva finds that her texts inflame the relationship, and her daughter begins replying in anger, Geneva can reevaluate. Because she has analyzed her goal, she has clarity about her intentions. She knows the goal isn't to text every other week, but rather, she intends to convey a message that she still loves her daughter, but without overdoing it. With such clarity, as needed and at any time, she can come up with new ideas and actions that will better support herself and the goal.

In hindsight, Laura recognizes that part of the frustration she and her husband felt derived from their lack of communication. "The doctor thought we wanted long-term therapy for our girls. We had expected him to mediate, so we could resolve our issues," says Laura. "Actually, I think we were looking for a miracle."

In contrast, Ginny had a goal in mind, and shopped around for help.

She called three therapists before making an appointment. "I asked what sort of experience they had, how long they'd been in practice, how they set up their meetings, and whether they thought they could help," says Ginny. Nervous when she made that first call, she used a short script. "I wrote out my issue in nutshell form, what I intended to achieve, plus the questions," she says. "It kept the calls short and businesslike." Ultimately, she felt comfortable with her therapist even before her first appointment, which alleviated some of her anxiety about seeking help in the first place.

A short phone conversation can help you judge rapport, and get preliminary questions answered. Consider making a short script to help you remain focused, and perhaps feel more confident. If you feel comfortable telling other people you're looking for help, don't overlook their recommendations.

As with many services, finding the right mental health practitioner may require trying more than one. Or you may opt for help that's outside the field of mental health. A life coach or pastor might help you with goals, for instance.

Several months after Laura and her husband returned home, and their daughters' sessions with the psychiatrist came to a halt, the couple sought assistance again. Laura instigated the idea, and had to talk her husband into going. "By then, I had confided in a few people, and a friend suggested a psychologist who had helped her move forward after a nasty divorce," explains Laura.

This time, the couple first talked their needs through together. Then Laura communicated those intentions before making the appointment. The psychologist agreed to help them outline a plan to disengage from their daughters and communicate their decision to stop paying for the girls' tuition. With the psychologist's help, they drafted a letter that communicated their love and disappointment, their hope for reconciliation, and also provided a timeline during which the girls would need to find their own college funding over the next two semesters. In just three sessions, Laura and her husband came away feeling empowered and supported. Laura adds, "It was also comforting to know we had a trusted professional to turn to in the future."

✈ Go For a Smart Goal That Supports You

In the midst of any situation in which you feel powerless, it's important to recognize that you *can* do something to help yourself. In fact, there is much you can do to start feeling better. You can begin to support yourself. You can take charge, even incrementally.

The first step is often the biggest, and you've already taken it. For some of you, reading this book was your first step forward. For others, it's one in a series of actions that, even inch-by-inch, are propelling you along on your healing journey. Take another step now. Create a sound goal, and commit to your success. This will begin to help you find solutions. Rather than feeling stuck, you'll begin to train yourself to look for the way forward. You'll begin creating your own supportive path.

Set a goal that helps you find the support you need or assists you in assessing your options for an online or in-person group. Or maybe your goal is to find a good match in a therapist, or make the most of your existing association with a mental health professional. Goals can help you face any estrangement-related issue, and help you create positive change around how it's affecting you.

Maybe you have a goal like Geneva's, which is detailed in *Setting Strong Goals*. Perhaps you need to break a habit that makes you feel bad. That's how Julia stopped reaching for her phone and waiting each morning for the call that wouldn't come. Do you need to reclaim your hobbies, and get back to focusing on things that make you happy? Or do you need to stop looking back, and learn to look forward to your life ahead, no matter how uncertain? A goal can help.

Refer to Geneva's example to see how she clearly defined the intent of her goal, the specific actions she would take to achieve the goal, how she built in a time factor, and measured success. Then use the smart steps below to create and achieve a S.M.A.R.T. goal for your own well-being. Choose one related to finding support, or anything else that's causing you to feel hurt, worry, anger, or any other negativity.

First, reflect on an estrangement-related problem, or a step you'd like to take. Maybe you need to stop looking at Facebook photos that only make you sad. Perhaps you keep asking, "Why?" And you need to focus on a question that better serves you, such as, "What now?"

Remember, goals are about things you can accomplish, not behavior over which you have no control. Make it specific, something you can easily state rather than a big problem with blurry boundaries. As you read through the paragraphs below, you'll work on honing your goal to a fine point that fits all the criteria. Get started now. Write down your basic goal.

_____

_____

_____

Be _specific_. Now that you've come up with an idea for a goal, let's narrow it down. A goal like, "I want to feel better." is too broad. "I want to look forward to my days again," is an improvement. Still, you can do better. Try: "I want to have a positive focus each and every day."

Look at your goal. Does it clearly and specifically state what you want to achieve? Don't set yourself up for failure. Break a complex goal into smaller goals. Starting small makes it easier to focus and follow through. Success fuels energy for more action, and more success. That's better than setting too many goals at once, and then feeling overwhelmed. Remember, you've been through a horrible trauma. Be kind to yourself. Be your own best friend. Using the example and its improved versions as a guide, expand your goal so it's more specific. Do that now. Write down your expanded goal.

_____

_____

_____

Make it <u>measurable</u>. Our more specific goal, "I want to have a positive focus each and every day," is decent but not so easy to measure. We need some actions associated with the goal. That's how to build in a way to quantify, or otherwise measure your success. Adding some measurable actions, the goal becomes: *"To have a positive focus each ꞏay, I'll reflect on an inspirational quote first thing each morning, plus ꞏo one special thing just for myself each day."*

In addition to holding these daily, action-based intentions, a tracking system helps you keep them up. How you track your action can be tailor-made just for you. You could place a checkmark on a calendar, find an accountability partner to whom you routinely report, send yourself a text, or jot a few notes in a journal. This last one helps with self-care ideas too. By recording what you have tried, you can see what worked. What felt right? What was easy on a busy day, and provided a boost, or let you take a breath, feel cared for, and consider what you might need?

While the intent behind the example is to have a more positive focus each and every day, the daily action items provide a structure to move toward the goal. You can also build in more measurability related to a time element. We'll explore that idea more below, in the section on making your goal timely.

Now, look at *your* goal. Have you included measurable actions? Add them now, or make them more concrete. Write down your complete goal.

_____

_____

_____

_____

Aim for the <u>attainable</u>. Analyze your goal. Is it dependent on someone or something else? If so, you'll need to make a change. To succeed, you must be in charge. Consider any factors that might prevent you from taking action. Then, further define or alter the language and focus so you're attempting something you can actually achieve. Just as Geneva's bi-weekly texts conveyed her intended message but did not depend on her daughter's response, your goal must not rely on another's actions.

Let's look at how else the example goal might face obstacles. A quotation book that's pulled off your shelf or purchased specifically for this task is a better option than relying on the dependability of an inspirational email list, or viewing a website that may not be functioning when needed. Such reliance can create barriers that are beyond your control. Goals must rely on you and only you.

We also didn't pinpoint the "one special" thing to be done each day. Set yourself up for success with a ready list of items to do. Making a list precedes attaining the goal. Keep it simple to start. *Enjoy a cup of my favorite tea. Paint my toenails. Sit for 10 minutes by the window and watch the birds. Moisturize my hands with a scented lotion. File my fingernails. Chew a stick of gum after lunch. Watch an uplifting music video. Throw out all my old cosmetics. Enjoy a glass of red wine. Try a new lipstick.* For the example, we would add a few bigger items, too, and take the time to plan them out for easy access and accomplishment. *Get a massage. Take a walk by the river. Spend a weekend away.*

Now, let's get back to *your* goal. On what or whom does your goal rely? Make changes if necessary. Write your goal again. Make note of needed support items. List required telephone numbers, supplies, or whatever else is needed to support your goal.

_____

_____

_____

Keep it <u>realistic</u>. With your available time, knowledge, and resources, do you have the ability to achieve the specified goal? That's a good question to think about and answer. If your goal was to have a positive focus each day, you might keep an inspiring book nearby, and get up earlier to read and reflect. One person might need time to journal about an inspirational quote she's read. Someone else may feel it's sufficient to incorporate reflection into another, perhaps more mindless task (doing dishes, riding the train to work, or taking a shower).

Think through any changes you'll need to make to your schedule. Consider just how the action items you've chosen for your goal will fit into your life. Make a note of these.

_____

_____

_____

Consider the <u>relevance</u>. In addition to standing for "realistic," sometimes, the "R" in S.M.A.R.T. goals is said to stand for "relevant." Because achieving goals takes effort, their _relevance_ is important. Take time to consider how useful attaining your goal will be to you. How will this action spur forward momentum, help you reclaim your health and happiness? Knowing this helps you stay motivated and on track. Take a few moments to reflect on the following questions, and then write down your honest and complete answers. Your thoughts get at the "why" behind your goal.

Why is achieving this goal so important to you?

_____

_____

_____

How will achieving this goal affect your life?

_____

_____

_____

Will achieving this goal affect people you care about? How?

_____

_____

_____

Now, using your notes, write out a couple of positive sentences that reinforce your ideas. Craft your thoughts as if they're already achieved. By doing so, you're creating a motivational statement that will help you succeed.

A positive motivational statement for our example goal might be:

Purposefully starting my day with a positive focus helps me look forward to my life, keeps me grateful for all the good, and helps me stay hopeful and present for the people I love. Doing something special just for me always makes me feel good, and helps me feel valued. By being my own best friend, I'm better prepared to also be a good friend to those I love.

Write your own motivational statement now. If you feel the need, take time first to ponder this while doing something you enjoy. Then come back feeling refreshed, and write a motivational statement you can believe in. Try a few even, and then settle on one that feels right.

_____

_____

_____

Once you've completed your motivational statement in a way that feels good to you, write it on a notecard and put it where you can easily refer to it for inspiration. Place it where it can remind you daily of the commitment you've made to your goal, and why you feel so strongly.

Keep your goal <u>timely</u>. Our example goal has daily actions, so a time element is built-in. However, there is no set duration for these actions to take place. Adding that element will help with measuring the success of the overall intent (a positive focus each day). Adding a span of time to try the actions associated with carrying out the goal allows for evaluation, changes, and refocusing if needed.

With the example goal, we might evaluate our feelings after one month. We could also track our feelings. In my writing work for a non-profit organization helping those with depression, I assisted in creating a monitoring kit for people to track their emotions. Two or three times a day, they could draw a happy or sad face, or write down a word or two to describe their feelings. Used along with a journal, they could then associate their emotions with what was going on in their lives.

For our example goal, using the awareness gained by doing the exercise, *Power Up A Positive Outlook*, at the end of Chapter Two will help. You could also reflect on your feelings at the end of each day or week, and then evaluate your overall outlook at the end of the month.

Whatever your goal is, factoring in a deadline or other time-related measurement is important. These sorts of questions apply: *By what date will you achieve your goal? For how many days/weeks will you continue before evaluating your success? On which days of the week will you do the goal-oriented actions?* Jot down your answers now.

_____

_____

Goals Are Transformative

Even when we craft our goals and create action steps to achieve them and to stay on track, heartaches, stress, and obstacles can slap us back. Staying motivated is a challenge. So, in my work as a life coach, I crafted another S.M.A.R.T. acronym that focuses on the prize: ***Stay Motivated And Realize Transformation.***

During my darkest hours, to ***Stay Motivated And Realize Transformation,*** sprang to mind, a beacon. It helped me put the experience in perspective and recognize the heartrending situation of my son's estrangement for what it was: an unexpected turn. While my life had changed, it wasn't over. I had overcome obstacles in the past. I had lived through horrendous experiences before—and I would live through this too. In fact, the hurt and loss provided me an opportunity to step forward, and prove again what I have witnessed in my own and others' lives: *The landscape of loss is fertile ground for growth.*

That realization helped me to accept my son's choices, and move forward with decisions for my own well-being. I could get on with the work of setting and achieving goals to rebuild my outlook and my life. In the aftermath of emotional devastation, I could search for building blocks to create an even better life and a more fully realized me. *And so can you.*

Among Friends: Plan Ahead

Turning to our friends for support may be second nature, but we may be embarrassed, or worry we'll be criticized or judged.

When Meg's 29-year-old son and his wife cut her and her husband out of their lives, Meg lost contact with her granddaughter too. All of the sudden, her whole life had changed, but she wasn't about to let it get her down. Meg says, "The day after my son emailed my husband and me what I now call our *termination letter,* I blew my nose, slathered tightening cream around my eyes, and used drops to get the red out." Then she attended her monthly business association luncheon where she serves as president and is friends with everybody.

Meg thought the normalcy would do her good. But once there, she says, "It felt like I'd entered the Twilight Zone. Before the meeting started, people chatted about all their fun. One gal was hosting a baby shower. Another was going camping with her son and his family. And there I sat gripping my coffee mug so tight I thought it would break."

While she did her best to nod and smile, Meg was overwhelmed with sadness. "And envy," she admits. "These women's lives were continuing happily on, while mine had fallen apart. It made me so angry I thought I'd explode. How come *they* were all so lucky?" Meg escaped to the restroom, expecting to take a few deep breaths and carry on. "I'm a strong woman," she says. "Instead, I locked myself in a stall and sobbed, all the while monitoring the bathroom door and praying nobody came in." Meg couldn't bring herself to go to the podium and run the meeting, so she texted her friend Lenore back at the table to take over for her. "Then I hid my swollen eyes behind sunglasses and left. On the way home, I got pulled over for speeding; my first traffic ticket *ever*."

Meg always believed that with friends, she could get through anything, but she says, "My son's rejection changed me. I resented people's relationships with their adult children and grandkids. It was too hard to smile and be happy for them." Meg isolated herself. To avoid interaction, she would go into her office only to review and sign paperwork.

Meg's feelings echo those of many mothers who tell me they're happy for their friends but the pain cuts deep. Seeing others content in their families reminds them of their own failings and sorrow. So, just as Meg did, they avoid friends and pull back from social commitments.

Because Meg and her family were active in her community, when Meg stopped socializing, people wondered what was wrong. When she began opening up, she felt judged. "I went from being a capable woman, a veritable pillar in the community, to a blubbering fool," Meg says. Unable to speak about the situation without crying, her lack of emotional control embarrassed her. But it was the shame of judgment she saw in others' eyes that hurt most. "I'd failed in a woman's most fundamental role . . . *motherhood*. I knew people wondered if they'd been seeing a public front.

Maybe I was an abuser who deserved my son's rejection."

Other than her husband, Meg's friend Lenore was the only person she trusted. To anyone else, she shared only the basic facts—her son had married, moved away, and wanted nothing to do with her.

And Lenore reminded her of her strength. "That was important," says Meg. "Lenore would sympathize, but she'd also remind me of other hardships I've been through. She'd tell me she knew I could get through this, that I was a powerful woman, an overcomer, somebody who has inspired her in her own life." With a laugh, Meg adds, "The best friends only let you wallow a little. Then they grab your hand and pull you out of the mud."

Meg has a point. When we've lost our footing, feel misunderstood, judged, and uncertain about our past and future all at once, a friend who believes in us provides a more realistic view than the one we see in the mirror.

Lenore's words helped Meg reclaim her strong identity. Confide in empathetic friends who help you feel empowered and remind you of your strengths. Or be your own friend. Remind yourself of your strengths.

Now, three years after the initial estrangement, Meg would advise moms who don't know what to tell people to pick themselves up and make a plan. "It's damage control," she says. "You know, like a food company with an E-coli outbreak. They plan how to present the facts but keep the public's confidence. Pretty soon, nobody even remembers there was a problem."

Many mothers fall into this naturally. When we're asked about our estranged adult children, we gloss over details on the fly. "He's doing well," we say. "You know those busy young adults," we quip—then change the subject.

While this works for some mothers, others end up saying more than they intend to, or don't tell the truth. Later, they regret their words. Those squirmy feelings leave them dreading social situations, which can further isolate them. With Meg's "damage control" idea in mind, let's look at how you can plan ahead for difficult conversations.

Foresee circumstances in which you might be compelled to talk about your child. Then plan responses that fit different situations and relationships. What you tell a previous co-worker you were close to but haven't seen in five years isn't equal to what you might say to the bank teller who points out her custom lapel button with a picture of her grandson on Santa's lap. You might indeed feel like sharing the truth of your disappointment with a co-worker you used to kibitz with about the trials and joys of motherhood—or not. If you've run into an old friend in a public place, you may not have the time or privacy to share the whole truth. Advance planning can help you feel prepared and in control.

In her rural town with its rumor mill, Trudy worked hard to get on with her life. In the beginning, her goals were short term. She knew she'd be seeing people. "I was embarrassed," Trudy says. "Most everybody knows something of everybody else's business, but I didn't want to talk about my son with very many."

Trudy wrote out the names of every person she might encounter around town. Then she worked to devise a scale that classified those relationships, and prepared some ready answers. Her scale weighted relationships by their history and level of trust. Edited for space and clarity, her scale consisted of four categories:

Level Four: High trust, reciprocal and intimate knowledge about one another's lives. Important what the person thinks.

Level Three: Not as personal. An intimate friend from the past, or a fellow mother from my son's high school years who will remember what a great kid he was—or who even sees him and his children on Facebook.

Level Two: A casual friend. Less personal connection, like with a fellow club or committee member. No reason to distrust.

Level One: An acquaintance with no personal connection, or someone who has hurt me in the past; a person I don't trust.

People in Trudy's *Level Four* received genuine responses that fit their knowledge of her situation, and her comfort with them knowing the truth. She felt at ease with these people. "But I was aware of time and other factors," she says. "I didn't share my troubles every chance I got."

Like many people do, Trudy worried she would be seen as a downer. If we go over and over our problems, there's a danger we'll take on a new identity: *the victim*. While our good friends do care, they also have limits.

For *Level Three* relationships, Trudy often relied on set answers. Consider casual quips that divulge little. A lighthearted comment like Trudy's might serve: "Our children are getting older, but we just keep getting better." A getaway statement can follow. Something about not having time to talk usually works in our busy world. Having ready statements doesn't mean you'll always need or use them. But at a time when you're feeling vulnerable or lack emotional control, being prepared helps.

For more casual relationships, people you don't trust, or people you're first meeting (Trudy's *Level One* and *Two*), come up with a few responses of your own. Or borrow from the examples I collected under *Ready Responses* at the end of this section. Then, when a casual acquaintance greets you in line or corners you in the office, you'll be ready.

Trudy's structured plan helped her go about her life in her small town. "I had a repertoire of sayings and I relied on it," she says. "I knew through the grapevine my son was doing fine, so when some people asked about the family, I'd say everyone was fine, and mean it."

Obviously, you may not need a plan as detailed as Trudy's. I share it here because the details may be helpful, and they represent how touchy the situation can be. Eighty-eight percent of my survey respondents had difficulty talking to others about their estrangement. Foreseeing potential encounters and planning how you'll respond helps you feel prepared. Preparation calms anxiety.

Unfortunately, not all friends will be supportive. Some friends may make accusatory statements, discount your feelings, or even dismiss them. Others may intend to offer support, but their comments don't help. Or because we're feeling so sensitive, we interpret the comments as criticism.

In my case, it became clear that one friend's unresolved anger toward her mother biased her judgment about my experience. She made excuses for my son, and referenced decades-old history with her mother. Looking back, I can empathize. She didn't intend to hurt me, but at the time, being around her caused me pain. Rather than discuss my feelings, I pulled away. Later, when I was past the shock of my son's rejection, we rekindled the relationship, and I'm grateful to count her as a friend.

Recently, she surprised me with an email about her past estrangement from her mother. Her explanations clarified the bias I'd sensed. I can empathize with the very real pain she feels, and sent a return email stating that. It's clear that seeing my pain poked at her sensitivities.

Do what works for you. If you have a friend (family member, or associate) that seems judgmental, consider broaching the subject. This may open a helpful discussion, or even deepen the friendship. Or, you may decide, as I did, that a conversation wouldn't help. You may need to pull back from certain friends to protect yourself. On the other hand, some friends may disconnect from you.

For fellow parents, your loss may prick up fears of losing their own children. In research that began in the 1960s, social psychologist Melvin Lerner demonstrated people's general belief that the world is just and fair. Today, it is understood that the concept of a "just world" is what's known as "cognitive bias." The thinking causes people to believe the world has a sort of built-in moral compass, and that we get what we deserve. Social scientists believe that this sort of thinking helps people to cope and carry on.

It works like this: When someone we know gets hurt, has a bad accident, becomes ill, or suffers some other misfortune, we try to make sense of it, confirming our belief that the world is just. *Uncle Phil got cancer because he didn't take care of himself. Aunt Claire's husband left her because she was too fastidious.* Some may go so far as to blame the victim. For example, some may reason that the people who lost their fortunes in the recent Bernie Madoff scheme were too trusting. Obviously, injustices *do* occur, and often. Despite any cognitive bias to the contrary, the world is not always just.

When other parents find out that our own child rejected us, they struggle to understand. *There must be a logical reason.* Otherwise, they are also at risk. Being around you may make them uncomfortable. Snubbing you saves them from fearing that their children could estrange them.

While I'm all for making known in our society the plague of adult children's estrangement, it isn't always in your best interests to speak out. When you're vulnerable and sensitive, it may not be wise to expend time and energy trying to convince people of the truth. Those who gossip or make you feel judged can hamper your confidence. A friend who raised her children with a stricter, or more lenient hand, may burden you (even unintentionally) with I-told-you-so thoughts.

While carrying on with life and keeping commitments is good advice for those suffering emotional trauma, grief, or loss, the advice isn't intended indiscriminately. Be selective. Limit your exposure as needed. As mothers, it's easy to imagine how we might protect a distressed child who has been through an emotional trauma. While a day or two off school might help, skipping an entire year would be detrimental. Imagine you're that child. Protect yourself. Even baby yourself for a time. But eventually, you'll need to take yourself by the hand as you would a child, and reintegrate. For now, be prepared for others' lack of understanding. Many mothers shared comments they called misinformed, ignorant, or of no help. Here's a sampling:

- "You must have said or done something to make him angry."
- "It's their loss. Good riddance."
- "You just have to get on with your life."
- "He may need you one day. Then he'll be back."
- "I'm sure it will blow over."
- "You raised your son right. This is just a phase."
- "You have other children. Consider yourself lucky."

Comments like these may be helpful in some situations, but they discount the emotional distress rejected parents experience. They also reveal how misunderstood estrangement by adult children is. People who haven't gone through this may relate it to their own experiences and equate estrangement to a misunderstanding, a stage that will pass, or a tiff with a clear-cut cause that can be fixed. These sorts of statements can make parents feel alone or feel guilty.

Soon after Dan's estrangement, I learned that when someone offered one of those statements, a simple "thank you" was expedient. Sometimes, people say hurtful things without meaning to. A "thank you" honors the person's good intentions (usually the case), and allows us to move on to something else.

Whenever I have felt judged, it helped me to remember that before Dan's estrangement, I couldn't have imagined this ever happening to me. In the throes of despair, faced with people's ignorance or uncaring words, it isn't easy to be so rational and giving. And I haven't always succeeded. In those rough moments, a silent prayer for strength and patience helped. You could also take a breath, imagine exhaling away the irritation, and politely change the subject. The reality is some people *will* be quick to make negative assumptions about you.

As mature adults, most of us have been in situations where we've had to move past irritation or others' lack of understanding. Draw from those experiences. Accept the awkwardness that may at times exist. Accept, too, that your feelings and sensitivity may be exacerbated by the depth of your loss. You may not like the situation, but get serious about accepting and working with it. Doing so helps you progress. And behaving in a calm, fair manner helps quell people's negative assumptions too.

Meg has stopped sharing about her son unless she's directly asked. "Most people are more than happy to leave it alone, even if it is sometimes the six-hundred-pound gorilla in the room!" Meg laughs. "The gorilla is shrinking. As the estrangement goes on, it loses weight. It's more like three hundred pounds these days." Maybe one day, the big gorilla will be a pocket-ape.

Making New Friends

Social connection is good for us, but meeting new people can be prickly for mothers whose children have rejected them. Meg has some ready answers. "If they ask about my family, I tell them I have a son and grand-daughter then change the subject back to them. They don't pry. Family questions are often just conversation starters anyway."

People like to talk about themselves. Ask questions. You may be surprised how easy changing the subject can be.

Some mothers choose a white lie for convenience, or even empowerment. One mother left a comment at RejectedParents.NET, saying that when she went in for surgery, she was asked if she had children. Already feeling vulnerable because of the medical procedure, replying with a simple "no," helped her feel strong. There was no son or daughter to drive her home, so why mislead the nurse and be forced to explain?

Here's another situation. When Esther and her husband retired to Florida, they had been estranged from their son for nine years. A few weeks after the move, Esther's husband died. Everyone Esther met there was new to her. Pretending she was childless seemed easiest.

"How could I explain something so humiliating to people who knew nothing about me?" Esther asks. "I know I was a good parent, but when George died, I contacted my son. He wasn't receptive, and it led me down a path of questioning reality all over again."

Unresolved conflict can give rise to a concept known as "innocent guilt," or guilt that is not based in fault or wrongdoing. Feelings of guilt lead to shame, which makes it difficult to tell new people about something so personal. A recent article in the *Journal of Applied Philosophy* examines the concept.[1] While they're still emotionally suffering, victims may feel guilt that arises from the conflict itself. Though innocent, they feel guilty, thus the term, "innocent guilt."

Parents of estranged adults know all too well the ongoing nature of suffering. Sadness, anger or other emotions can persist or spring up when we least expect them. What we experience as guilt may be a natural emotional reaction to the unresolved conflict.

When Esther contacted her son and was rebuffed by him again, her sense of guilt was re-triggered. She thought she was over that, but began going over his childhood again, and focusing on every little mistake. Esther explains, "If *I* still wondered what I did wrong, how could I expect a new friend not to wonder."

Not being forthcoming about her son eventually backfired. As a new friendship developed, Esther felt compelled to tell the whole truth. The earlier deception sometimes interfered with the relationship. Some assumed she hadn't told them about her son because she was at fault.

Since that time, Esther has made many new friends. She now chooses honesty "I do have a son. Unfortunately, he chooses not to have me in his life," she now explains. "Being truthful allows people to get close to the real me. Honesty requires trust, but isn't that what friendship is all about?"

Esther's question makes the point: If we don't trust people enough to let them in, we don't allow them the opportunity to show they care. In short, we don't let them be friends, and they can't provide us with friendly support. While some draw close, others may turn away. We can't let their behavior darken our outlook.

As Pam did, Esther met other estranged parents. Esther feels she can help, so is quick to share her insight and offer a kind word. "We can have a happy life," she says.

Like these women, I made a conscious decision to openly share my situation. Telling people was a breakthrough. It was like going from being a "vict*im*" to a "vict*or*." That empowering little word, "or," implies there's another choice. I chose something better—and you can too.

I knew being open wouldn't always go well, so tried putting myself in others' shoes as a way to prepare for any negative response. Because conversation often turns to family and children, opportunities quickly presented themselves.

At a professional meeting, when I shared my son's estrangement with a woman I'd just met, she immediately looked away and drew her arms up over her chest.

"I know," I empathized, leaning a little closer. "It must sound like I'm an abuser. But in doing research, I've discovered that the numbers of estranged adult children from loving families is on the rise."

To my surprise, my new friend unfolded her arms. "Well, that must be hard to talk about," she said.

Her comment made me laugh. "It used to be," I said. Owning the truth felt freeing. Accepting her initial judgment, then pushing past it to acknowledge her feelings and even guide her response, challenged my fears that nobody would understand.

Since then, talking about my situation has gotten easier. Still, not everybody is accepting. While I can understand judgment, and even empathize, I won't allow people to humiliate me.

Avoidance can reinforce feelings of shame or embarrassment, but sometimes taking yourself out of harm's way is the most self-compassionate solution. To illustrate, at a different table at that same professional meeting, the conversation circled back to children. I tried honesty again. This time, a new acquaintance grew suddenly cold—and remained so. If I see her again, I won't choose to sit by her. Doing so would only cause us both discomfort. Besides, in time, with continued proximity through those professional meetings, and with my efforts at polite acknowledgment and congeniality, maybe she'll come around.

In these cases, limiting contact honors you, and doesn't allow others to shame you. Creating healthy boundaries aligns your behavior with your positive view of yourself and your history as a caring parent.

Resources for Support

- MentalHealth.gov—Web guide with a variety of information and support, as well as how to find local assistance.

- MentalHealthAmerica.net—Comprehensive site for help, definitions, and treatment options.

- NAMI.org—Information from the National Alliance On Mental Illness with fact sheets and research.

- Local county offices (in your telephone directory or online) can direct you to services and support.

- Meetup.com—Site that matches people with local groups of all sorts.

- Ask your physician.

- For faith-based support, call places of worship or search the Web. Using a plus sign and phrases enclosed in quotation marks connects a spiritual discipline with estrangement. You may be surprised what pops up in your locale, so be creative with your searches. Examples:

- *"estranged parents"+Catholic+Pittsburgh*
- *"parents of estranged adult children"+Jewish+New York*
- *"estrangement"+Buddhist*
- *Yoga+"forgiveness"*

Ready Responses

Parents tell me they've become masters at changing the subject. In the lists below, you'll find that some of the examples do just that. Others are blatantly honest, or more like put-offs. Some parents expounded on their motivation or reasoning for the responses they shared, so I've included their offered explanations. Use the lines as is, or as idea-starters for your own ready responses.

For first meets when people ask if you have children/grandchildren:

- "I have two grown children. They're busy and career-minded. I'm hoping one day they'll give me more than kitties as grandbabies. What about you?"
- "Yes, but they live far away. How about you?"
- "I do, but I don't. It's a long complicated story. Believe me. You don't want to hear it."
- "No. No children."—*This mother explains:* "After so many years, I have no hope of reconciling, so for me, the statement is true."
- "Yes. I have grown sons. They don't want anything to do with me."— *This mother explains:* "It's brutally honest, but stops questions. Nobody wants to know the gory details. And I don't want to lie."
- "Yes, but we're not close."
- "I'm estranged from my son, but maybe one day he'll come around."— *This mother explains,* "The person will rarely ask me anything about my children again, so that takes care of it."

- "I do but we're estranged."—*This mother explains*, "It's sometimes awkward. But once in a while, the person is relieved, and tells me a similar story, or about some other heartache. It brings me closer to people quicker."

- "Yes, but there's not always a fairy tale ending. Our kids aren't close to us, but we wish them the best."

- "I have three children, but my oldest won't talk to me."—*This mother explains:* "This way, I'm telling the truth. Sometimes the person will ask what happened or say my daughter must be mad about something. In that case, I continue the honesty with 'yeah, but she won't tell me.' That's usually as far as the conversation goes."

When people know your child, but may or may not know of the estrangement:

- "Well, you know how busy things are with small children and working parents."

- "Thank you for asking about my girls. They're not ready to reach out. I'm moving on with my life, but I do have faith. The door is always open."

- "I prefer not to talk about it, but thank you."

- "She's doing fine. Thanks for asking."

- "The whole family has exploded. You don't want to know. . . ."

- "That's a difficult question. Here's the truth. . . ."—*This mother explains,* "Until I opened up, I didn't know some of the people I thought were a little weird or hard to get to know had estranged children. Once I shared, they did too. Some had been hurting alone for many years. I ended up helping them get something horrible off their chests, which made me feel better too."

- "She's fine, and her two-year-old daughter is a delight. How about yours?"—*This mother explains,* "If I know something specific, I will add that to ensure the subject changes. Something like, *'How's your son's baseball going?'*"

Faith Based Support

Adversity often draws people closer to the comfort of their faith, or motivates some to seek spiritual guidance for the first time. In the loving care of a like-minded congregation, they may feel especially safe. Dropping defenses and asking for others' prayers may even be encouraged, and help people heal. Others, however, haven't found help so easily, or have been emotionally hurt. In faith-based groups, expectations may be higher than in other support situations, making it especially hurtful if help and understanding don't come.

Daphne grew up attending what was then the only church in her small town in the Southwest. As a teenager there, she met the man who later became her husband. After college, they were married in the same church by the pastor whose sermons they had grown up listening to. People she'd known since babyhood gathered to celebrate the union, filling the worn wooden pews draped in white lace and flowers for the special day. When Daphne's two sons were born, they were welcomed into the church family and, for a time, were what Daphne calls "church babies." Congregants loved and spoiled them.

The town has grown over the years, sprawling toward neighboring communities where other churches, synagogues, a temple, and a mosque have sprung up. But Daphne and her husband stayed close to the center of their original town. Their sons grew up attending the same church.

"My oldest son, William, was always a little man," says Daphne. "He helped at every church function, delivered food to the poor, and played the lead role in the Christmas pageant even if it meant giving up his fun to practice every night for a month. William took a girl with Down Syndrome to the prom. That's the kind of kid he was."

William studied hard in college. When he entered medical school, church friends said things like, "We knew that boy would go far." Daphne was so proud. "But when William got his M.D., everything changed," she says. "He stopped calling home, and eventually told us not to bother him anymore." Daphne still doesn't understand why her son disowned his family.

Daphne and her husband endured some church gossip. People

speculated he might be gay and didn't want to tell his parents, or that he was negatively influenced in some way while he was away at college. "We forgive people for their talk," she says. "He was one of the church babies. They were proud of him, too. They're as puzzled as us."

Daphne's world was in tatters. "I carried on," she says. "But the fabric of our very lives was torn. And as the months passed without him changing his mind no matter how many times we tried to talk, we got discouraged. We were angry at God. How could He give us such a beautiful son then take him away?"

In their shame and anger, they stayed away from church. In hindsight, Daphne sees that they were insulating themselves from humiliation. At their younger son's urging, they spoke to their pastor. "I'm so glad we did," says Daphne. "He couldn't fully understand, of course. Who can really get it unless it's happened to them? But he tried. He has known us for so long. He knows we're not monsters."

With their pastor's encouragement, Daphne and her husband attempted to contact William again to try to resolve the conflict. When he wouldn't budge, the pastor helped them come to a point of acceptance.

"I now see that God didn't *cause* this to happen," says Daphne. "William is exercising his free will, as God allows us each to do. My husband and I supported William and loved him. We took out a loan on our home to pay for his education. We're not to blame, but we're hopeful one day he will come back to us. And we're comforted by our faith."

Now in their late sixties and estranged from William for many years, they're thankful their younger son remains close. They love his wife and enjoy their grandchildren. "Every once in a while I look at hospital news on the Internet and will see something about William," says Daphne. "He's a successful doctor, still helping people. We're thankful he's apparently happy. We'll never understand, but he's independent and well. We had something to do with that."

Occasionally, somebody at church will still ask about William. Daphne knows they mean well. "After all this time, it makes me feel good to know they still remember him."

While Daphne is glad they shared with church members and were supported, others don't feel as comfortable divulging what's happening in their lives. Celia, whose only daughter severed ties eight years ago, vividly remembers the fear that kept her from confiding in fellow worshippers at her Connecticut synagogue. "Jewish traditions include rituals that honor the family," says Celia. "I didn't know anyone else whose adult children were estranged." Feeling like an outsider among her spiritual family, three years passed before Celia finally approached her rabbi. He helped her to study families in the Torah, and look for parallels.

For Celia, the Genesis account of Joseph whose brothers left him to die, stained his coat with animal blood to convince their father he'd been attacked by an animal, and caused many years of estrangement, was particularly helpful. Not only does Joseph become successful, but the story ends with forgiveness and love. Celia found hope. At her rabbi's encouragement, she began to share her grief with others. "He reminded me that people are imperfect," Celia says. "And to forgive, just as Joseph did."

Celia is quick to add that forgiving doesn't automatically mean forgetting. "Joseph tested his brothers," she explains. "It wasn't until he knew they had changed that Joseph trusted them fully again. After so many years, that's how it would be with my daughter, too."

Not everyone who turns to a faith-based group for support has a positive experience. Estrangement is complex and can be confusing. Kathleen remembers feeling ostracized and disheartened. "I thought we had a great group of friends through the church, but when things became difficult for us, I quickly learned that it made them uncomfortable if I was too honest about what was going on in our family. I felt utterly alone and deserted by people I thought were our friends. People just quit calling, quit inviting or including us in social events."

Looking back, Kathleen speculates that people in the church were likely fearful. "Some people believe that if something this bad is happening to you or your family, then you are not walking closely with God, and Satan has gained a foothold in your life." While hurt by the lack of empathy and support from those she felt close to, Kathleen recognizes they are just people, too. Every church is unique. The stigma she experienced doesn't exist in all churches, and not even in those of the same faith. Her trust in God is still a big part of her life.

Kathleen's daughter has now been estranged for seven years. Her younger three children are in various stages of college or careers, and are doing fine. Relocating to a new town surrounded by mountains and natural beauty that, in Kathleen's eyes, reflect God's perfection, was a healthy decision. "I needed to move on and make a new life in order to heal," she says. "I'm focused on helping my children who still want me in their lives. This has been the best thing for us, as a family, to be able to move forward and continue to experience joy."

Sometimes, spiritual help comes from unexpected places. Earlier, we met Theresa, whose only daughter, sandwiched between four sons, believes Theresa loved her brothers more. Theresa attends mass regularly, but she didn't seek support through her church. She found comfort in a weekly women's Bible study at a nearby Protestant church. The women there have grown close. Theresa prays for each of her children daily, and says, "You have to find help where it feels right for you. And you'd be surprised how many people are going through family breakups."

Recall Georgia, whose two daughters' sibling rivalry led to estrangement. Georgia believes there's a divine purpose working in her life. Though heartbroken, she looked for that purpose. Georgia has found meaning in her volunteer work with single mothers, which she sees as a sort of calling. The young women and their babies have filled a void in her life, and she has done the same for them. Other than her daughters' petty arguments, she doesn't understand why they have abandoned her. But she has accepted it, and believes her work with the young mothers is somehow related, or even meant to be. This gives her peace.

Like Georgia, many mothers speak of acceptance as part of healing. The idea can have spiritual roots. Through her secular work, Celia had the opportunity to sit in on a Buddhist lunch group. "They talked about accepting what is," she says. "You acknowledge and admit, then find a way to live your life anyway, or even better. It's about detaching enough that you observe, even observe yourself. That way you can take responsibility for your response." Celia sees the Buddhist way as complementary and similar to her faith, and says, "Acceptance makes getting to forgiveness and hope even easier."

If you're a person of faith, the teachings can empower you. In the Christian faith, for instance, the Bible is full of people whose lives took sudden turns—yet they overcame their troubles, and lived on to do great things. So can you. Spiritual *practices* also help. Prayer, yoga or meditation can lower stress, anxiety, irritability, and depression.[2]

Whether or not you currently belong to a religious group or are spiritual in your own way, I hope these mothers' stories will help you find the support you need. Theresa's words bear repeating: "You have to find help where it feels right for you."

Suggested Reading

It's A Meaningful Life: It Just Takes Practice, by Bo Lozoff. A variety of spiritual practices mingle with the author's experiences in an enlightening mosaic that guides readers toward meaning in their everyday lives.

An Empowering View

We are social creatures. Study after study confirms that people who are socially connected are healthier, happier, and live longer. Even a single trusting relationship can positively affect your life. Good friendships are worth the effort. But be aware of "support" that pigeonholes you as a victim, or encourages you to wallow in self-pity. Helpful, quality support empowers.

When Meg's friend reminded her she was a strong woman who had weathered many storms in her life, Meg felt more like her old self, and confident she could get through this heartache too. Likewise, when you reach out for help either privately or in a group, make sure the "support" doesn't enable self-pity, delay healing, or stigmatize you.

One mother who answered my survey likes the idea of online support groups, but has found them limiting. "Some are nothing more than 'bitch-and-stitch' forums," she says. "The group becomes a bunch of poor, pitiful parents whose children left them. And judging from some of the long-term members who regularly relive the drama and pain, you can get the idea that a pitiful rejected parent is what you'll *always* be."

How we see ourselves is important, and may help—or hinder—our recovery. Studies have shown that people's opinion of themselves and which groups they identify with influences behavior. In a Harvard University study, researchers found that when Asian women were reminded of their gender, and the stereotype that women aren't as good at math, their performance on math tests was poor. On the other hand, Asian women reminded of the stereotype that Asians are good at math, performed well.[3]

See yourself as strong. You can buck the stereotype of the "pitiful rejected parent." Rather than wallowing, stuck, and at the mercy of our adult children's decisions whether or not to return to us, let's empower ourselves. Let's be part of a new stereotype: parents who, though rejected, purposefully shape our lives and reclaim our happiness.

Early into Dan's estrangement, I imagined how things might be if he returned. My thoughts went to how he might feel if he found me wallowing in self-pity, a crying old woman, stuck in the emotional mire of losing him. The last thing I would want is for him to feel responsible for ruining his mother's life. And if he had purposely set out to do so, I wasn't about to give him the satisfaction. But mostly, I knew I must take care of myself. And in doing that, I would set the example I have always striven to set, as an optimistic person who succeeds despite struggles.

Ask yourself: *If at some point we truly reconcile and put this behind us, how do I want my child to find me living my life?* Or perhaps even better: *A year from now, how do I want myself and my life to look?*

Be strong. Step forward. Live.

Depression and Guilt

If you have ever suffered from depression, differences in how your brain works may make you more susceptible to guilt than a person who has never been depressed.

In 2012 research, two groups of people were studied: those who had previously suffered from depression, and those who had not. The brains of those who had previously suffered from depression showed communication gaps, while those in the other group did not.

The subgenual cingulated cortex and an adjacent region that's been associated with guilt, together known as the SCSR, communicates with the anterior temporal lobe, which is active during thoughts about morals. In the study, functional magnetic resonance imaging (fMRI) revealed that in individuals who had never been depressed, both regions were active during thoughts about guilt. However, in those who had previously suffered depression, the SCSR and anterior temporal lobe did not sync. Participants with the greatest tendency to blame themselves for everything showed the largest gaps in this communication path.

The two brain regions studied are known to be influenced by learning, which offers hope. Researchers believe this indicates that people who routinely self-blame could benefit from cognitive or talk therapy, in which they can learn new thinking patterns to replace unhealthy ones. If you suffer from intrusive feelings of guilt that interfere with your well-being, you may benefit from seeking help from a professional specializing in these types of therapy.[4]

At Your Best

Reflect on how you've successfully dealt with problems in the past. Reliving those satisfying moments can break a habit of self-blame or self-pity, and trigger more positive feelings about the future. In fact, writing about a time when you were at your best, and then reflecting on the memory daily for a week, has been shown to increase well-being.[5]

After reading through the next few paragraphs, use the lines to describe you at your very best. Perhaps you are a sunny person, even in times of trouble. Or you prioritize what's important, and focus on the present moment. Maybe you are caring and careful of how your speech and actions affect others. Maybe people or pets are drawn to you. Maybe you can make anything grow, and see things from every possible side.

In your written description, remember a time when you were at your best, or create a story in which you use your strengths. Perhaps imagine you're stranded on an island. You don't waste a moment crying. You befriend island natives, wow them with magic tricks, and gain their trust. Your attention to detail allows you to quickly learn their survival skills, and you lead the stranded group off the island without a hitch.

In my work as a life coach, some clients wrote poems to describe themselves at their best. Others made up songs, hymns, or created a simple list. Descriptions ran the gamut. The exercise works well when you do what feels right to you.

Describing yourself at your best, in writing, can reconnect you with your values, your strengths, and your accomplishments, and provide you with bolstering words that you can read through on another day. Remembering who you are at your best will boost your self-respect, and spur your interest and energy into activities you enjoy and do well.

Me at my best: _____

_____

_____

_____

_____

_____

_____

_____

The next logical step is to think about using your best self to conquer the heartache and prevail in your life. Reflect on what you've written about yourself.

Now, concentrating on your strengths, imagine a year has passed. Enter the future now, imagine your best self, and describe what you see. What are you doing with yourself and your life? Are you happy? Have you moved ahead? Do you feel free? Using the lines on the next page, write about it now.

One year from now—me at my best: _____

_____

_____

_____

_____

_____

_____

_____

_____

_____

CHAPTER FOUR

Ready, Set, Prepare

When a loved one dies, there's a funeral, a memorial that celebrates the person's life. We're typically not embarrassed to tell others we've lost someone we loved. And helpful social terms—widow, orphan, survivor, bereaved—are instantly recognized, and help others to empathize. Grief after a death is expected. For parents of estranged adult children, the loss is similar, but others don't recognize the depth of their emotional pain, which may persist.

Often, the future includes some contact with the child due to family commitments or practical matters. The contact rekindles parents' hopes that then bring disappointment. Or parents may suffer renewed anxiety and sorrow during important events, when an estranged child's physical absence may be so keenly felt that her psychological presence looms. Parents try to mourn, but say they can't achieve closure. They hold onto hope, but have no control.

Despite the uncertainty of what's ahead, you can prepare for the ups and downs. Here, you'll discover ways to prepare, cope, and thrive.

How Has Estrangement Changed You?

Faced with the pain of an adult child's rejection, even moms who pride themselves on their ability to calmly assess situations and take necessary action can feel as if they've stepped into someone else's skin.

During the first holiday season, shortly after my son's departure from our family, I still looked like the capable person I have always been. Inside though, my emotions seethed. My self-worth had crumbled. And what's worse, I didn't recognize what was happening to me. By the second week of December, while the Earth outside stilled into winter's quiet, I scurried about, determined to keep the family's spirits bright. I cleaned, cooked, and shopped. I raced around, creating a Christmas to remember—and perhaps to forget. My heart wasn't full in it.

Looking back, I can see there was an anxious pitch to my behavior, as if making everything picture perfect for the holiday would make *me* picture perfect—and prove to myself and others that I really was a good mom.

In the silence of night after Christmas was done, I wasn't satisfied or content. I remember lying in my bed in the dark and wondering: *Did I do enough?* I imagined myself old and alone. *Is that how I'll end up?*

My eyes opened in the darkness. No matter how silly and self-indulgent, the thought rang true. I had told myself my holiday frenzy was normal, but fear was at the root. Fear had me working my fingers to the bone to make the best holiday ever, to hang onto my remaining family.

As midnight fell, and the timed on-and-off Christmas lights faded, I imagined Dan spending the holidays with his new family. Had he thought of us? Had his new mother's food been as tasty as mine? Had her gifts been as heartfelt? Dan's wife had once told me that her mother goes all out for the holidays. That she brings out ornaments that commemorate her children's births, and every year afterward. That she decorates with trains, makes gingerbread houses, and sets up miniature towns with carousels and churches and thousands of lights. After Christmas, she packs everything neatly away, ready for the next season an entire year away.

Then there's me, with some decorations tucked away to spots so "safe" I may not find them. At our house, as late as summer, you might see the odd Christmas candle still on the fireplace mantle where a ceramic snowman has a permanent place.

I had only been to her house once, right after her daughter moved in with Dan. Every inch of her wall space was filled with framed mementos. Portraits memorialize her family throughout the years. Snapshots captured perfect poses and smiling perfection. I remembered her yard with its squared off hedge, her flawless lawn, and the statue cranes posed to greet guests as they meandered up the flower-lined walk. Her home was perfect. Was that the atmosphere I'd been trying to create?

Tears welled, and I felt powerless. Dan had made choices. No matter how hard I worked, I couldn't change that. No matter how wonderful our Christmas had seemed, no one in my family expected me to wear myself out providing it. I enjoyed all the cooking and shopping, but only to a point. This year, I had gone too far.

That night in the darkness, I realized that all the presents and favorite foods in the world wouldn't hold the rest of my family together. We were individuals. We had never been about things, about decorations, or a façade presented to the outside world. We were imperfect and real. So, why had I gone so far?

Dan may not be physically near, but psychologically, he was always present. Meanwhile, I'd been absent. Focused on my failings, I'd been so busy proving myself that I'd missed the point. I hadn't enjoyed the holidays or my family much at all. As often happens in the aftermath of rejection, I'd experienced a sort of rebound effect, stretching to fill a void, to recapture what had been lost, and to protect the future from uncertainty.

Especially when rejection lacks a definitive cause, studies show that women will work extra hard to recapture a sense of belonging. When someone you've been so very close to and expected would share your life forever walks away, your foundation crumbles. *All* relationships then look uncertain. Women will exert all sorts of effort in a struggle to preserve those relationships and keep them stable.[1] Being aware of that tendency is important.

Consider how you have changed since your child abandoned you. What are *you* doing differently? Perhaps you're rushing about, quashing your pain behind a façade of perfection. Or like Meg in the last chapter, maybe you're isolating yourself, leery of socializing because you're embarrassed, and afraid of judgment. Perhaps you're protecting yourself by not getting close to anyone. After all, if your own child could desert you, whom can you possibly trust?

Take a conscious look at your thoughts, feelings, and behavior. What do you do since your child's rejection that you didn't do before? What have you stopped doing? How do you interact differently? Or don't you interact at all? What fears exist? What thoughts repeatedly come to mind that you previously wouldn't have harbored?

Whether you are newly estranged, or have suffered through years of estrangement, the experience has changed you. Whether outwardly, inwardly, or a combination of both, you've been affected.

In the following exercise, you will have the opportunity to take stock of those changes. Knowledge is power as the saying goes, but what we do with knowledge is where real power lies. The next exercise will move you toward harnessing that sort of power.

✈Take Stock

Take a few moments (or even a few days), to consider how the estrangement has affected you—your life, your relationships, your mood, your habits. Consider these effects in writing. You can use the space in the boxes here, or make headings on paper and expand your thoughts.

You may decide to read through and ponder the questions without writing. But your notes will be useful to you as you continue forward in the book. Taking the time to examine what's going on in your life will provide awareness (knowledge) and insight that can help you take positive action (power). For now, simply take stock of the effects by recording them. Don't worry about getting too meticulous, but be as detailed as feels right. You're becoming more aware, and forming a solid foundation for positive action toward solutions.

Let's Begin. Use the categories listed to reflect on your life since your child has been estranged. *How do you feel? What is missing? What are you doing well? How can you improve?* The headings are in no particular order. If one area feels easier than another, feel free to work in the order that best suits you. Be honest. Don't censor yourself.

Avoid the urge to answer as you would have before the estrangement, or how you'd like to be. Your candid reflections help you examine your life as it stands right now. Later, your notes will help you create achievable goals to move forward. For now, quickly jot down ideas that might be of help to you.

At the end, there's an optional section where you can add an additional area you choose, such as your physical environment or career.

Emotional Well-Being/Happiness: *How has the estrangement affected your attitude and happiness?*

What can you do to feel better?

Health & Fitness: *Since the estrangement began, has your health & fitness level declined? How?*

In what ways can you take better care of yourself?

Friends, Family and Social Connection: *Since the estrangement, have you neglected, lost, or maintained relationships and social commitments?*

How can you improve in this area?

Personal Growth/Dreams: *Since the estrangement, have you given up something important to you? How has the estrangement affected your outlook?*

How can you begin to make changes for the better?

Leisure & Fun: *Since the estrangement, do you still have fun and enjoy leisure time?*

How can you do more to enjoy yourself?

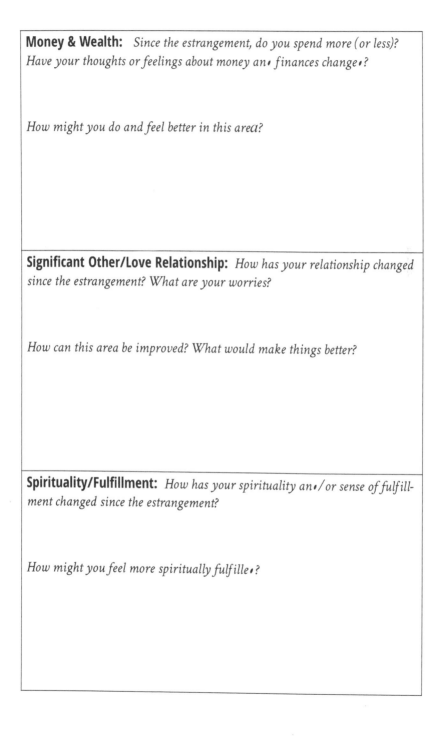

Money & Wealth: *Since the estrangement, do you spend more (or less)? Have your thoughts or feelings about money and finances changed?*

How might you do and feel better in this area?

Significant Other/Love Relationship: *How has your relationship changed since the estrangement? What are your worries?*

How can this area be improved? What would make things better?

Spirituality/Fulfillment: *How has your spirituality and/or sense of fulfillment changed since the estrangement?*

How might you feel more spiritually fulfilled?

Self-Image/Self-Esteem: *Since the estrangement, has your self-esteem/ self-image changed? What is different? Why?*

What can you do to feel better about yourself?

Optional: *Add an area you define.*

The *Take Stock* exercise is intended to create a foundation for you to build upon later. We'll return to your notes in Chapter Nine.

The Pain of Hope

When my son first disowned us, he was living in a small rental house we own in the historic district of our nearby city. We had offered him the alley cottage because it seemed like the right thing to do. After a year-long period during which Dan had dropped his internship and lacked direction, he had regained the steady footing we had always known him to have. Dating the young woman he later married had seemed to spur him forward, and we were glad she'd come along. We were proud of

Dan. Offering the rental with its gated privacy where bougainvillea spills a bright flame along the fence seemed a natural way to express our love. Dan had been working steadily again for several months. We trusted him.

We discounted the rent, and were excited that Dan was the first person to move into the property since we'd remodeled and upgraded its kitchen. Soon, his girlfriend moved in with him, and we were happy for them. About a year later, when Dan rejected us, what had begun as an extension of our love and trust quickly disintegrated to a tense business arrangement.

Previously, Dan paying his rent meant we'd share a friendly visit or a meal. Suddenly, he would drop the rent in our mailbox at the end of our long driveway then text to tell me it was there. I had asked him to hand it to me personally, hoping we could talk, but he refused.

On one of those rent days, I was sandwiched between people in the bank line at the grocery store, and I spotted Dan a few feet away. He was paying at the food cashier, in my direct line of sight. Moments later, pushing his cart with bagged goods, he passed right by me without a word.

Humiliated and angry, I drove home in a daze. Once there, I crumpled on my bedroom floor, a sobbing heap. Then I heard his car. Swiping my eyes, I rushed outdoors, but he was already backing away. As he raced off, the whine of his car engine split the air. The rent was in the mail box.

I sent a text: *The next time you pass your mother in the grocery store, you could speak.*

He texted back: *I didn't see you.*

At the time, I didn't pursue the conversation further, but I also didn't believe him. How could you walk right past your mother, a woman you had seen every day for more than 20 years, and not see her? Especially when I saw *him* everywhere, the way people grieving a loved one who has died often say they do. A pair of broad shoulders, sandy hair, a familiar stance . . . the angle of a chin in profile at the traffic light, and I would do a double take, often, and everywhere.

My attitude about that day in the grocery store has since changed. I suppose I've softened. The truth is, I didn't jump out of line and run to greet Dan either. My heart had leapt to my throat. And as he'd neared, I looked away, uncertain. Even if he did see me, maybe he had felt as awkward as I had.

Days later, Dan sent a text giving notice for a mid-month move-out. We were sad but relieved. We prorated the rent, and asked Dan if he would meet us with the keys. When he agreed, we were elated. Other than the grocery store sighting, we hadn't seen him for 11 weeks.

When that morning finally arrived, I remember driving up the alley with my hopes in flight. But the reunion I imagined ending with hugs, didn't take place. Instead, my husband parked the car and, along with another one of our three sons, we got out. Feeling uneasy and awkward, we approached our Dan. He stood near the porch where the entry and security doors gaped open.

He gestured to the house. "I lost the key," he said, his eyes hidden behind dark glasses. Even so, I could see that his face looked lined, as if he hadn't slept. Sunlight glinted at the red-blonde stubble on his firm square jaw, and I was struck by how handsome he was. I wanted to hug him, but defiance fenced him in. His rigid posture warded me off.

From there, my hopes evaporated. The little rental house was in disarray. There were holes in the walls. A beat-up dresser, an abandoned bed, an old television, and ratty couches were left for us to haul away. The yard was unkempt. The peach, lemon and fig trees looked shriveled and dry. Dan told us he had also lost the keys to a classic truck we had given him to use. It stood with the hood up, half primer gray, half chipped white paint as if abandoned mid-project. Weeds grew up all around.

The way the place had deteriorated reminded me of a phone call with Dan a few months earlier. He had referred to the location of the little rental house we'd been proud to acquire in this quaint historic neighborhood as "the slums."

Maybe I should have overlooked the condition of things, but my anger flared. All I could see was the work that lay ahead. At a time when my husband's business had taken a nosedive like so many others in the dismal economy of the time, we couldn't let the house sit empty for long. We needed renters to help pay the mortgage, but getting the house in shape for new inhabitants would take time.

I had planned to hug Dan and tell him how much we missed him. Instead, I stated the obvious, "We're expected to clean up all your messes."

Dan didn't miss a beat. "I never signed anything."

His words stung. And seconds later he was brushing past us, his shoulders square and solid as he walked away. I called after him in frustration, my voice cracking in the dry air of that mid-September day. "I want you to know," I said, stepping forward as he opened his car door. "I'm going to cry every day for the rest of my life." And then he was gone, my hopes for a tearful reunion dashed.

These disappointments were firsts in a series of deflated hopes that I now know are common. The cycling of hope and pain is often a major part of the ongoing trauma mothers experience after an adult child's estrangement. Unfinished business like our rental arrangement with Dan may make interaction inevitable. Or, our children may contact us when we're least expecting them to, and bring us hope. Or, they open wounds we thought were finally healing. The simple passage of time, the holidays, family events, and even tragedies, can bring up new dilemmas and ongoing pain.

Vicky, a divorced mother of three, let her oldest daughter, Danielle, live in her basement to save money during graduate school. They had previously had a good relationship. Then Danielle began avoiding Vicky, who describes the estrangement as an emotional roller coaster.

"I assumed her despondency had to do with stress," Vicky explains. "Or perhaps she felt bad having to lean on her mother." Danielle had divorced, and was starting over. So, like many parents do, Vicky had helped out with housing.

The trouble between them escalated after Danielle received her Master's degree, went to work for a university, and moved out. "She left the basement a mess," says Vicky. "She hadn't told me about a leak in the bathroom, so there was mold. Extensive repairs took a lot of my savings." Vicky also added a kitchenette and a separate entrance. Then she got a paying renter. "That's when Danielle flew off the handle," says Vicky. "She was mad I hadn't added a kitchen for her, and claimed I'd been chomping at the bit the last six years to get her out."

Stunned, Vicky assured her daughter she'd been happy to help, but now needed rent money. She'd lost her job and was only working part time while supporting Danielle through graduate school.

Soon after Danielle's blow-up, Vicky's other children planned a party for her sixty-first birthday. Danielle volunteered to bring the cake, but never showed up. Instead, she sent a text telling her mother she no longer wanted to see her. "There I was, waiting in my front room with pink paper streamers strung all around. Danielle's siblings were there, a few neighbors, and even my pastor's wife. Then I got the text."

Vicky tried to call, but Danielle wouldn't answer. Her brother and sister also phoned, but Danielle ignored their calls. Over the next several weeks, they tried to see her in person, but she refused to open her door. She also blocked them all on Facebook. "We thought about showing up at her work," says Vicky. "But we didn't want to embarrass her in her new job. Besides, she'd made herself clear. We had no choice but to accept her decision."

Months later, Vicky received another text from Danielle. When she read the words, "I love you, Mom," her heart leapt with joy. Vicky immediately texted back, "I love you too." But Danielle didn't reply, so Vicky texted again. "For two days, I kept my phone in hand," says Vicky. "And finally, Danielle sent another text . . . *Was just thinking of you, and always hope you're well.*" Vicky remembers feeling angry then. "If she was always hoping I was well, would she leave me hanging for two days?" Vicky swallowed her irritation and texted a single word: *Thanks.*

A week later, Vicky received another text, this time asking for childhood vaccination records. "She gave me a post office box where I could mail them, and of course, I did," says Vicky. "I also drove by her house a week later, and saw that it was empty. She'd moved away."

Since that first exchange six months after Vicky's birthday, a pattern formed. "She'll text me an 'I love you,' lure me into a little conversation, then a few days later ask for something," explains Vicky. "Sometimes it's money, sometimes it's something else. Once, she asked if I could get the antique jewelry my mother had left her from the safe deposit box and leave it with her friend."

Each time her daughter contacted her, Vicky's hope surged. "I was in denial for years. It's hard to accept that you raised such a self-serving person, but eventually, you can't deny the truth."

Vicky refers to the woman she calls her "old self" as gullible. "Danielle played me for a fool. She still contacts me right before her birthday, talks about growing older and hoping one day we can reconcile. I used to wonder, *what in the world?* It wasn't *me* who cut *her* off. But for four of those birthdays, I actually sent her money and gifts." Vicky adds, "That's not the new me. My trust is forever changed."

Now estranged for nine years, Vicky will soon celebrate her seventieth birthday. "I've given up hope of reconciling," she says. "And I've told my younger son and daughter the gift I'd like is a new smart phone with a brand new number." Vicky sees time moving ever faster. "How many years do I have left?" she asks. "If I could tell another mother just one thing, it would be to get on with her own life. If a daughter or son comes back, so be it. If not, you haven't wasted your life waiting."

Just as Vicky mailed her daughter's vaccination records, when my son contacted me about his, I sent them along. The shock of an adult child's abandonment can leave self-esteem in tatters. Choosing to behave like a mature adult strengthens you, and helps you reclaim self-confidence and maintain your self-respect. Helping Dan in such a basic way was the only response that lived up to my old self-image as a good mother. I had decided early on that when it came to items such as phone messages and mail that arrived for him, or documents he needed to get on with his life, my humiliation, anger or hurt—my ego—wouldn't get in my way (or his).

In Chapter One, I shared one of my own and others' impulsive acts in the wake of shock that led to consequences or regret. Here, I offer the alternative. A slower course allows you to act with dignity, wisdom, and from a place of strength.

Like a picked-at scab, wounds that are opened and reopened don't quickly heal. That's why I urge you to plan ahead. Making choices now about how you'll handle potential contact will help you act wisely, hold onto self-respect, and avoid snap decisions that spring from anger and pain. Reflect on how you handled previous contact or requests. Could you have done something better to maintain your integrity and support your well-being? Imagine how you might best handle future situations.

Many years ago, I had trouble saying no to people's requests. Knowing their needs made me want to help—and clouded my judgment about how much energy and time I could devote. That's when I learned that stalling gave me time to make sound decisions. If your child contacts you with a request, give yourself a buffer of time to tend to your emotions, and then provide a wise response.

If your son or daughter texts, distance is built in. While delaying your response by days or weeks may come across as insensitive or purposely dismissive, a few hours are reasonable. If your child calls directly, you still have choices. You can tell your child you'll have to call them back or that you'll have to see if you can find whatever it is they want. Make some other excuse if you feel the need. As was said in Chapter One, don't be hasty. Give yourself the gift of time. Allow yourself the distance you need to maintain your integrity and self-respect. Behaving in a manner that allows you to move forward without regret helps you recover more quickly from any renewed pain.

Some mothers say their adult children surface around the holidays, and then disappear again. Many of these parents eventually identify the behavior as manipulative rather than cause for hope, and refuse to participate. For mothers who have grandchildren, such a decision can be much more complex. Nurturing those tenuous relationships with their innocent grandchildren can be particularly trying and bittersweet.

In this book's opening pages, we met Evelyn, whose son cut all contact for nearly a year, and then brought her grandsons over for Christmas. She had missed them very much, and was thrilled to visit with them. But when they left, she stood waving for so long that her tears froze. She had no idea when, or even if, she would see them again.

Evelyn attempted to make contact a couple of times the following year, but her son and daughter-in-law were not receptive. She sent the boys birthday gifts, and her son mailed them back. Even so, before

Christmas, he called to tell her they would come. Evelyn was surprised, but agreed. Using holiday paper, she rewrapped the returned birthday presents she had saved, and then even purchased more gifts. The visit lasted only a few hours, but Evelyn loved seeing her grandsons. They came the next two Christmases, and the visits were much the same.

Evelyn hates what she calls the "dishonesty" of their relationship, but is glad to see the boys. Still, each year, the emotional distance between them grows. This past Christmas, she also gave her grandsons their birthday presents. "I told them if I'd seen them on their birthdays, I'd have given them to them then," says Evelyn. Then her son shot her a disapproving look, so she didn't say more. "Who knows what he'll do now," she wonders. "Come again next Christmas, or not?" She hopes the holiday visits will continue. "If I can keep a thread of connection, maybe one day the boys will be old enough to understand what's happening. Maybe they'll come see me when they're adults."

Evelyn loves her grandsons. She isn't ready to call it quits, but with only short yearly visits to try and forge a bond, she suffers no illusions either. Evelyn's hope may not pay off.

In Chapter Two, we met Sondra. Her granddaughters are old enough now to understand that their father is the only one who doesn't speak to their "Gran." She enjoys a good relationship with them despite her son's disdain for her. But Sondra is one of the luckier ones.

Remember Ruby, whose estranged son asked her to take a road trip with him, and then immediately turned the radio to Howard Stern? For many years, Ruby and her husband mailed gifts for every grandchild's birthday. Despite no responses, and failed attempts throughout the year to arrange time with the grandchildren, Ruby sent cards and letters, trying to stay present in their lives. For many Christmases, Ruby and her husband went along with their son's idea of a yearly visit. They agreed to meet him at a fast food restaurant to see the grandchildren and present them with holiday gifts in person.

Two Christmases ago, they realized their efforts were a losing battle. Already burdened by her husband's recent diagnosis with prostate cancer, the visit was hurtful, and added to their stress. When Ruby slipped and fell in the parking lot, her son and his wife laughed at her. Following their example, the older grandchildren snickered. Then, in the restaurant, the grandchildren hid her cane in the adjacent booth as a joke.

After later discussion, Ruby and her husband decided they could no longer suffer their son's abuse. Enough was enough. This past year, when their son called the day before Christmas to say they could meet for the grandkids' gifts, Ruby told him that would no longer work for them. When she hung up the phone, she cried. Not so much for sadness, but more from relief. Strapped into an emotional roller coaster for so many years, she finally felt free.

Some may judge Ruby for disengaging. Others may take Evelyn for a fool. However, situations of estranged adult children take many forms. Likewise, the people within those situations are unique. Handling these difficult relationships while retaining our dignity and self-respect is a fine line of balance each of us must walk. Despite the common ground of estrangement, each situation is unique. It's best not to judge. However, looking at others' situations may assist you in better analyzing your own, and taking action to support yourself.

As you read about these women, did you feel strong emotions? How do those feelings relate to your own situation? Keep your own estrangement in mind as you contemplate the questions below.

Can you identify with Vicky's shock when the daughter she supported through graduate school turned on her? How about her surging hope each time her daughter called? Do you recognize yourself in her story? Perhaps, as her daughter continued to disappoint her, you found yourself pitying Vicky. Did you cheer her eventual decision to disengage? What does Vicky's story tell you about your own?

When you read about Evelyn and Ruby, were you angry on their behalf? Did strong words and emotions come to mind? If Evelyn saw her son and his wife's behavior as "abuse," do you think she might change her own actions? If you were Evelyn, would you do more to stand up to your son? He won't allow her to take photos. Would you risk installing a hidden nanny cam to record your grandsons' Christmas visits as Evelyn's friends suggested she do? What else might you say or do?

For many years, Ruby and her husband were always giving. Eventually, they identified their son's behavior as a form of abuse, and realized their grandchildren were following suit. Because of her husband's illness, Ruby also experienced the sense that time was fleeting, and they'd wasted too much of it. How does your own situation relate?

Ambivalence often goes with uncertainty, but no decision you make today must forever bind you. Plan ahead, but remain open. You can take one holiday, one birthday, or one big bit of family news at a time. Not sending gifts one year doesn't mean you can never send gifts again. Reaching out for holidays and birthdays this year, does not mean you're required to reach out the next.

After Christmas, Evelyn knows she'll feel down. She lets herself cry some. Then she makes a practice of remembering the good moments they shared. She writes down what her grandsons talked about, and records their cute sayings. Doing so helps her memorize the boys' faces as they said the words.

Then, on New Year's Day, Evelyn shifts gears and moves on. She hangs new calendars with feel-good sayings, and starts fresh with a new set of goals. "I can't control my son's behavior," says Evelyn. "But I always say a prayer for his family at the start of the year. And I *will* control what I can . . . myself, my moods, and my life."

For now, Evelyn has come to accept what she calls her "lot in life," and fosters a grateful attitude. She will reevaluate as time passes. Ruby made a decision that supports herself and her husband, who is recovering. They hope he's soon well enough to take the vacation they put off for years. Like Vicky, who is getting a new phone number, Ruby's change of heart is an example of how our feelings can evolve. Decisions we at one time believed in may no longer fit. These women like so many mothers, recognize that throughout the years, we worked hard to nurture our babies, reassure our toddlers, guide our children, support our teens, and encourage our young adults. Even in estrangement, when we maintain our integrity and behave as mature adults, we can have the satisfaction of knowing we've done, and are doing, our best.

Pause and Reflect

- Each of us must decide what's best for us.

- Decisions are not set in stone.

- Our feelings may evolve.

- Our best is good enough.

- We have the right to take care of ourselves.

- We deserve to be happy.

Life Can Bring Dilemmas

I often hear from parents who face a choice to acknowledge a birthday, a wedding, or some other big event, or simply let it pass without comment. Sometimes sad or tragic events cause a parent to consider communicating with an estranged child, even if they haven't spoken in many years. Extended family may tell of a child's illness or divorce. Perhaps there's a death in the family, or some other event. Let's look in on four mothers' lives, and learn from their choices.

Mother of one son, Petra, recently confided that a family member had told her about her only grandchild's Christening. She hasn't spoken to her son for more than a year, but the baby's Christening weighed on her heart. "The mom in me says to send a gift," Petra says. "My faith is important to me, and I'm pleased my son is honoring tradition. But I doubt he'll reply. Why set myself up for disappointment?"

Then there's Andrea, whose son was getting married. She'd already sent a generous check when she heard he was engaged. She was not invited to his wedding. Still, Andrea's moral compass told her she should send him a congratulatory note on the day of his marriage.

In another example, Lauren remembers watching TV news that showed hurricanes very close to the faraway location where her daughter had moved. Lauren felt cornered. They hadn't spoken in two years. "After all the hurt she had put me through, her silence was actually a reprieve," Lauren admits. But when the hurricanes hit her area, Lauren imagined her daughter caught in one, and hurt or even killed. Lauren wondered, "What would people think if her own mother didn't call to inquire about her?" Lauren worried about opening old wounds, but was also concerned what message *not* calling might send. Would her daughter think she didn't care enough to call?

Lauren did try to phone, but was relieved when the calls wouldn't go through. "I went ahead and texted too, and after a couple of weeks, my daughter sent a return text saying she was fine. I sent a quick reply that I was glad. And then I held my breath, wondering if she'd text back again."

When no more texts or calls arrived, a familiar agony dragged at Lauren. After so much hurt and pain, she hadn't really been ready for her daughter to make further contact. But she'd also gotten her hopes up. Lauren quickly reminded herself of the real reason she'd reached out: "To make sure my daughter was safe."

In Chapter Three, we met Pam. She struggled when her daughter's husband passed away. "I felt for her," says Pam. "And even though she'd hurt me so much, I imagined she might need her mother's support."

Petra, Andrea, Lauren, and Pam faced a dilemma that's shared at some point by a great many parents: What is the *right* thing to do, when either choice can backfire?

Parents whose children have been ungrateful, cold, or vicious often feel conflicted. Rather than letting your emotions get the better of you, ask yourself a few pointed questions. Your answers can help you make decisions you can live with later.

Lauren solved her dilemma after the hurricanes in her daughter's region by answering these two questions:

- "If something happened to my daughter, can I live with people thinking I didn't care enough to call?"

- "Can I live with my daughter thinking I didn't care?"

Lauren's answer to both questions was, "No." She explains, "There's still a tiny piece of me that hopes for reconciliation someday. I think calling her when those hurricanes hit let my daughter know this."

Pam had similar feelings when her daughter's husband passed away. Would her daughter view a phone call as intruding? Or, if she didn't reach out, would her daughter think she didn't care? Pam ended up sending a card with a short note. Her daughter didn't respond, but Pam felt better for expressing concern.

As a life coach, I often ask questions to help clients clarify their feelings, make decisions, and move confidently forward. Lauren and Pam's questions were helpful ones. Here are a few more for you to use as is or tailor for your own circumstances:

- If I call, text, or send a gift, and my child doesn't respond, will his failure to reply hurt me?

- If I don't call, text, or send a gift, will I worry that I should have?

- Which is worse?

- Will I be able to live with myself if I don't do the "right" thing?

- What really is the "right" thing to do? And is my view based on fear, or what I truly believe or feel is "right"?

You can benefit from fully considering your situation and examining your feelings. If guilt comes up, re-read the discussion about "innocent guilt" in Chapter Three (Under the heading, *Making New Friends*).

Lauren had worried what other people might think. While allowing others' possible opinions to rule our lives isn't healthy, being honest about concerns that may influence our decision-making enlightens us.

Andrea's thoughts boiled down to worrying that her son hadn't told his fiancée's family the truth about the reasons behind their estrangement, and had blamed her. Andrea realized her earlier decision to send money for her son's engagement stemmed from that worry. But her gift hadn't changed their relationship. She realized that in letting fear dictate her actions, she was letting her son control her. Andrea decided that her earlier gift was the end of her obligation with regard to his wedding. She would not to reach out on her son's wedding day. "He has not been a good son to me for a long, long time," she says. Drawing strength from acceptance, Andrea decided she would no longer pursue a relationship with someone who doesn't want one. "I wish things were different," she says. "But so do a lot of people, about a lot of things."

In essence, Andrea was taking an important stance for moving forward in her life. Her affirmative thoughts went like this:

- "I will no longer allow him to control me. Nor will I enable his hurting me. I will not make contact."

Explore your feelings, and then come up with some confident and affirmative thoughts of your own. Here are a few examples:

- Because I would like to open the door to my daughter's possible return to me, I will congratulate her about her new baby.

- Even though texting my son on his wedding day feels like the "right" thing for me to do, in light of the animosity he has expressed toward me, this may not be the best time. If I decide to make contact, it will be on another day.

- I will text (call, send a card) because this is the only decision I can feel good about later—regardless of my child's potential response or lack of a reply.

After considering her situation from several angles, Petra sent her tiny granddaughter a beautiful Bible in honor of her Christening. "Inside was a family tree," Petra says. "I filled it in with our side of the family, and wrote a personal note." Petra's son didn't respond, but her actions felt right. It was the only decision she could live with. Petra knew she'd feel anxious after sending the gift, so she made plans with people she cares about, got her favorite healthy foods, and occupied her mind.

Lauren, Petra, Andrea, and Pam each faced unique dilemmas. When your child is estranged, experiencing damned-if-you-do damned-if-you-don't situations is common. These mothers made decisions that honored their feelings in different ways. While they recognize the future may hold trials, they are seizing the present, and moving forward.

Emotional Triggers

Family photos, a box of childhood mementos, a baby book, or a stash of well-played board games we come across in a disused cupboard can bring up memories when we least expect them. Memories of good times in the past can then turn sour, and remind us of loss.

We still live in the home where Dan grew up. In the hall, a series of black lines labeled with the children's names rises up a door frame. Dan's name first appears knee-high, repeating higher and higher until he towered above me. The reminders have been endless. In those early months of estrangement, I saw evidence everywhere of the boy who grew into a strong young man. Dan's capable hands had been on everything. In his late teens, he was the one who hung the wood shelves in my room, and the lightweight racks in my closet. In one bathroom, I could still see him crouched in work clothes, positioning the veined rock tiles above the tub. And every time I got into my youngest daughter's car, a sedan that Dan used to drive, I remembered him coming to our rescue on the side of a busy freeway one day. Dan had answered our desperate call.

In my home, Dan's life with us spilled around me like paint—in his childhood artwork, in photos, in our family history, and in the memories we share within these walls.

If mementos and photos become too much to bear, adding to your sadness and confusion over what happens now, what you did wrong, or even who you are without your estranged child in your life, consider packing them away. For many though, this can feel as if they're giving up hope, saying a permanent good-bye to the child they once knew. But many also confide that boxing things up frees them. Putting away the constant visual reminders removes a trigger to their feelings of failure, anger, sadness, and even hopes that, thus far, have been unfounded, so may seem futile, or even foolish.

After a couple of years, I did box up mementos, take down artwork, and pack away some photos. Others remain. Often I don't even notice the photos of Dan. As often happens with the things around us, they fade into the background. But when I do stop to look at them, pictures of Dan in collages or photo groupings remind me of happy family times we shared. He was a part of that, a part of the family. I can't erase him from our lives. Regardless of what's transpired, or the state of things now, I wouldn't want to. And rather than tear down shelves, redo the bathroom tile, or insist my daughter get a different car, I've shifted my perspective. Those reminders of Dan as a capable young man also remind me of my own strengths. They're physical evidence of what a decent mother I have always been. Even to Dan. Even now.

Stay Mindful

A family member recently asked me if it's normal to feel angry and upset each year around the time of a past traumatic event. His wife had noticed his cyclical short fuse. Until she brought his yearly foul mood to his attention, he was unaware of the connection. The passage of time, special dates, the mishaps of life, momentous events, or even someone else's joy, can trigger distress. It's important to consider what your potential triggers may be, your reactions, and how you can recover.

Staying mindful is the first step in combatting emotional triggers. And the easiest association to make is a date or time of year. For me, the days of early summer hold emotional landmines. Our family bonfires may remind me of a lonely evening when we were still in shock. Though Dan had abruptly halted the rehearsal dinner, our family still gathered beneath the trees we'd threaded with pink lights to honor the bride's wedding colors. With the bonfire blazing, we stuffed ourselves with catered Greek food, and lightly joked as if nothing was wrong.

For the first two years after my son's estrangement, on the actual date of his wedding we didn't attend, I imagined Dan and his wife celebrating. Now, the date passes without notice, but I do hope my son is happy.

As each year marches into autumn, the falling leaves and crisp night air bring sweet back-to-school memories that I can cherish. But if I'm not mindful of the direction of my thoughts, those memories could mix with thoughts of another autumn day when my son moved out of the rental house—and remind me of my disappointment.

For most of us, an estranged child's birthday can be difficult. The anniversary of our child's birth holds more than the history of surprises, cakes, and celebrations. Burned into memory is the image of that tiny newborn's face after waiting so long to see him. Mothers recall with clarity the way a newborn's eyes gazed up at theirs. I can still hear Dan's first cry, muffling to coos as he snuggled close to feed.

For me, thinking of the pop 1960s Lesley Gore hit lightens my mood. Maybe it was *her* party in the song, but I always change the words as I sing them aloud: *It's* your birthday *and I'll cry if I want to, cry if I want to, cry if I want to. . . . You would cry too, if it happened to-oo you!*

Whether your child's birthday, Mother's Day, a holiday, or any day that holds significance, consider possible associations that may trigger emotional distress. Perhaps even mark important dates on a calendar. Then, make a plan. After identifying potentially troubling times when you may feel angry or worry you will have a case of the blues, brainstorm ideas for what might help. Planning helps you take a sensible approach. Here are a few ideas:

- Alert a willing friend or family member who will check in on you or be on-call to talk. Choose someone with whom you can freely share your feelings without feeling judged, rushed, or embarrassed.

- Take vacation days to cut down on stress around times you know will trouble you.

- Organize your closet, get rid of clutter, or participate in other activities that keep you occupied, and help you feel productive.

- Recall an uplifting phrase, find a go-to song (like mine), watch a funny movie, or do something else that picks up your mood.

- If marking dates feels too much like commemorating negative events and loss, plan fun activities that help you form new and positive connections—and note *those* things on your calendar instead.

Despite good intentions and planning, if you still feel unsettled, or find yourself angry or in tears, please remember, you have not failed. The pain we feel over sons and daughters who have abandoned us runs deep.

We'll talk more about feelings and seeing them in a new light in Chapter Five. For now, be realistic. Forgive yourself. You're only human. But don't let yourself wallow forever. Pick yourself up and start again.

Also, keep in mind that no matter how much you make yourself aware of potential triggers, some may take you by surprise. With a plan in place, you can quickly recover.

At 61, Vera responded to an ad for a free kitten. Excited to adopt a furry friend, the last thing she expected was a reminder that her only son is estranged. But the woman with the kitten was concerned. "You're getting up in years," she told Vera. "Will someone take the kitten, a son or daughter maybe, if you become indisposed?"

Shocked, Vera mumbled that she did have a son, but he wasn't around to help. After a few more questions, the woman refused to give up the kitten. Vera says, "What started as a happy pet adoption became a sad reminder that I'm orphaned myself."

That's how suddenly life can turn your emotions upside down. An unrelated event or a person's unwitting words can take you hostage—if you let them. *Don't.*

One, Two, Three . . . Get Free

First, when an emotional trigger pulls you down, tell yourself to stop. Take a few calming breaths. Then recite a few simple phrases to get you back to the present. Like these:

- *What's happened is* done. *For now, I cannot change things. I can only change my response.*

Second, focus on something more positive. Think of anything that you're grateful for, or appreciate the good memories for the enjoyment they once gave you. Perhaps you can pat yourself on the back for the good you did in your estranged son or daughter's life (return to the exercise of that name in Chapter Two to refresh your memory).

Third, take back control. That might mean soothing yourself with a few kind words. Something like this:

- *I've lived through the worst of this. I am rebuilding my life in a way that pleases me now. I choose to take charge of my thoughts, my feelings, and my future. No longer will I allow my estranged adult child to hold me hostage to hurt and pain. I am healing and moving forward on a positive path.*

Making the decision to move forward despite the hurt that has been inflicted on you is empowering. Emotional triggers hold the potential for setbacks, but you can overcome them. Turn the triggers into strength builders.

One afternoon, my husband and I were catching up after a few busy days of work. He rattled on about a new client, a local gal who was having some work done on her house. She told my husband she had three sons like us, and she wondered if they'd gone to school together.

"One of her sons is in the military," Brian related. "Another is in his late twenties with kids. And her third son's getting married in a month. She was excited because they'll all be traveling cross country to go to the wedding. I guess he's marrying a real nice girl."

"Well," I said, anger trickling out of me like acid. "Isn't her life perfect?"

My husband's jaw dropped. "I'm sorry, babe," he said.

Tears splashed from my eyes. "I guess *she's* perfect, and so are her sons." I scooted back my chair and stood, glaring at my poor husband. "Sorry *I'm* not so perfect, and neither is our life." I stormed out of the room, muttering as I went, "She makes it sound so great, but I bet the truth is she's stressed about the wedding, and wishes she didn't have to traipse across country to get to it."

I slammed the back door as I left the house. Outdoors, I looked up at the sky. Puffy white clouds floated in a tranquil sea of blue. A Mockingbird fluttered by, stopped on a garden pole to flick its tail, and then lifted its head to sing. I took a breath, realizing what had just happened.

Back inside, I found my husband where I'd left him, his chin in his palm. He looked up, his green eyes uncertain.

"I'm not mad at *you*," I said. "I'm just mad. You know, three great sons, a wedding. . . ."

His face lit with understanding. He raised a brow, and in his best old-timer imitation, teased, "I reckon I'm insensitive."

And then we both laughed.

Staying mindful includes recognizing when an unexpected trigger has struck. But triggers aren't always so easily identified. When your emotions take a sudden turn for the worse, or your reactions seem too strong for the circumstances, investigate. Something may have prompted bad feelings without you even realizing it. Maybe a coworker raved that day about what a terrific relationship she shares with her adult children. Busy at work, perhaps you didn't make the connection. But later, you find yourself reaching for comfort food, or grousing at the family pet. Once you recognize what's happened, don't dwell on thoughts that bring you down. Admit what's happened, and then move on.

On that day, I could have blamed my husband. How could he be so insensitive, talking to me about a woman with three terrific sons, and even one who was marrying a wonderful girl? Her life seemed perfect, while one of our three sons had disowned us. But my sensitivity wasn't my husband's fault. I shouldn't expect him or anyone to tiptoe around me, forever self-censoring. I also could have been angry at myself that day, and slipped into unhelpful thinking that made things worse: *After more than two years, something as inconsequential as a chatty woman's happy family still throws me for a loop. I'll never get over this. . . .*

Whether you feel angry, sad, frustrated, or find yourself repeating a futile, *what's the point?* sort of thought, awareness allows you to take a breath, and take control. Remove yourself from the situation if you need to. Give yourself a pep talk. Regain your composure. For me, getting outdoors, and then purposely taking note of my surroundings always helps. The vast sky, the magnificence of a stately tree, the pleasant rustling of wind in the leaves, or the trill of a songbird raises my spirits, and connects me to something bigger than me and my sorrows. I can turn to nature quickly, even if that means looking out a window and imagining my bad feelings drifting away with the clouds. You might recall a favorite scripture, open a book full of inspirational quotes, or remind yourself of a silly joke.

Vera turned to friends in an online support group whom she knew could empathize. She got the story off her chest, out of her mind, and then moved forward. There were other kittens needing homes.

Whatever you do, don't get down on yourself. Acknowledge your feelings, so you can deal with them. Remember the utter shock you felt when your son or daughter first cut you off? Don't think of triggered emotions as setbacks. They're aftershocks—a normal occurrence that relieves pressure. Think: *Forward. I'm adapting. I'm healing. I'm moving on.*

Lovely Path, or Rut of Despair?

When faced with triggered hurt, imagine the serenity of a natural space. Sunlight filters through a leafy canopy. Birdsong fills the air. A pleasant breeze whispers against your skin. Don't let intruding thoughts bring you down. *Why did this happen? Am I a bad person? I'll never be happy. Just when things are going well, something reminds me, and I'm right back where I started, hurting. Will this pain ever end?*

Following a negativity path only digs a deeper groove, a rut that blocks your view of what's good in your life. Positive questions can help pull you up and out. Consider these:

- *Which would I rather be? Upset, angry, and sad? Or optimistic, grateful, and glad?*

- *Is there* anything *I can do to change things now?* If yes, make a plan. If no, accept that reality.

- *Are my thoughts stuck in the past?*

- *What can I focus on right now that will make me feel better?*

Come up with your own ready menu of feel-better sayings or questions to positively deal with triggered emotions. Add actions to your ready list too. Go for a walk, take a bath, clean out a drawer. . . . Sometimes, just getting out of our heads and actually *doing* something helps.

Focusing on what makes us happy feels good. Developing a positive outlook may have health benefits too. A 2006 study in the journal, *Psychosomatic Medicine,* showed that a positive emotional style reduced the likelihood of contracting a virus. With a little advance planning, self-control, and determination, we *can* conquer our emotional triggers.[2]

Pain Management

In today's culture, the idea of closure is bandied about like some mythical desert oasis or place of bliss. People believe that without closure, we can never move on and heal. However, such completion, or "closure," is a myth.[3]

Even when a relationship ends in the finality of death, closure isn't full and complete. We often experience guilt, i.e., wishing we'd spent more time, hadn't argued, or had taken that last vacation together. Even after resolving those feelings, we're forced to adapt to our loss, and learn to live without the person and the roles they filled. Despite moving forward and finding joy after loss, we must adjust in practical ways, such as taking over the tasks a person once did for us. Also, we still miss the individual who has passed. Losing an adult child to estrangement is similar. Letting go is gradual. In fact, "closure," in the sense that we reach completion and eradicate all pain like an exterminator killing pests, may be unrealistic, and perhaps unwise.

Motherhood has been a big part of your identity. Suddenly closing off feelings might feel like abandoning your child or even yourself. Who are you if you're not Susie's mother? How do you tuck away all those years of nurturing Bobby as if they never happened? You don't. Rather, you embrace the memories, cherish the joy you shared, feel proud of the hard times you saw your child through, and remain satisfied with the support and love you offered. Mothering is a gift you freely gave. You did well. Hold that thought—rather than let a hurtful thought hold you.

Rather than "closure," defined as a final resolution about our loss, we learn to adjust—in both our physical and our emotional life. This more realistic goal, to adapt, is something we all do in varying degrees throughout our lives. As normal, healthy adults, we have all experienced loss, and most of us have found ways to adjust. This is true whether our losses were material and concrete such as a high paying job, or more idealistic, such as accepting that because of time, money, or for some other reason, a longed for dream will remain unrealized.

Wise people often look back on the storms of life that once seemed pointless and find meaning or in some way come to terms about them. Over time, perspectives shift. It's not unusual for parents who wondered what they did to cause the break to later believe their child's cutting-off had nothing to do with them. While the loss of the relationship and the dream of a shared future still hurt, they reach a new observation point on the journey. Often, such new perspectives help us find meaning, which further helps us adapt to the change.

For me, despite the shock, confusion, self-blame, shame, anger and fear, I now look upon my time with Dan as a gift. I value those years as a mother who cared for a son. He was a child who brought me heartache, joy, and pride. When he grew up, he took possession of his life, and forged a path of his own making. In losing him, I have found meaning, if only in the awareness that I cherish treasured people even more. Just as a survivor might say after a loved one's sudden death that our lives are fleeting; cherished relationships are precious few.

At first when the pain is fresh, or the relationship's break particularly hateful, such a shift may seem impossible, but you too can adapt. Find some purpose or value in the loss, but don't insist on something momentous or earth-shattering. Finding meaning doesn't have to mean changing the world. It may be as simple as realizing your life is more peaceful without an abusive adult child's presence. Perhaps your bank account is gaining without a selfish taker's constant drain. Or perhaps you have more time and energy to devote to something important to you, to your community, or even to the world. Life doesn't stand still, and neither should you.

You didn't fail because of your adult child's choices. Don't remain forever a hostage, waiting for some mythical finality of closure that may never come. Free yourself now to step forward and try.

As loving mothers, we surely made mistakes. All parents do. But as kind and supportive parents, we did our best. We must recognize that no matter the choices our adult children make, their behavior doesn't diminish the good we did or continue to do. Someone's inability to see our value does not detract from our worth.

Another Perspective: Kids Who Don't Fit

At the age of 10, my son told me that when he grew up, he would change his name and move away. I thought it was a phase, just words, like so many plans kids make. He wasn't angry. The words came out of nowhere really. But he said it several times. Now, in light of his estrangement, those words hold significance.

Much is written about temperament, and how children's personalities can mesh, *or clash*, with parents, other figures of authority, and even peers. But compatibility goes deeper than personality traits. We didn't have power struggles or arguments. My easygoing son was well-adjusted and happy. But in light of his childhood words, I wondered: *Did he feel as if he didn't fit?*

One woman related, "I must have been switched at birth." Growing up, she felt like the "ugly duckling" from the story of the same name. Just as the hatchling swan didn't fit until he found his own kind, she didn't feel she belonged until she grew up, moved away, and found a different home among different people.

If that is what Dan needed, I hope he found a place to belong, and realizes his full potential. I hope he becomes a swan.

✈Visualize Your Child's Happy Life

Though angry and hurt, thousands of mothers share the hope that the children they nurtured will do well. This loving thought that's so common among supportive mothers can be put to good use for themselves. To free yourself, adapt, and embrace your future, wish your child well. Visualize your child happy, healthy, and living a meaningful life.

Before Starting: Keep in mind that if you are forever checking in on your child through Facebook, Google Plus, or some other social network, this exercise may not be successful. Seeing details in online photos can upset you. If your son has lost weight, you may worry about his health. If beer bottles cluster on a table behind your daughter, you may fear she's drinking too much. Speculation can be endless, and defeats the purpose of this exercise. Honor your adult child's wishes to separate from you. *For your own good*, stop lurking in his or her life.

Be aware that the positive results of this exercise are for *you*. Your thoughts don't have an effect on your child's life, and don't magically fix your relationship with him or her. The results follow the spirit of this book: acceptance, and moving successfully forward in your own life. By wishing your child well, despite his choices or whether or not her path leads back to you, you set the stage to let go of worry, anger, pride, or expectation. You set *yourself* free to embrace the present.

Let's Begin: Choose a quiet space: in your bedroom with the lights dimmed, in a comfortable outdoor setting, or as you close your eyes before falling asleep. Then, using the tips below, visualize your child as happy, well-adjusted, loved, and content.

Tips For Success

- **Resist the urge to overthink details.** If your child dreamed of becoming a doctor but quit school and rejected you, don't create a detailed drama that chronicles her recapturing that goal. This isn't about specifics that feed abandoned expectations or fulfill your hopes. Don't visualize detailed scenarios that set you up for further disappointment. Imagine your child happy and satisfied, period.

- **Frame this visualization to fit your beliefs.** My first iteration of this exercise was a prayer. A peaceful visual of my son and his life in a loving Creator's hands. A blessing of sorts. If using your belief system feels right to you, then utilize that to provide some structure. Or simply imagine without any specific beliefs in mind. Visualize your child as a kind adult, engaged in meaningful activities such as caring for animals, playing music, or cooking.

- **Repeat this exercise and allow it to evolve.** My initial prayer progressed into helpful snapshots, fleeting but intentional imaginings like my son walking out a door, golden sunlight shining on his path. Create and recreate this simple exercise. Turn to it when you're worried or you long for the child you so miss. Use positive visualization whenever needed, in a brief yet meaningful way that lets you let go.

- **Remember, this is not an exercise to control results in your child's life.** Visualizing your child well and happy will help *you*.

- **If it feels right for you, use your physical body to support this exercise.** Open your hands, and imagine letting tension go, and also releasing your child. Do what works for you. Close your eyes, open your palms to the sky, or assume a meditational pose. Make this exercise yours.

- **Add powerful thoughts and images to support you.** Breathe deeply. Imagine inhaling peace, confidence, and love. When you exhale, visualize worry, anger, and all negativity swirling out and away from you.

- **Make it real.** Picture your son's laughing eyes. See your daughter's flawless skin or shining hair. Imagine welcoming faces, a table spread with healthy foods, a cozy living space, and a life full of hugs and joy.... Create imagery that feels good and makes you smile. Whether you're ever part of that wonderful life, want that for your child. Believe in it.

As you heal from the harrowing pain of estrangement, you may find, as I did, that these positive visualizations become briefer, but also more fulfilling: a fleeting picture you can conjure up at any time to strengthen you; an image that helps you to trust that all will be well. And then you can turn to your own life, your own sunlit path.

Notes

CHAPTER FIVE

See Your Feelings In a New Light

Mothers often contact me in desperation. They ask: *How can I get over the loss? Why is this so difficult?* Or worse, they say they *never will* get over it or that they just *can't*. They have lost their sense of self-worth, purpose, and pride. They are baffled, often hopeless, frustrated, sad, angry, confused, guilty, and feel as if they failed. Some say the things that used to bring them joy don't hold the same radiance. Many no longer trust.

Smart women, who run the gamut from homemakers to doctors, elementary school teachers to college professors, tell me they've lost their confidence. Accomplished, successful women tell me they now live in dread and fear. They long for their prior self-assurance, but don't know how to get it back. They mourn not only the loss of their child, but the loss of themselves. Maybe you can relate.

A child's estrangement includes the loss of an ideal, of a vision perhaps carried even before we ever thought about having children. But because the loss is so ambiguous and embarrassing, it can feel as if we have no right to mourn. Because friends and relatives don't know what to say, or don't understand how difficult this situation really is, we may feel like an outsider with a shameful secret. We may never openly grieve at all.

Because motherhood is such an important part of life, it can't be discounted. It's not like a promotion you can say you're relieved you didn't get because it would have required too much travel. Or a contest you didn't win, because the odds were against you anyway. You can't say about motherhood that you're glad it didn't work out. If you did, people would think you're horrible, and not believe you anyway. And you wouldn't believe yourself. Sure, that's why you changed all those diapers, spent all those nights waiting up for your teen, helped with homework, and growing pains, and did so much to do your best.

The loss that occurs in an estrangement involves much more than a single relationship. The family we've created implodes. In the safe, and understanding company of others who have suffered this trauma, parents confide the far-reaching effects, and how much it's changed them. In this chapter, we'll explore the loss, examine emotions, and take a practical stance. Self-nurturing and coping strategies are sprinkled throughout. It's time to fully grasp the loss, look at its every detail, and try to lay it to rest.

Life Includes Loss

Each of us experiences loss in our lives, even though we may not think of some of the things we lose as worthy of grief. Recognizing some common losses can help us understand that coping with loss is a part of life.

I'm fortunate to have lived in the same house for thirty years. This home is my way of controlling what I couldn't control in childhood, and creating that stability for my children. In a way, having a place to call home is my way of grieving my childhood loss of many homes. Some of you can relate to moving as a form of loss, even though we don't typically grieve the homes we've left, the lives we've led in them, and the familiar surroundings we grew used to.

Other common losses include the death of a person or pet we love, a job, a romantic relationship, a promotion we didn't get, a bet of some sort, or the loss of a dream we come to realize we will never achieve.

Each loss causes others. Losing a job means the loss of income, perhaps prestige, and the sense of security. The end of a romantic relationship may include the loss of a future ideal. When people divorce, they not only lose a partner but sometimes friends, and an entire family of in-laws who were once so much a part of their lives.

Maybe as a child you entered a talent contest but didn't win. Tried out for a part in a play, but didn't get it. Did your best at almost anything, but didn't achieve the grade, the reward, or the prize. Each situation has related losses, yet we aren't typically taught to grieve. These sorts of things are seen simply as *change*. But change includes loss, and is part of living.

That's not to say any of these things is on par with losing a child, either by death or to estrangement. But it's a way to start considering specifically how much the loss has affected you. The *Take Stock* exercise in Chapter Four began this process. In it, you considered things you used to do but now don't, and how the estrangement has affected your relationships, monopolized conversations, created new habits, and stopped you from doing things you've loved. Now, let's look at the losses more specifically, and what can be learned from them.

The Landscape of Loss Is Fertile Ground For Growth

Portrait artist, Barb, used to have long talks with her daughter while sitting on the porch. In vivid memories, she described wisteria growing up the porch columns, and scenting the air as they chatted. The brilliant sun dipped over the horizon, painting the sky orange and pink. Barb had expected those intimate talks would continue. So, when her daughter walked away, Barb's future sunk with the sun, leaving her vision dark. She'd lost her closest relationship, as well as the practical roles her daughter once played in her life: a friend, a confidante, a shopping buddy, a personal stylist, someone who helped her plan parties and outings.

Our children fill roles beyond that of sons and daughters. Among other things, Dan is a computer whiz, and we depended on his talents. What about your son or daughter? Did he or she cook, fix the car, or do home repairs? Maybe your son always encouraged you. Or your daughter instigated and planned family outings.

Reflect on all the roles your child fulfilled, both tangible and intangible. Then, think of how you've filled those roles with the skills of other people, or took them over for yourself. Also think about the vision or ideals that crashed down with your child's rejection. These are losses too.

Maybe you can relate to the family ideal I set out to achieve: the happy, secure and stable family in the cozy old homestead. But the Hallmark card reality doesn't fully exist. Maybe not every mother has a child that leaves the family, but they have other problems. No family is perfect, of course, even if a few appear so to the outside world. And I realized I could learn from this experience. I could share my sorrows, and help others. It's like a friend's house that's cluttered when you arrive. You feel relieved to know that your own housekeeping may not be perfect, but it's not that bad. That's why I'm sharing with you here.

Dan's leaving required me to learn more about computers. To calmly read instructions, hook up cords. . . . When it came to wireless connections, hardware, and software, I had to learn how to research, study product reviews and tutorials, and hire help. That's how I've continued my career as a writer, relying strongly on the Internet and email to get jobs done. And I learned how to create a website, add a forum, and bring mothers of estranged adult children together to heal.

It was frustrating and difficult, but Dan's leaving required me to stretch and grow. Now, I can help other people with some technology. Just yesterday, I showed a friend how to find the emoticons menu on her new smartphone. Before, I would have thrown up my hands and called on Dan. Now, my other children step up if I need them. They're willing to help. In fact, the estrangement has drawn our family even closer.

You may find help in unlikely places. One mother told me she called on a young neighbor to help her set up and use her new electronic tablet. Most young adults love technology and, as this mother discovered, enjoy the opportunity to play with others' new toys, and to help people.

Barb made new friends. She has grown closer to her younger daughter, who has taken on a bigger family role that she might not have had the opportunity to if her sister was still around. Because Barb's estranged daughter used to help her stay stylish, Barb found another way to fill the need. She started a closet-swap, and holds fun quarterly parties at a rented hall. Women bring their designer clothes and make trades.

Whether you've thought of the loss from this perspective or not, every one of us can think of ways we've dealt with the estrangement, and grew because of it. Even mothers who say they have lost so much of themselves can find good ways they have changed. As you do the next exercise, see yourself in a capable light.

✈ *Help Wanted?* Help Yourself

What's Missing? Start with a list of the roles your estranged son or daughter fulfilled. These can be practical things like cook, gardener, and computer assistant. Or less tangible roles, like the person who filled the house with live music, or lifted the atmosphere with all their friends.

Roles Your Child Filled:	Making Up For The Loss:

Once you've made your list, take note of which activities you now do for yourself—and feel proud. Or, if you've sought outside assistance, grown in some way as an individual or as a family, give yourself credit for the change. While loss hurts, there's also a positive side. It provides room to grow, and teaches us new things.

If you can't think of many things you now do for yourself, don't worry. Identifying where you can make positive changes is helpful. We'll deal with filling those roles in a moment.

Give yourself some love. Now, come up with a few statements to explain the growth. Even if you can only think of one small thing, give yourself credit. You've adapted to change! You'll use the lines below. Here are some examples:

- I have the patience and intelligence to learn how technology works, and can set most of it up. Because of this, I'm more independent. It feels good to know that I can adapt to change.

- I now know that I can look for, and even hire help. Hired help, in fact, is more prompt, dependable, and takes less time.

- I have learned to ask friends for help. There is always someone who *wants* to help. People enjoy being needed.

- I've learned more about letting go, realizing that even if I do my best, some things are beyond my control. This has helped me worry less about outcomes, and enjoy the present more.

Now, write down a few positive statements of your own about how you have grown, adapted, or positively changed.

_____

_____

_____

Fill in the blanks. Some of your child's roles will remain empty. Notice them. They're part of the loss. Think of ways to fulfill the roles not yet occupied. If you enjoyed that your child played music, you can buy show tickets, attend free concerts, play CDs, or learn an instrument yourself. If you haven't already done so, go back to your list of roles, and fill in how they're being filled, or ways you might fill them.

Shift perspective, and acknowledge positives. What *don't* you miss? Be honest. If your son or daughter had friends over all the time, you may now enjoy the quiet. Did your child often initiate deep discussions that you weren't ready for, or that became combative or frustrating? You probably don't miss those talks. Was your child verbally abusive? It's fair to admit you don't miss the volcano you feared would explode, the ugly words, or the arguments.

Right now, think of a few things that you *don't* miss. Do you have more space, more time, or more money? Is there less overall strife, or are there fewer distractions? Are you glad you aren't put on the spot? Called to be available when you already have plans? Perhaps you're relieved not to walk on eggshells around your child's unkind spouse. Although born of heartache, it's okay to recognize that some things are better. There's no need to feel guilty for those feelings.

_____

_____

_____

_____

Estrangement is a force you must reckon with. Just as you have done with other losses you've experienced in life, you can learn and grow. You can choose to live a happy and fulfilling life. Look at the lists you've created here. You can get past this. In some ways, you already have.

The Waiting Game

Recently, a woman in her sixties told me she frequently sits alone and pets her cat. She has put herself, her needs, and her very life on hold while she waits for her son to return to her. But even after several years of no contact and no replies, she won't allow herself to believe he may *never* return. Doing so, in her eyes, would be giving up. She has set the bar at reconciliation, and believes that until she achieves the goal, she can't move on.

Many women have suffered for years, holding onto the belief that unless their child returns, they will always suffer. It's almost as if they've martyred themselves to an ideal of motherhood. I feel for these women, because I understand. I once tied my happiness to my son's behavior. The trouble is that while a parent waits in this way, time passes. Opportunities come and go. Unfortunately, for many nothing changes. The adult children go on with their lives as they please, not likely even thinking of the mother who waits for them.

Since our future relationship with an estranged child is uncertain, perhaps it's helpful to think of their absence as a sort of hiatus. We already likened loss to change. Mothers whose children are away at college, or have moved to another country to pursue a career, face similar challenges. Obviously, the idea of no relationship, maybe forever, is different from a child who is simply away. This won't work for everyone, but could you learn from the empty nesters? Could you use this time and space to your own advantage?

Parents *can* get on with living, even while they wait. Particularly with the support of others, mothers paralyzed in the mire of undue guilt, and pressured by ideals of mother-child relationships, *do* end up letting go. It's a rational decision. And at a time when they feel so vulnerable, permitting themselves to move on and live empowers them. Many parents tell me they wish they would have done so sooner. They regret having wasted precious time.

I've read the writings and quotes of people considered experts in the realm of estranged adult children, who tell parents we should never give up. That we should keep reaching out to our children forever. That someday, *someday*, perhaps they will return. Some suggest that parents should continue to financially support these children who are adults. That we should pay for their education, and do for them whatever we would do for their siblings with whom we're still close.

To these opinions, I'll pose a question: *When does childhood end and adulthood begin?*

Each of us may have a different answer. My son was 24 when he became estranged. To me, age 24 held more accountability than age 18. Just as age 26 is different from age 31, and so on. Only you know the maturity level of your son or daughter, the specific circumstances surrounding the estrangement. Only you can decide whether financial arrangements should change. Some parents conclude that providing financial support to a daughter or son who wants nothing else to do with them is tantamount to attempting to buy their love. Others continue to support their children through college or beyond.

We've already explored the value of careful deliberation, rather than making snap decisions or quick comments we may later regret. It's the same with financial matters. In Chapter Three, we met Laura and her husband, who worked with a therapist to devise a plan for gradual financial disengagement from their twin daughters. These parents are at peace with their decision to pay for two more college semesters. Giving such notice allowed their daughters time to make other arrangements.

All anyone can do in the face of loss and change is to consciously adapt. You can alter your perspective. You can come to see giving up more as giving in, and even giving honor to your adult child's decision. Moving on doesn't mean you turn a tit-for-tat cold shoulder that can never grow warm again. In giving in, you allow yourself to live. You're not a quitter. You're a starter—in a new phase of life.

Sadness Hurts, So Take Care

Since physical and emotional pain show up in the same areas of the brain, let's look to physical injury as a guide in caring for emotional hurt. When you're in physical pain, the natural response is to rest the injured area, and provide support. You might take the pressure off a hurt leg by using crutches, support a painful wrist with a brace or a sprained arm with a sling.

How can you similarly heal from sadness and hurt? Below, I've provided a few self-nurturing ideas that worked for me and other mothers who have moved on while still holding out hope. These are not meant as absolutes. Rather, they are suggestions, jumping off points for your own healing wisdom.

Take time for yourself. Time off or away can help you reenergize and recoup. Getting out of our own environment provides a different perspective that can trigger new ways of seeing ourselves in the world. With intention, you may get the same feelings of anticipation, optimism, and excitement from a planned afternoon out as you might from a long trip. Whether you spend three hours or three weeks, don't stress over perfectionistic ideals.

Choose destinations and make plans that don't require many details. Consider visiting quiet places of serenity in your own city, or your own backyard. Tranquil views or natural settings can feed your soul. Immerse yourself in their healing energy. At the ocean, listen to the rhythmic breath of the waves, and feel connected. In the shadow of mountains, appreciate their strength and beauty. Notice how the sky reflects even on puddle water, and imagine yourself reflecting only beauty.

Make your days off days of rest. If you work outside the home, use your days off for what you enjoy. If you work inside the home, schedule days off on your calendar. Allow yourself to rest—if not for days, then for hours or moments. People fill their time off with must-dos. Try ordering in, and explore online buying options for food and goods. Leave your work at work. If you must check-in then make a plan that manages stress and supports you. Check email or voicemail at set times. If you can, put your mobile phone away or turn it off.

Make moments meaningful. Clear a relaxation space. Put up pictures that please you or fill you with awe, or place a comfy chair to enjoy a lovely view. Use your terrace, patio, or an area of your yard to create a peaceful place. At work, adopt a space. Add a potted plant or freshly cut flowers, and bring a book with inspiring photos. Or, you may find an outdoor spot near trees, a water feature, or a view of interesting architecture. Take a tea or lunch break there. Talk with a friend. Watch the birds outside the window. Or, read a book that lifts your spirits. Something like Nancy Thayer's funny book series starting with the novel, *The Hot Flash Club,* might make you smile. Or maybe a spiritual book or one that's filled with encouraging quotes. Even the smallest homes can make room for a restful space for moments of recuperation, meditation, or meaning. Moments are what make up our lives. Make them good ones.

Take care of your physical body. If you suffered a physical ailment, you'd be wise to eat gentle, wholesome foods, drink plenty of fluids, and get enough rest. Your mind and your heart, where your emotions are seated, are part of your body. Support your physical health, and you support your emotional health.

Get moving. Moderate, regular exercise has been shown to aid recovery from depression. While there's no need to run a marathon, moderate exercise such as walking for half an hour can boost your mood and support your well-being. Even physical ailments benefit from some movement. Give yourself a little physical therapy and get moving.

Indulge in things you love. Think of a few activities that make you happy. I love gardening. So after my son's estrangement, the hobby took on new meaning for me. Nurture yourself. Take a long bath, get a pedicure, go to the library, watch a movie, walk for a cause, stroll along the beach, take a class or take a sick day. What you do love? Make a list. Turn to it often.

Get involved. Join a book club, volunteer at a library, work at a food shelter, try out for a bowling team, or take your dog to obedience class. Opportunities to get your mind off yourself and onto activities and other people abound. Take advantage of one or two, with the intention of having fun, or helping in some way. If you're worried about fielding questions about your family, prepare ahead. Turn back to Chapter Three for some reply ideas. Or, make this a turning point with all out honesty.

Do something new. Trying something new engages the mind and creates excitement that can influence feel-good chemicals in the brain. Also, by doing something new, you step toward the adaptation that's required with any loss. Among other things, for me that meant trying a hobby I had always intended to but kept putting off: beekeeping. What new activity might you try? You could go back to school, learn a new language, try your hand at painting, learn how to sew, knit, or just try a new hair color. What's something you've always wanted to do, or something new you can try now?

What else might help? I'm a firm believer that we each know what's really best for us. If you were asked that question, what would you say? If it's easier to help someone else, step outside yourself and imagine you are a beloved friend. What would you suggest to help her? Now, give yourself a gift: your own wisdom.

Kat, whose two sons in their forties have been estranged for more than 15 years, decided to quit living in sorrow and reclaim her old self. She looked back to the time of life *before* what she calls, the three B's—boys, bras, and babies. "I remembered the sense of self and purpose I had back then," says Kat, who used to love tap dancing. "After 40 years, I bought an expensive pair of tap shoes, and stomped and shimmied emotions out and on their way."

Your Feelings: Coming to Terms

Emotions help us to communicate and understand what we like or don't like, alert us to changes, and motivate us to take action. Feel fear, and you may run or get set to defend yourself. Feel lonely, and you may realize you need to seek out a place to belong.

Many of us have been taught we shouldn't feel some emotions, such as envy and anger. These may have gotten tangled up with shame or associated with punishment. Although these emotions may be unpleasant, they're innocent bystanders to our action. It's how we respond to them that can help or hurt us.

People start forming positive or negative views about emotions as children. You may have been sent to your room for your anger. Maybe that was because you threw toys, hit a sibling, or put someone down. It was how you expressed anger that got you in trouble—or maybe how a parent or teacher feared you *might* express it. Because of that, you may have learned the emotion itself is one you *shouldn't* feel. This may be especially true for women because the nursery rhyme "everything nice" girl behavior may have been positively reinforced. So now, when you have every right to feel angry, it's intrusive and unsettling to you.

No matter what you've been taught, it's better to acknowledge your anger than to pretend it doesn't exist. Mary, whose middle child is estranged, says the anger she felt was scary, so she pushed it down. But later, it roared out. She'd yell at her 10-year-old for spilling his juice, cuss at her husband for leaving the toilet seat up, or find herself being impatient with a co-worker in a subordinate position.

Mary's examples demonstrate what often happens when people feel angry about situations that make them powerless. Anger rolls downhill. That's an urban phrase some say started in the military, only I've substituted "anger" for a four-letter word. When we're helpless to fix a situation, our anger and frustration may roll "downhill," onto someone or something with whom we feel safe, or perhaps *can* control: someone lower on the work rung, a child, a pet, or a devoted spouse.

If you're like Mary, you may benefit from a technique I've introduced to some of my coaching clients. Use the word "rage" as an acronym for steps to deal with anger that gets expressed where it shouldn't. It goes like this: **R**ecognize. **A**dmit. **G**ratitude. **E**xpress.

Mary already recognizes her roaring rage isn't really about spilled juice or the left-up the toilet seat. Those things only trigger the rage she has bottled up over her daughter's estrangement that she's powerless to change.

The next step is to admit what's going on—and apologize to the person she's hurt. She can tell her 10-year-old that she's sorry, that the spilled juice isn't really what's bugging her, and then give him a hug.

Next is gratitude. Mary is thankful her sweet 10-year-old is in her life, and her husband is so patient. Did you yell at the dog? Give your pooch a pat. Instead of focusing on your mistake, be grateful your dog loves you even when you're a jerk. Switching to gratitude helps people feel stronger and lightens the mood.

Finally, express. Extending yourself by expressing your feelings to people who can empathize or face similar challenges helps you feel less alone and bad. Support communities like the one I started online provide a safe place to share. Telling family members can help them understand what's going on. Even expressing your thoughts to yourself can help. Acknowledge to yourself that you feel angry, admit how it shows up in your life, and reinforce the recognition of any need to change. Doing so gives you back some control—and when it comes to estrangement, lack of control may fuel the rage. Nobody likes to feel powerless, without a choice or a plan to fix something they feel is broken. But admitting that it's true, and makes you angry, can be a turning point.

Being cognizant of your feelings helps you to recognize them sooner, and alter your response. Take a few calming breaths, tell yourself the situation at hand isn't a big deal, make a joke to defuse emotions, or imagine yourself with horns and smoke coming out of your ears (not a pretty picture). It isn't fair or healthy to take your anger out on your child/husband/dog/co-worker. Don't let your anger roll downhill.

Another emotion we may feel bad about is envy. Remember Meg, the self-assured real estate broker who was upset at her monthly business meeting when all the women talked about their happy families? You might not lock yourself in a public bathroom stall and curse like Meg did, but at some point, you may feel envy. How can you avoid being envious when your own son or daughter has dashed out the back door of your life—and everywhere you go, friends, relatives, and even strangers pull out their brag books and share their happy family plans? Even if you stay home, Facebook reminds you how happy and connected everyone else seems to be. Envy calls attention to what's missing for you, but that all those other people still enjoy. Feeling envious of other people's intact families is natural. *Why are they so lucky?* But envy may clash with moral teachings, or maybe you were taught to be content with what you have.

Let's talk about guilt too. Maybe you were *told* you should be ashamed of yourself for something you did or didn't do. Guilt might have been expected when you didn't meet someone else's standards for right or wrong. Guilt can stir up anger, frustration, or even resentment.

Guilt is especially common for mothers. Work long hours, and then feel bad about being away. Devote whole weeks to our children, and wonder if the time spent was quality enough. Do you give in too much, or not allow enough choice? Make home cooked meals, and then worry about the bit of sugar added to the squash. Oh, and was it organic?

The guilt trips can go on forever. So, it's no surprise the self-blame that arrives with an adult child's departure pulls out the sofa bed and fixes to stay. That doesn't mean you have to give it a room. Don't forget the concept of innocent guilt, as explained in Chapter Three. By virtue of its lack of resolution, estrangement can *cause* feelings of guilt. And as was also mentioned in that chapter, if you have ever suffered depression, you may be guilt-prone.

While it's crucial to accept our emotions, rather than to pretend they don't exist, you may fear that acknowledging anger, envy, or sadness will lead to losing control, breaking down into tears, or saying things you will regret. The idea of recognizing and accepting powerful and even scary emotions like frustration, anger or envy can seem like jumping into the open sea, and drifting. Perhaps the feelings will sweep you up and away in an uncontrollable tide that lands you on the shores of Bad Mood Beach. You might even find yourself on a rendezvous with rage—a date you don't enjoy. So, you may ignore the emotions, and stuff them down beneath extra work, overeating, or some other numbing activity—which is not healthy.

But you can take charge. You can notice the feelings, be aware, and accept that your emotions are alerting you to a change that must be made. Then you can channel the energy into a focused behavior that helps you heal. As you work toward positive change, you're adapting.

Earlier in the book, we have already explored emotions including humiliation, hopelessness, shame, embarrassment, disbelief, and fear—of judgment, of never reconciling, of going on in a life that's vastly different than what we wanted. As the shared experiences have shown, emotions are natural, and nothing bad. *They simply are.* So, let's work to accept the feelings, find effective ways to manage them, and get on with living.

Later in the chapter, you'll find a long list of how-tos for effective strategies to try. First, let's more fully explore the intensity of feelings that can go with estrangement, and how other circumstances can pile on—as well as how to deal with them.

Distrust and Cynicism

Sometimes, our disillusionment can lead to a gloomy outlook. A pervasive sense of dread can creep insidiously into every area of life.

Lila, a mother of two estranged sons, used to sit by the window and watch the world go by. When parents passed with children in strollers, she would cluck bitterly, thinking they had bought into the same promise of family she once did. Since the estrangement, she had come to think of the concept of family as some cruel joke of God or the universe. And those young mothers and fathers didn't have a clue.

Previously happy, optimistic, and engaged in friendships and hobbies that brought her joy, Lila's whole outlook had changed. If the fabric of such a fundamental system as the family could unravel, then anything could. She became less trusting, and much more cynical.

I can relate to Lila's feelings. At a social gathering several months after my son's estrangement, a friend mentioned a book she'd read about finding happiness.

"Oh yeah," I blurted. "Happiness is the big catch phrase right now. Everybody's looking for a simple answer, but there isn't one."

My friend looked surprised, and a little deflated. In the pause that followed, I glanced around to find similar expressions on the other women's faces. Books and articles on the subject of happiness had swept the nation. The topic was popular, and important to my friend. My snippy comment dismissed her feelings, and previously, I was sure I'd have supported her.

After that horrible pause, others asked her more about the book she'd found. And I tucked my proverbial tail. Who was I to rain on her parade?

I went home that night feeling bad about myself. My insensitivity proved what I'd been feeling: I wasn't the same anymore. Maybe I never would be. Instead of seeing the world with a hefty dose of optimism that had sometimes gotten me labeled a Pollyanna, I'd become suspicious, and even critical. The world looked different, and I no longer fit.

To make matters worse, I wondered if my friends thought maybe they were getting a glimpse of the *real* me. Maybe they questioned what face I'd been displaying to the world. Did they wonder if my son was *right* to leave me? My feelings mirrored this mothers' concern:

- *"Sometimes, I even wonder if my closest friends doubt me, like they're measuring everything I say or do against the estrangement, and wondering if it was really my fault."*

Over the next several months, I caught myself in similar situations. All around me would be the tinkling of glasses, the bubbling of conversations, the rise and fall of laughter. Rather than joining in the fun, the surface tone of life, people, and their interests irritated me. Like Lila, I was disillusioned. I knew my crotchety outlook was related to Dan's estrangement. My changed attitude stemmed from distrust, which I now know is common after such a deep emotional wounding from someone so close. See if you can relate to these mothers:

- *"I've closed my heart. I've put up walls. Being hurt like that again would kill me."*

- *"I keep people at arm's length now. No getting too close."*

- *"I'm much less open to making friends, or getting involved in groups and causes. I'm more cautious about everything now."*

Take a look at your own attitude. Have you become more suspicious or guarded? My distrust had spread into an outlook that bordered on cynicism. The admission itself feels foreign, and dreadful. But it's also honest. Though embarrassing, maybe sharing here will help others who have built up cynical walls to protect themselves.

Cynicism is defined as distrust of human nature and people's motives, a belief that humans act out of self-interest, and as skepticism. While a moderate measure of skepticism can be a healthy way to protect ourselves, pervasive distrust is not.

When I took a hard look at myself, I had to admit that I'd grown skeptical of almost everything, and much less willing to take things at face value. I looked beyond what would have once brought me joy, and predicted gloom or ascribed impure motives. It was difficult for me to see the good. Here's how a few mothers described comparable feelings:

- *"I'm impatient, and much more questioning of motives."*

- *"I've always tried to see people's good side. Now, I'm immediately looking for clues as to who they really are and what they really want from me. That way I can write them off before they hurt me."*

- *"It's as if I see beyond what's presented, and question everything. I'm expecting, and ready, for the other shoe to drop."*

Nineteenth-Century author and social reformer, Henry Ward Beecher, defined a cynic as a human owl, "Vigilant in darkness and blind to light, mousing for vermin, and never seeing noble game."

In response to their disappointment that led to disillusionment, some mothers shared a pervasive distrust that fits Beecher's dark description. Women that used to give people the benefit of the doubt had changed. They became impatient, intolerant, and unwilling, as one mother said, "to take any crap from anyone anymore."

My feelings were similar. I had become crabby, disagreeable, and no fun to be around. As if I had slipped into a saltier, more tell-it-like-is woman's skin. Looking back now, I can laugh. I was becoming a little like John Wagner's cartoon character, *Maxine*—only *not* funny.

When a son or daughter walks away, it's as if your foundation shifts, cracking open the beliefs you've held so close. There's no solid ground. But when you allow those feelings to make you critical, you hurt people. You hurt yourself.

An emotional wounding such as this can have far-reaching effects. You may feel like you will never heal, and your family will never be the same.

Earlier, we met Kathleen, a mother of four whose oldest daughter is estranged. Kathleen described the feeling like this:

- *"When my daughter left seven years ago, it tore a huge hole in the fabric of our family. We are like a tapestry, all our lives intricately and tightly woven together. When my oldest daughter removed herself, our family tapestry was horribly torn and damaged. We can try to cover up the hole, but it never goes away. We can try to hide the ugliness of the damage and focus on the beautiful parts, but the hole is still there."*

The mothers quoted here are honest about what's happened to them, how they've changed, and who they have become. But they feel powerless to regain themselves. They feel like I once did. Over the days, weeks, and months after an adult child's rejection, it's as if little bits of you are torn off and dragged away.

At first, the missing pieces are so small, gnawed away when you are in such shock that you hardly notice. Then over time, as your edges grow ragged, you find you've become overly sensitive, and more abrasive. While you used to glide in and out of crowds and social situations with ease, suddenly you're caught on some thought, snagged on someone's words, or blurting out things that surprise and alarm you.

You realize just how much you've changed, but it feels like those missing pieces are so far gone you can never find them. How can you begin to look for and reclaim bits of your old self? We face a choice: Resign ourselves to accept the negative changes and hold onto hurt, or work at letting go, recovering our old selves, and growing from the experience.

Notes

Should You Forgive?

Doreen asks, "Why should I forgive my son? He hasn't apologized. And he's not making any effort to reconcile."

Another mom explained her thoughts this way: "Forgiveness comes when the person wants to make things right. My estranged daughter *doesn't*."

What does it mean to forgive? For some, forgiveness holds deeply spiritual roots, and may imply a divine sense of the word that erases past errors. Therefore, forgiving someone who has hurt us deeply may seem impossible, or even wrong—particularly if the person hasn't apologized or changed. For others, substituting a phrase such as "letting go," in place of "forgiveness" more accurately expresses feelings. The intent has less to do with the person who has wronged us, and is more focused on dropping unhealthy responses that can hold us back.

Does forgiving mean forgetting? Not necessarily. If we're lied to, stolen from, treated with indifference, subjected to angry outbursts, or in some other way hurt, *forgetting*, and completely letting down our guard, is probably not the wisest course. That sort of forgiveness may come across as an invitation: *I'm a doormat. Walk on me!* Forgetting bad behavior can make us vulnerable. If a dog bites us, we'll be wary of that dog in the future. That doesn't mean the dog will definitely bite us again, but believing the dog will *not* bite is illogical.

Does forgiveness erase the consequences of bad behavior? A crime victim may "forgive" their assailant, but that doesn't mean the jail sentence gets reduced—even if the perpetrator confesses, and promises to change. An excessive gambler may stop betting, but the havoc wreaked on finances doesn't disappear with a changed mind. If a person borrows money but doesn't pay it back, their reputation suffers. These situations are analogous to our relationships with estranged adult children. Our forgiveness doesn't instantly restore our trust.

Is forgiveness wise when there's no apology? In a 2001 article in the *Journal of Counseling & Development*, the term "forgiveness" is defined as ceasing to feel angry or resentful. The meaning focuses on letting go of emotions that can cause distress.[1] It's the definition intended in most discussions on forgiveness today.

Doreen's anger toward her son made her miserable. She was frustrated, hurt, and consumed by thoughts of him, their disappointing relationship, and her rage. Guilt about her anger became overwhelming.

Letting go of deeply embedded emotions and resolving unhealthy resentment can be beneficial. Forgiveness can help you move beyond troubling emotions such as sadness, guilt, and anger. That's why the concept of forgiveness, regardless of the wrongdoer's presence or attitude, is so often suggested by helping professionals. Forgiveness, for your own benefit, is therapeutic.

Can forgiveness empower you? In refusing to forgive, Doreen couldn't quite let go enough to move forward in peace. Harboring blame and anger gave her son power over her emotions. Holding him accountable, even from a distance while he was off living his life, was like allowing him to hold her hostage.

If you believe forgiveness is impossible, unjust, or are angered that the topic is even proposed here, don't feel badly. Perhaps in the future you will feel differently. Or perhaps substitute another word such as "releasing."

Eventually, Doreen accepted the idea of letting go, without pardoning her son's bad behavior. She decided that if he ever tried to come back into her life, she would have to hold him accountable in order to make a reconciliation work. But concentrating on his wrongs had imprisoned her in rage. Making a decision to "forgive," and release her anger, freed her. She was then able to get on with her own life.

When the Bad Outweighs The Good

The impact of estrangement may be compounded by other difficulties, and arrive at the worst possible time. You may have also lost a loved one in death, been diagnosed with a serious illness, or been injured in a car accident. Along with estrangement, some parents find themselves coping with job loss, divorce, lawsuits, painful injuries, and other difficult, or even life-changing, events. Some face several crises at once.

That's how it was for me. So I know this can feel as if you're under attack, standing in a maze with fires starting at every possible path. Negative clichés about life may come to mind, blot out hope or become a mantra. *Kick 'em when they're down. When it rains it pours.* And then there are the questions: *Why me? What now?* And *what else could go wrong?* Suddenly, there's proof of Murphy's Law. Do you recognize yourself here? If so, take notice. In Chapter Two, we talked about observational bias. When we're focused on something, we find evidence of it. Being aware of how the mind works can help you combat negative thinking. Acknowledge that giving in to negativity does no good.

Rather than share all the muck that went on in my life, let's see how one mother turned her circumstances around.

Rowena's only daughter had become distant, and occasionally, even hostile. Still, when Rowena was diagnosed with breast cancer, she asked if she'd drive her to and from the chemo treatments. Her daughter refused, even blurting out that she hoped her mother would die.

The next two days piled on even more distress. Rowena was sued by a neighbor who had tripped in her yard. Then a pipe broke in the night, and she woke up to a flooded house. To top off her aggravation with more sorrow, out in the driveway, the plumber who came to fix the pipe backed his truck over Rowena's old deaf dog.

For several weeks, Rowena did little more than shuffle through her work days in a haze of robotic motions. She would chirp the expected *please, thank you*, and *fine how are you?* Then she'd drive back home on autopilot, and crawl into bed.

When Rowena could barely open the front door past the pile of mail that had gathered beneath the slot, she stooped to pick it up. She let the sliding pile loose on the kitchen table, and sat in one of the sturdy wood chairs. A charity envelope with a child's hungry face caught her eye. The picture reminded Rowena of what her mother used to say: *Be grateful for any blessings.*

Rowena imagined her mother saying that now. She was right to focus on the good. Maybe Rowena's daughter didn't want a mother's love, but Rowena still missed her own mother, who had had a tough but encouraging nature. She recalled her mother sitting down with a pen and paper. Rowena needed a plan. She made herself a cup of tea, grabbed her magnetic notepad from the refrigerator door, and got to work.

When problems mount, it's vital to create a plan. For my coaching clients, I created an easy-to-remember tactic that lightens the mood and makes issues more manageable: *P, B, and J.* No, not a peanut butter and jelly sandwich—although that might be comforting. The initials stand for: *Prioritize, Break* into slices, or *Just* leave alone.

Here's how *P, B, and J* works. First, you'll need to stop seeing your life like a mine field, even if it feels like one. When multiple issues, hurts, and problems get muddled into an oppressive pile, you need to examine and work on each issue individually. That way, you can *prioritize.* Some problems are more important than others. Some you can *break* into more manageable slices. And some you can *just* leave alone.

Using Rowena's circumstances as an example, let's fully explore the concept of *P, B, and J.*

P: Prioritize. Determine the most important issue. Order other issues in terms of what needs attention first. Then begin to take action. Rowena prioritized her health. She'd already missed two of her treatments. She phoned to reschedule them. The next most urgent matter was the lawsuit. She left a phone message for her homeowner's insurance agent to call her back. Next were her rusty pipes. That one needed more thought, and to be handled in stages, as did a few more things on her list.

B: Break into manageable slices. The plumber had insisted her old pipes needed replacing. Rowena didn't want another flood, but the prospect required money and time. She'd break that prospect into more manageable pieces. First, she'd get other opinions and estimates. If she did need to replace the pipes, she'd choose a plumber who could work in stages that fit around her cancer treatments.

To grieve the loss of her beloved pet, Rowena planned a garden memorial to honor him. The old terrier had helped Rowena through the dark days after her husband left her years ago. Training a puppy might be too much right now, but she could find an older dog. Maybe one as lonely as she felt just now. The thought of a new old friend to sit with her—two peas in a pitiful pod—made her smile. She made a note to call rescue services soon.

She looked at the mail on the table. It wasn't going anywhere, and more arrived daily. She began to make piles: junk mail to shred and toss, magazines and other items to read at her leisure, important bills or other items needing attention. She'd make time the following day to continue organizing all the mail, then go through and prioritize for further action.

J: Just leave alone. At 32, Rowena's daughter was hardly a child whose behavior Rowena could excuse. Her daughter had wished her dead. The memory made Rowena nauseous. She must put herself first. She would not put herself in a position to hear such verbal abuse again. For the time being, there was no solution. She'd just leave that situation alone. She circled her notes about her daughter with a wavy line.

Strategies

During my children's growing-up years, mothers were advised that when their children were upset, they should say, "Use your words." Not the four-lettered ones, of course. We told the kids to calmly explain why they felt the way they did, and to negotiate what they wanted rather than use aggression, sulk or cry. It is good advice, even for adult children, but yours may refuse to talk, or use words that are hateful, accusatory, and definitely not meant to facilitate reconciliation. The only negotiating they do may be to tell you to stay away.

We may also have tried to talk things through, but as much as it hurts, our children may not care what we want or how we feel. Some mothers explain their children's point of view like this: *They just don't give a damn.*

At least these mothers are voicing their thoughts. We can't do that in every situation. We may not be the type to frequent forums or support groups, or we might get tired of doing so. We may worry our friends and family members are tired of our whining. Frankly, maybe we are too. That's where strategies come in. Having tools to turn to and employ can be empowering. Strategies help us step away from the pain, and regain ourselves. Use the helpful strategies listed earlier in this chapter under the heading, *Sadness Hurts, So Take Care*, as well as the additional ones below

Write it out. Some mothers have pages and pages of letters they've written to their estranged children but have never sent. They may have already sent numerous emails, cards, texts, and letters with negative results. Frustrated, they then use letters as a one-sided conversation, and feel better after expressing their emotions. Similarly, a journal provides space to release feelings. Some find that reading the entries later helps them understand their feelings too. Journaling is known to help relieve stress, so if keeping a diary feels right, do it.

In the early months, Julia wrote letters daily. Doing so helped her discharge her emotions and feel as if she was sharing experiences with her son the way she used to in their morning calls. At first, she intended to keep all the letters in a folder and, if estrangement persisted, leave instructions that they be given to her son after her death. But Julia has since decided to destroy them. "I realize now those letters were for me," she explains. "Writing them helped me cope."

Keep a record. Many mothers worry about how much their child is missing out on in the family. Some also believe that medical history, genetics or ancestry-related information might be useful to their child later. Recording life events, health facts, and other items they feel are important creates a record. These mothers can release their concern, and feel secure that should their child need or want it, they can provide the information at any time.

Be mindful. Fully experience the present. This can include simply noticing and accepting your thoughts and feelings. That sort of curious observation may alert you to sensitivities around certain people or certain subjects, and that sort of information can help you in the future. After observing, you can let the thoughts and feelings drift away, and get back to the present moment and whatever you were engaged in before the feelings intruded.

Recognize, Analyze, Regroup, Adapt. The old saying about knowledge being power is only half true. It's what you do with the knowledge that can really make a difference—and that second, vital step is included in this strategy with initials pronounced like a cheer: RA-RA. I originally created this strategy for my life coaching clients, who successfully utilized it in many scenarios. You can, too. If you find yourself avoiding situations or people, are fearful, or disturbed by a specific emotion, then you already recognize that something needs your attention. Take some time to analyze, regroup, and then come up with a plan to adapt.

Meg avoided people because she was afraid she would lose control. A strong leader in her community, she *recognized* that the idea of others seeing her as weak repulsed her. When Meg *analyzed* her feelings, she understood she derived self-esteem from being strong in others' eyes. Her feelings stemmed from childhood. One of two sisters, Meg was always the strong, capable daughter. In her teen years, her level-headed persona solidified. Friends went boy crazy, and suffered teen angst, but she was the rock they came to for advice. With her self-worth tied into her strong leadership, crying in public was mortifying to Meg.

Once she recognized how an idea of herself—how she should act, and how she needed other people to view her—was holding her back, she knew it was time to *regroup*. She began to take small steps. Instead of allowing her "damage control" philosophy to restrict her to spending just a few minutes in the office to sign papers, she stopped avoiding everyone. At first, she forced herself to spend just five minutes chatting with agents who worked under her. As she interacted more, and widened out to be seen more around town, she began to *adapt* and feel more confident. She might need to cry, but not every moment. And she could excuse herself. Or, if someone did see her tear up, she realized that didn't change who she was. No matter what, she was a strong, capable woman. Her estranged son and his wife couldn't take that from her, but she was also human. Maybe eventually, that chink in her armor would even improve her leadership skills. Maybe she could better empathize.

The initials for this technique (RA-RA) don't correctly spell out the cheer, but since they make the same sound, let's give Meg a *Rah-Rah!*

Laugh. The healing powers of humor are irrefutable. Studies support the cliché that laughter is good medicine, but when it comes to loss, some feel guilty about humor. They believe they *should* be sad.

When Dan was around eight, we attended a military funeral. There, Dan and one of his brothers got a case of the giggles. When the young sailors in their dress uniforms marched out and pivoted, one raised his bugle, and others performed a rifle salute, their robotic drill movements struck my young sons as funny. I shushed them, of course, but after a few moments, they sank to the ground, covering their mouths against peals of laughter.

Guiding my boys to the back of the crowd, I looked around. Thankfully, the family of the deceased was much like the man had been—always teasing, with his eyes always twinkling. His relatives and friends smiled through their tears, obviously tickled at my sons' reaction. As family members got up to talk about the man whose life the ceremony honored, they cracked jokes. They were lighthearted like he had been.

In some families, laughter at a funeral might be seen as disrespectful. A family's culture influences the use of humor as a healing tool in times of pain. In my sadness after Dan's estrangement, I was thankful for the humor my family shared. One example was our alteration of a shared family joke.

Over the years, we had often blamed a non-existent person we named "Not Me" for every broken glass, spilled drink, or other mishap that no one owned up to. After Dan's dismissal of us, we blamed him instead. Every mess, every break, every problem became "Dan's fault." This may sound harsh to some, but we weren't being mean-spirited. We were coping. Humor is a good way to defuse anger, melt sorrow, or simply acknowledge the elephant in the room. Every time Dan was blamed, we smiled. And if Dan knew about us doing this, I believe he would smile, too.

Even if you're not accustomed to laughing through pain, humor still may come naturally, and catch you off guard. In the early months after a loved one is lost in death, people often say that a spark of amusement brings the death to mind, and then triggers guilt. They realize that for just a moment, they forgot the deceased was gone. Be aware that you may have similar experiences after estrangement.

If you catch yourself laughing, and then feeling guilty for it, take notice. Or maybe the joking of your spouse or other family member disturbs you. By recognizing and analyzing the distress, you can then regroup and adapt (RA-RA).

One mother of two estranged sons says that once she allowed herself to laugh, her wit grew sharp. She sometimes poked fun at her situation, and faced her embarrassment head-on. She explains: "It was kind of like wearing a big sandwich board placard that boldly read, 'REJECTED MOM.' My ability to laugh broke through tension, so others felt more comfortable, too."

Reappraise. Another way to begin adapting to the loss is through reappraisal, a process in which you reevaluate how you view an event, a memory, or circumstance. You reinterpret the situation, seeing it in a more positive or less threatening way, and then change your thoughts about how well you can deal with its emotional impact. One example of reappraisal would be choosing to view estrangement more like an empty nester might see their child's absence. From that perspective, the situation can be approached more like a new phase, or for some of you, even as a new adventure. Like anything, the ability to reappraise is strengthened with practice, as are the benefits.[2, 3]

If you're doing the exercises in this book, you've already begun to see your situation in new ways that support you. Altering defeatist beliefs about your inability to cope, and changing them to more empowering beliefs and statements, is a form of reappraisal. A few other reappraisals we've tried include seeing loss as part of life, and viewing acceptance as giving in, and honoring your son or daughter's decision, rather than giving up. We have also talked about recognizing how you have already grown because of the estrangement. These sorts of shifts help you accept the circumstances. You can find a new way of life, celebrate the time you have, and find more meaning and joy.

To practice reappraisal, take a few moments to look over the parts in this chapter on ways to support yourself including making moments meaningful, trying new things, and taking time just for you. With these suggestions, and with ideas of your own in mind, you can take a few moments each night to make some notes, and answer the question: *How can I improve my life, my outlook, and myself?*

You can view the question based on your feelings about each day, and any events or emotional triggers you encountered. Or, you can answer from a general perspective since the estrangement began. Or shift from day-to-day. It's up to you.

Think of yourself as the dynamic being you truly are. If you declined an invitation out of fear you would be asked about your son or daughter, how could you reappraise? You could expect that no one would ask. Or, you could prepare ready responses like the ones in Chapter Three. If a co-worker talked about her family plans, and in your distress you made a statement you regret, how might you have better handled the conversation? The idea is to use your imagination to practice handling things in ways you can look back on and feel good about. There is much wisdom in planning ahead.

Practice gratitude. While the practice of gratitude may sound all gooey and wonderful, it does work. Just as observational bias can influence our thoughts about our parenting and any perceived mistakes we might have made, gratitude attunes us to finding the good. A grateful outlook helps us appreciate the things we value but perhaps take for granted. Gratitude helps no matter how long your child has been estranged, whether you're in the throes of disbelief, or years past the separation. Focusing on good can shift your perception to a more abundant outlook, making each day a new adventure.

As is the case with reappraisal, gratitude requires repetition. It's the *practice* of gratitude that provides lasting benefits. Starting more than a decade ago, Robert Emmons, Ph.D., and his colleagues repeatedly witnessed that people who make a practice of gratitude reap many rewards. Their health is improved with lower blood pressure and stronger immune systems. They sleep better, and suffer less pain. People who make a conscious practice of appreciation and gratitude feel more optimistic, more alert, alive, and joyful. They also have better social connections—perhaps because they're more outgoing, more forgiving, and more generous as a result of those positive feelings.

Try this easy practice: Write down a few things you're grateful for each night. Maybe you'll promote happy dreams and restful sleep. Or, do this in the morning like I sometimes do. Use gratitude to set up your positive focus for the day. What have you got to lose but a dreary mood?

Forget struggling to write down things that are earth-shattering. A practice of gratitude is about noticing the tiniest things that bring you joy. For me, that may be the way my dog wants to snuggle up to me—no matter what. Maybe you appreciate the warmth of the sunlight after months of snow, feel glad your husband tells you look nice on bad hair days, or are thankful the neighbor's cat visits you for a pat but then goes home to eat. Perhaps you're thankful your boss was out all day, that there was one tea bag left in the box, or that you found a fresh pack of gum you'd forgotten about.

You can go very small and specific: *The tea was sweet and warm on my throat. The gum burst with minty flavor.* Or, you can take a more general approach if that feels right: *Everyone was cheerful at work today.*

To prompt appreciative thoughts, try sifting through your memories for joy. One memory that always makes me grateful is that of a dreary morning when I was five. The rain had finally stopped. Out in the yard, a big pink lily had bloomed. Its frilly petals were spotted with rain droplets, and it filled the air with a scent like baby powder, candy, and even my mom. For a five-year-old cooped up inside all morning, the moment held magic.

Although practice is necessary, you don't need a formal journal. Use a white board in your kitchen, Post-it notes you stick up around the house, or a jar you drop coins or a bill into with each good thought—then donate the money to a charity once full. You can even use a smartphone app.

Come up with your own ideas to make this practice yours. Make the art of gratitude part of your daily life, and see how good you will feel.

Ask yourself what a wise person would do. Remembering her mother's words motivated Rowena to crawl out of the doldrums. Can you think of someone who has overcome obstacles? Who do you admire for her tenacity? Think of a successful businessperson, a modern, historical, or spiritual figure, or a friend or family member you look up to. Faced with your circumstances, what might this wise individual do? Getting outside ourselves frees up energy, and helps us look for and find solutions.

Visualize. Don't underestimate the power of your mind. Champions know that to imagine taking calm, purposeful action, and then execute the action pays off. Picture yourself as flexible, resilient, and strong. You tackle problems, and come out ahead. Imagine marking a folder "done," then stuffing it into a drawer you shut and lock. Whatever has piled up in your life, see it as settled. Visualize signing the last payment check, walking out your door with a spring in your step, or turning the calendar page with a satisfied smile. Imagine the joy of knowing problems are in your past. Winning thoughts feel better than losing ones. Train your mind to hope for the best.

Gain perspective. "This too shall pass." The wise old saying is true. You've been through tough times before. You may have been overwhelmed, but you solved problems, found ways around them, or learned to let them go. In your future, current troubles will also be in the past.

Ask for help. Some problems need a team. Challenges may require expertise. Get a specialist—a plumber, an attorney, a doctor, an accountant, a therapist, a tutor, a contractor, a handyman, a life coach, or whatever expert makes sense. Maybe a friend can help. Don't rule out help for daily routines either. Stress can make you more forgetful. Juggling extra plates can throw you off balance. Help with chores lets you get your footing. Get a neighbor to watch your pet, hire someone to mow the yard, enlist family members to take over some chores. You can also lower your standards a bit. I'm not advocating letting trash pile up, wearing dirty clothes, or going without a bath. But in times of distress, having a floor clean enough to eat off is overrated. Spend your energy wisely.

Declutter. You don't need frustration like the inability to find a tool, a fashion accessory, or important papers you've tucked someplace "safe." Especially in times of stress, hunting for keys yet again can make you feel like a failure. And living in the midst of chaos magnifies any feelings that your life is out of control. Put a few systems in place and repeat actions to create helpful habits. Put keys in a bowl or on a hook by the door. Do laundry when there's time to finish the job, and actually put the clothes away. Put a shredder or trash bin in a convenient spot, then immediately dispose of junk mail. Take the extra steps to put shoes in a closet rather than kick them off and leave them where they lay. You know your habits, junky drawers, and repeated misplacements. Whether it's a frustrating clutter spot, disorganization, or too much stuff for the space, pick one area and work at a solution. Don't add road blocks. Clear the way.

Make room. Another aspect of decluttering involves paring out activities that no longer support you or that add stress at this time. I have encouraged my life coaching clients to imagine life like a bouquet. Even the most balanced and beautiful flower arrangement eventually needs pruning. Bedraggled blooms need removing. Fresh water must be added. Stems must be snipped with a fresh cut so they can soak up renewing moisture. Our lives are similar. Interests and commitments that at one point filled us with joy may later drain us. In your life bouquet, what can you prune back, remove or shift? Make room for fresh, restorative blooms: uplifting people, restful activities, engaging hobbies, and fun.

You *Can* Manage Adversity

When my son was newly estranged, and I was hit with a bunch of problems, I remember identifying with the saying: *Stop the world, I want to get off!* Unfortunately, our life journeys don't pause to let us catch up. As Rowena's did, your road may fill with obstacles, spike strips, and unwelcome hitchhikers you're forced to pick up. Don't rush ahead without a map. Park yourself in a chair, gather energy and create a plan. Then climb back into the driver's seat. You can dodge some road blocks, patch up your emotional tires, and drop unwelcome travelers at their destinations. Make a plan. Remember, *P, B, and J*. Prioritize, break into manageable slices, or just leave alone. With a take-action focus, you can use strategies such as the ones explored in this chapter to support your wellbeing. You can get started on solutions that shape your future now.

Depression and Suicidal Thoughts: Do You Need Help?

Years past the estrangement, when I explained to a friend how dark my outlook had once been, she told me I must have been depressed. I wasn't surprised. At the time, I had wondered myself. But I had also stopped to analyze, and do research about depression. While I was sad, I wasn't in danger. I hadn't lost interest in most things. My participation in some activities had waned, but I had started others. And although I was tempted to isolate myself, for the most part, I didn't do that. While I may have let the phone go to voicemail more often, and even dreaded some events, I would eventually come around. I returned phone calls, and although I pared down my commitments, I socialized. I was still getting most things done, still participating in life—and still wanting to.

Like many people do at some point in their lives, in my darkest moments, I wondered if my family really loved me, and whether they would miss me if I was gone. But I wasn't suicidal. I didn't ponder ways to kill myself. I didn't have a plan in place. *And I didn't want to die.* What I wanted was to come to terms with my feelings and heal. I wanted to regain my optimism and joy. I wanted to be me again.

It's completely normal to feel down after an emotional trauma. But if you continue to feel stuck, can't seem to shake the blues, and find that those feelings interfere with your life, you may need to seek help. As time goes on, and you work at taking care of yourself in all the ways we've talked about here (and more), if you still can't shake the looping thoughts that bring you down, do recognize the wisdom in asking for professional help.

There is no shame in seeking assistance. If you can't seem to get past your situation, or feel you're getting worse instead of better, that does not mean you are sick, crazy, or in any way weak. A great many of us have trouble asking for help, and may even feel ashamed. But recognizing your own limitations is a sign of strength.

See Chapter Three for strategies to find the right therapist for you. The resource box in Chapter Three can also help. So can your physician, a pastor, your spouse, a trusted friend, or family member.

I cannot say this strongly enough: If you find yourself thinking about committing suicide, and particularly if you have a plan, it is imperative that you get help immediately. If you're feeling unsafe, get help *now*. Here's how:

- Go to an emergency room.

- Call a suicide hotline. Try: 1-800-273-8255, which is the hotline from www.suicidepreventionlifeline.org

- If you're in immediate danger, call 9-1-1.

Finding Strength in the Process

The challenges we face and live through can either break us, or mold us and help us grow. I wanted the dark period after Dan's estrangement to shape me for the better. Rather than allow the situation to debilitate me, I sought a sense of meaning, and a way to move ahead. But, the task seemed daunting, almost impossible. How could I reclaim what was forever changed? Could I muster the strength? You may feel the same.

Going through some old books one day, I came across a photo-heavy textbook on Japanese art. As I flipped through the book, I remembered learning about a Japanese view of happenstance that had instantly intrigued me: *Wabi-sabi*.

The idea of *Wabi-sabi* is embracing mistakes, artfully incorporating the happenstance, and making strength from weakness. In Japanese art, this might mean that when pottery cracks during the firing process, it is mended with seams of gold. The artist makes beauty from an ugly crack, and generates strength in a once-weakened point. Rather than discarding the imperfect piece, the artist utilizes mistakes, which are woven into the final product, and even admired.

Many of us use the concept of *Wabi-sabi*. Perhaps as I was, you were taught not to waste. For me, that meant that if a jacket got a hole, I might embroider a design around the ragged spot, and apply lace to peek out from the underside. When redoing my kitchen, incorrect measurements left us short of a specific ceramic tile type for our countertops. So we found a colorful edging to artfully take up space. When overwhelmed after my mother's sudden death, I turned to writing, filling in the jagged seams of my life with meaning by working toward fulfilling unrealized dreams as her early death taught me to do.

The sorrow and pain of estrangement are much the same.

If we allow the broken trust from one very close relationship to extend a lack of trust to *all* relationships, we're making the choice to hurt our-selves. Our emotional scars victimize us, just as our children have. Caught up in fear, we attempt to protect ourselves by shutting out the possibility of pain. But we also cut ourselves off, and hinder forward momentum.

Like Kathleen realized, I knew that the tapestry of my life and family had changed. But I could choose to make beauty from the flaw. I could choose to see the estrangement as a point of strength, and perhaps even beauty, rather than a raw and gaping hole. I chose to heal, finding beauty and strength in the process. So can you.

✈The Good Life: Yours

In Chapter Four, we explored the idea of wishing our children well. We visualized him or her in a happy life. We reflected on what that would look like and mean, and saw our children successful, well, and content. In order to adapt and embrace our own future, now let's turn to our own sunlit path. Visualize yourself happy, healthy, and living a meaningful life.

Before Starting: You may want to look at your notes from the *Take Stock* exercise in Chapter Four. Doing so will provide insight into how you've changed since the estrangement, and enable you to see yourself on-the-mend, fortifying deficits, and getting back in touch with yourself, your dreams, the activities you enjoy, and the people who are important to you.

The positive results of this exercise are for *you*. Your wishes cannot magically fix your child's life or your relationship with him or her. Please make this about your life, separate and apart from any possible relationship with your child now or in the future. Imagining what a satisfying life looks like on your own, and perhaps with others who choose to be with you, follows the spirit of this book: acceptance, and moving successfully forward in your own life. Earlier, you wished your child well. Now wish yourself well. By letting go of trying to control another person's choices, or making your happiness dependent on what they may or may not do, you strengthen yourself. You set the stage to let go of worry, anger, pride, or expectation. You set yourself free to embrace the present.

Let's Begin: Choose a quiet space such as in your bedroom with the lights dimmed, or in a comfortable outdoor setting. Or you could try this as you close your eyes before falling asleep at night. Using the tips below, visualize yourself as happy, well-adjusted, loved, and content. What does that look like to you?

Tips For Success

- Resist the urge to overthink details. This isn't about detailed scenarios. We're going for impressions here. Blissful images, wishes, and dreams.

- Allow thoughts and images to drift in, and then analyze how you feel about them. If something causes tension, makes you angry or sad, direct yourself to let the image go. Then refocus with a clear intent. Ask yourself: *What makes me feel happy?* Do you see yourself all smiles, sharing time with your partner? Are you outdoors? Successful and engaged at work? Walking along the shore? Imagine yourself in the scene.

- Frame this visualization to fit your beliefs. Perhaps you say a prayer. Maybe you imagine yourself in a loving Creator's hands, or ask for a blessing. Or simply imagine without any specific beliefs in mind. Visualize yourself as contented and engaged in meaningful tasks.

- If it feels right, include your physical body too. Close your eyes, open your palms to the sky, or assume a meditational pose.

- Use your breath. Add powerful thoughts and images to support you. Imagine inhaling peace, confidence, and love. When you exhale, visualize worry, anger, and all negativity swirling out and away from you.

- If words or phrases come to you, let them. For me, the phrase "dancing through life," was immediately prominent. The words felt good, and allowed positive imagery to fall into my mind and heart. Whatever dark clouds or full-on storms came my way, I could weather them. I could still feel joy, see the good, and cherish the beautiful—I could dance through life.

Make It Tangible: Now that you've imagined yourself happy, contented, and moving on with your life, make it real. Using a computer program or magazine cut outs, make a collage. Or draw what your visualization looks like. My creation depicted me (as a clip art figure, much like a child). I danced along a path lined with wildflowers and other items I love. The words "dancing through life," are prominent. So is sunlight, and spiritual imagery—to provide me with energy and strength.

Six months after my son first became estranged I printed out and shared my creation with friends as part of a goal-setting meeting. If it helps you, then share your creation with people you trust to support you. You might also hang it in a place you'll see it often. If you tuck it away in a drawer or some other safe, *out-of-sight* place, don't let it also be *out-of-mind*. Pull it out now and again, and allow the imagery to strengthen your beliefs. You can be happy. You can be whole. *You can be dancing through life.*

Notes

CHAPTER SIX

Managing Effects On The Family

If you think of your family as a circle, a cube, or some other geometric form, then you'll understand that each part holds the shape together. What happens when you remove one section of a triangle? A third line no longer joins the two. Take out part of a circle, and it's no longer closed. Remove the top plane of a cylinder, and what's inside is no longer contained.

That's how it is for the family when a member becomes estranged. Your circle no longer smoothly rolls. Your square has a missing side. Your triangle is reduced to two lines, connecting at a single point. How you close the gap, leave it gaping, or come together in a brand new form is what this chapter is all about.

In the pages ahead, you'll find the real life stories of couples and families as they manage their fears, and work through struggles in their committed relationships, with children and extended family, and on social media. They are shared here to help. Don't settle for a broken triangle. You *can* close the gap, assess and reshape your family, and develop into a new and even better form.

A United Front

In a series of recent television commercials, a father takes the kids on adventures, leads his son down a dangerous ski slope, and lets the children eat fast food in the car. Then he says, "Don't tell Mom." We laugh at the parent-child alliance that leaves the mother out, but it's not funny when one parent talks with an estranged child on the sly. The left-out parent can feel betrayed. Let's see what we can learn from couples where one parent's alliance with a child hurts the other parent, jeopardizes the marriage, and does nothing to present a united front. Then, we'll talk about how to best handle contact from an estranged child.

After Pauline's husband had a heart attack, he secretly reached out to their estranged daughter with money and gifts. When Pauline found out, she was angry. Her husband had been in touch with their estranged daughter for months. Among other things, he had bought her a car. Because of her husband's recent heart attack, Pauline tried to remain calm, and to understand his reasons. His illness had changed their relationship. She saw her husband as frail, and worried she would lose him. Therefore, she often tiptoed around rather than confront him on anything.

But when their daughter sent a wedding invitation addressed only to her father, Pauline's patience grew thin. "My husband already knew she was getting married," says Pauline. "He was paying for a fancy wedding I wasn't even invited to." She insisted they see a marriage counselor.

In those sessions, Pauline learned that after his heart attack, her husband was fearful he'd die without reconciling with their only child. But he had also come to realize that he'd been buying her love. He admitted their daughter only called when she wanted something. The couple then laid some ground rules, and worked at rebuilding a healthy relationship.

The husband told their daughter that he had been wrong to contact her and to support her financially without her mother's knowledge. He explained that his heart attack had clouded his judgment, and asked their daughter to join them in counseling so they could all reconcile. But she refused. Soon after, she contacted him again to ask for money. When he wouldn't give it to her, she slandered her parents on Facebook.

They blocked her, and refused to engage. Three years passed, but Pauline recently received a Mother's Day card. She replied with a short thank you note, and invited their daughter to call for her father's upcoming birthday. "His birthday came and went with no word." The couple still hopes to one day reconcile, but they have gone on with their lives. "We're actually quite close now, and are in a good place," says Pauline.

Some couples come to a mutual agreement that one spouse's contact is more acceptable to them than complete estrangement. So when does contact with one parent and not with the other become a problem? The key word is "mutual." If you face this sort of exclusion, use the questions discussed with examples below to analyze whether it's working for you.

Is your spouse sharing updates and information about your child, and considering your interests? When the spouse who is still in contact is open about what they know, communication between the parents may make the situation tolerable. Factors such as your child's age and maturity level may also influence the decision to allow contact with just one parent. Never hesitate to reevaluate the situation together.

In the case of Diedre and her husband, their son began to distance himself from his father soon after he went away to college. He was angry that his father expected him to live with relatives, or work to pay for an apartment. By the end of the first semester, his anger had spread. He thought his parents should provide him with a car and pay for related costs. He also developed a deep disdain for his father's overall worldview, and was intolerant of him.

Their son would call Diedre but didn't want to speak with his father. Occasionally, he asked her to drive up for lunch. She worried about her husband's feelings, but he encouraged her to go ahead. At least one of them was talking to their kid. Because their son had also changed his appearance, the couple assumed this was a phase. For two years, Diedre kept in touch, and the couple paid their son's tuition. Then, when he graduated and got a job, he tried to turn Diedre against her husband. He asked her why she stayed with such an annoying man.

Diedre was incensed. She informed him that she loved his father. Soon afterward, their son stopped contacting her, and ignored her calls.

Then he moved five states away. He left a forwarding address with relatives, so for two years, she continued to send occasional cards and letters. They all went unanswered. "He's gone on with his life," says Diedre. "It's time for us to do the same."

Is your partner taking "sides" with your child? If so, longstanding family patterns may be at work. Or, as in Pauline's situation, your spouse may be acting out of fear or emotional distress. Family dynamics, cultural influence, or ideals from your upbringing may have shaped you, your spouse, and your marriage—thus your response to the situation of estrangement.

When Jennifer's husband sided with her estranged son, she insisted they see a marriage counselor. They were still raising two daughters. Unfortunately, they couldn't work things out. Her son had been increasingly disrespectful since his early teens. Jennifer believed he was following her husband's example. She says her husband had put other people ahead of her throughout their marriage. When the couple divorced, their son took his father's side, which she had expected. Father and son now live together, and their son remains estranged from Jennifer.

In Jennifer's view, the men in her husband's family are disrespectful of the women. She hopes to break the pattern for her two daughters, who were eight and nine at the time of the divorce two years ago. "Time will tell," says Jennifer. "But it's a tough road when my husband and my son are working to turn the girls against me." Jennifer joined an online PAS forum, which has been a good source of information and support.

Is your spouse keeping the contact secret? If your spouse speaks to your son or daughter in secret, work at responding with forethought that takes your goals, happiness, and well-being into account.

Louisa's oldest son is estranged. She was surprised when her husband let it slip he'd been in fairly regular communication. He informed her that their son had asked him not to tell her. When she said he was wrong to bow to their son's request, her husband became angry.

Though distraught, Louisa also knew her husband was confused. Their children had always been the center of their lives. And their eldest had been very close with his father. But his secret contact felt like betrayal. She wanted to talk more about this with her husband, but knew she would be too emotional. Then her husband would interrupt, and probably even walk out.

Louisa wrote her husband a letter, and left it on the seat of his car so that he'd find it when he left for work. In the letter she first asked that he please read it through to the end. Then, she used bullet points to lay out the hurt their son had caused in the last few years. She asked her husband whether he believed she was a good mother and wife, and whether he believed she deserved their son's alienation. "How would you feel if the tables were turned?" she wrote. She added that she loved him, and hoped they could work this out. Her husband arrived home late that night, but he apologized.

Since then, Louisa's husband has begun sharing the details from his phone calls with their son. Obviously, the situation is not perfect, but having their contact out in the open has helped. Louisa still feels slighted, but is willing to tolerate the circumstances for now.

If your circumstances are similar, can you tolerate them as Louisa has? Or will you need to take a different stance? How can *you* best approach the situation and your partner? Set yourself up for success. Plan the best way to engage in conversation. Consider when might be the best time to talk. Also consider your approach. Accusations may not be as effective as a positive or even curious stance. Think back to other issues at other times. How did you confront your partner? What did you learn then that you can bring into the present situation?

Even if you are not currently excluded, a conversation about expectations can ward off future issues. Talk with your spouse. Try to come to a *mutual* decision about how either of you will handle any contact.

In our household, my husband and I decided from the start that any communication with one of us would be disclosed to the other. While our son had never tried to pit my husband and me against each other, we weren't about to let him start (even unintentionally).

For us, full-disclosure is the best tactic, but every marriage is different. You must decide what's appropriate, tolerable, or works for you and your spouse, and then negotiate as needed. If you are communicating with your child and excluding the other parent, feel as if your spouse sides with your estranged child, or are in any way distressed by one parent's contact, address the issue. Don't allow resentment to take root.

For obvious reasons, marriage counseling is most beneficial when couples work together. However, if your spouse refuses, an insightful counselor may be able to provide some individual guidance. Positive changes in one partner can still positively affect the relationship.

When your son or daughter wants to maintain contact with only one parent, work with your spouse to arrive at an agreement. Also recognize that deciding something now does not mean it must be a final decision. Circumstances that are tolerable now may not be tolerable later. The uncertainty of estrangement and its duration may influence your decisions, which may change over time. Do what works for you and your spouse now. You can always re-evaluate later.

Couples Tips

- Think things through before assigning blame.
- Check-in with your partner.
- Talk things through. Share your feelings.
- In social situations, plan some code words or cues.
- Beware of emotional distancing or numbing.
- Keep your partner's relating style in mind.
- Find a friendly way to convey your understanding.

The Blame Game

In the early period of shock, when parents are searching for answers, blaming is common. Some sort of relationship pattern, favoritism, or another issue may very well have contributed to a child's ability to cut ties. However, the haze of pain and shock can distort our thinking. If we're trying to make sense of the unthinkable, we're under duress. We may not be as discerning or empathetic as we normally would be.

Blaming one adult for another's bad behavior lets one person off the hook. Ask yourself whether doing so is fair and helpful, or perhaps creates more problems. What does blaming solve? Think things through before assigning blame. Only you can decide whether your feelings toward your partner's culpability in the estrangement outweigh the good you see, or the value of your marriage as a whole. Perhaps the couples' stories shared here will shed some light on your own situation.

Candace, a mother of three boys, believes her husband's leniency with their two younger sons is partially to blame for their estrangement. She says her husband expected more from their oldest child, the same as his family did from him. Although it may seem counterintuitive, Candace believes her husband's high expectations for their oldest son may have helped shape him into the kind and responsible adult he is today. Their oldest son remains close to them, while the younger ones are not.

Though Candace at first blamed her husband, she has come to terms with those feelings. "Kids grow up," she says. "Our younger sons were twenty-five and twenty-four when they left the family. *Adults*. They chose their ways."

Let's look at another example. Marla, a mother of two, got all the blame when her youngest daughter walked away at age 21. "I had gone back to work when our two girls were teens," Marla says. "When our younger daughter cut us off, my husband accused me of not being there for the girls when he said they needed me the most." Hurt, Marla went to live with relatives.

Meanwhile, Marla's husband reached out to their estranged daughter. After a few months, their reunion ended. He came to Marla and apologized, asking her to come home. Marla says, "Apparently the reconciliation only stretched as far as his wallet."

Marla admits there's still work to do in the marriage, but she has forgiven her husband, and has recommitted to him. "Forgetting the way he turned on me is a tall order," she says. "But I do feel for him. He was looking for something or someone to blame. Our daughter's betrayal was confusing, and uncovered existing issues between us. Now, we get to try and solve them." Marla is looking for positives in a bad situation.

She came to understand that when she went back to work, her husband had been reminded of his childhood with a mother who struggled as a single mom. Marla's husband had always idealized the concept of a man caring for the mother of his children so she would never have to work. Rather than seeing Marla's career as her success, he'd seen it as his own failure. The couple had never explored those feelings, but their daughter's estrangement brought them to the fore. Understanding how his history influenced his feelings, Marla could empathize. She says, "Maybe we'll come out of this with an even stronger bond."

Both Candace and Marla have coped by attributing their husbands' behavior to causes with which they can empathize. Candace believes her husband's leniency toward the younger boys stems from his upbringing, which helps her to forgive. Marla attributes her husband's blaming of her to his need to make sense of the unthinkable. Their empathetic reasoning helped them remain committed to their marriages. Such thinking moderates the effects of stress on a committed relationship, while more negative thoughts can have the opposite effect.[1]

When people dwell on the negative, things always look worse. Negative memories pile onto current disappointments. During emotionally-charged periods, it's easy to allow our feelings to bleed into other areas of the relationship and our lives together. Whether your spouse blames you, or you find yourself blaming your spouse, be aware of your thoughts, and work at keeping them fair, focused, and in perspective.

How Fathers Relate

As I read through the responses from the small percentage of fathers who filled in the survey boxes with details of their own stories, two things became clear: Men worry about their partners, and want to protect them. And when it comes to estrangement, they're not so different from women.

Over and over, fathers said they were ashamed of the hurtful way their adult children treated their mother. They worried less for themselves than for their mates, and expressed anger, disbelief, and disgust at their adult children's behavior.

Many said that they minimize their own pain to remain strong for a mate. They worry that their partner will be burdened if they show their own emotional distress over the estrangement. Even widowed and divorced fathers, who have remarried or entered committed relationships, express concern on behalf of their mates. They worry the new partner will get caught in the middle of the conflict. Therefore, some said they refuse to talk about the problem, and discourage their new mate from getting involved.

Fathers suffer the same worries over other relationships that mothers do. They ask: *If your own child can walk away, who can you trust?*

They also worry about judgment, and say the estrangement affects their other relationships. Many avoid friends and social situations to keep people from finding out.

Leaning On One Another

Some couples pull together and grow closer after a child's estrangement. We can learn from successful marriages where couples feel equally important, and are in tune with one another's emotions.[2] After a child's estrangement, respectful, loving communication can keep partners aware of one another's feelings, which helps reinforce their bond, and weather unexpected emotional triggers like those we'll explore here.

Virgie said that when her son rejected them, she asked her husband to please check in with her—often. "I was going through hell," she says. "And my husband is not the most emotional man. The rejection didn't hit him as hard. I was going forward, doing what I needed to do, but it hurt. I didn't want him to think I was handling it as easily as he was."

The checking-in process worked. Just knowing her husband cared helped Virgie to feel loved, supported, and more secure when everything that seemed so solid and everlasting had broken apart. But five years later, her emotional response to a situation that reminded her of the estrangement caught them both by surprise. When their other son got serious about a young woman they liked very much, they were thrilled. Then they were invited to meet the woman's mother at her home (which became an emotional trigger).

While the woman was kind and inviting, Virgie found herself feeling uncomfortable. She began mentioning their need to get back on the road, but her husband seemed oblivious to her feelings. Later, she clued him in. "He was apologetic," says Virgie. "But it would have helped if I'd known meeting another potential in-law for one of my sons would bring up such strong feelings. We could have talked about it ahead of time, and planned some cues to keep us connected while we were there. Then my husband would have been attuned to me. We could have left sooner, which would have saved him the grief of my laying into him for his insensitivity, and me feeling powerless and stressed. Maybe just anticipating my feelings would have helped me feel more comfortable."

Talking the experience through made the couple realize that post-estrangement, their communication is more important than ever. While they have gotten on with their lives, and are quite happy, they realize the estrangement holds residual effects. Virgie's advice echoes mine from Chapter Four about the ambiguity of the loss and the potential for emotional triggers: *Be aware of strong emotional responses, because they might be related to the estrangement.*

Brian and I can relate to Virgie's experience. We recently met the parents of one of our other adult children's romantic interest. While marriage is not yet on the table, meeting the family made me quite anxious. It helped to acknowledge to my husband that the prospect was scary to me after what happened with Dan. To my surprise, he agreed. I felt better knowing he understood. Are the feelings irrational? Maybe, but that doesn't mean they don't exist. Putting them on the table makes them manageable. I could then practice RA-RA (recognize, analyze, regroup, and adapt).

Couples might also take special note when one or both want to avoid certain situations. If you or your spouse no longer wants to attend social events in general or even specific places or people, talk about those feelings. Bringing feelings and the thinking behind them out into the open can help couples to make informed decisions rather than simply react.

Working together, couples can provide one another with support and advice, and perhaps more easily regain a sense of normalcy in their lives. For instance, prior to a social event, a couple could decide to share a cue or a code word when one wants to leave. In times of distress, an escape plan can help husbands and wives feel more secure.

Another possible situation is one parent's emotional distance or emotional numbing. Wives complain that their husbands are impatient with their sadness, and don't seem as hurt as they are. Their husbands don't want to talk—or to listen.

While mothers may need to express their profound hurt, doing so forces husbands, who may be used to finding solutions, to face something they can't fix. Maybe seeing their wives in such pain, and knowing there's nothing they can do to solve the problem, makes these men feel powerless. So they then shut down their own feelings as a way to cope. It's stereotypical man-woman behavior, but it's often true.

In the fog of such grief, empathizing with a husband who seems out of touch with your feelings may be difficult. Find a friendly way to convey your understanding. I remember telling Brian that I knew there was no answer, but that as my husband and Dan's father, he was the only one who could truly understand the situation and my distress. We were in it together, just as we have been in so many life trials over thirty years. It was hard on him to see me cry when all he could do was hold me, but knowing my needs, he did.

That's not to say that I didn't work at moderating my talk. When free in the safety of our shared experience, the raw emotion would pour out of me. But knowing how powerless he felt to help, I would stop myself, and say aloud, "Okay. That's it. I don't want all our time together to be about Dan." Together, we worked at focusing on other topics, the present moment, and anything we could look forward to.

In monitoring and moderating my expression of pain, I was better able to listen for my husband's feelings, though rarely expressed in the form of a direct statement about his emotions. But from our mild climate, he often noticed the wild weather reports from the area of the country our son moved to. Obviously he thought about Dan, and missed him, too. Did he need me to acknowledge those feelings? Not necessarily. But by calling attention to the weather, he shared them in his own way. If I wasn't always talking about my feelings, I could better listen, so was open to hear.

In a committed relationship, bringing feelings out into the open can feel scary, but doing so in ways that respect each partner's communication needs and styles, paves the way for a deepening bond. In all relationships, the vulnerability of communicating distress, fear, and need allows committed partners the opportunity to demonstrate understanding and love. No matter how trite it may sound, difficult times do provide opportunity for growth.

Due to circumstances such as divorce, some parents are not a couple when their adult child becomes estranged. In these situations, many mothers fear their emotions will unduly burden their current partner. They fear their sadness will ruin the relationship. A spouse or significant other who is not related to your children may not have the deep feelings for your son or daughter that you have. But your feelings, and your partner's understanding of your feelings, are important.

It may be helpful to ponder your partner's potential support and emotional understanding if it were some other distressing situation you faced. If you were devastated by some other loss, would your spouse be attentive and helpful? Would you be as worried about the relationship failing? Examine your thoughts and feelings. Why does your son or daughter's estrangement cause you such worries about your committed relationship? Would you feel as threatened if distressed over something else? Sometimes it's feelings of shame or the pervasive distrust mothers say they often feel that make the situation touchy. Other times, individual personalities, and relationship dynamics come into play.

Leilani dealt with a sort of *I-told-you-so* attitude from her husband, Tom, whom she married when her children were young adults. He said he'd seen her daughter's estrangement coming on for years, and had tried to warn her. "My daughter had been insensitive and uncaring for a long time," Leilani says. "Tom was right about her, but his attitude did not help."

Leilani knew her husband's heart was in the right place. He had witnessed her daughter's verbal abuse, and had tried to get Leilani to stand up to her all along. He did have her back, but reminding her that he was right about her daughter didn't help. "He has a big ego that sometimes covers his vulnerable side," Leilani says.

Feeling isolated, Leilani confided in one of her sisters-in-law. "In a moment of frustration, I told her Tom always had to be right," says Leilani. That's when her sister-in-law reminded her that she'd been in the family of six brothers long enough to know they *all* had big egos. The women shared a moment of levity, and Leilani went home feeling light. Her husband may need an ego stroke, but she also knew that he could laugh at himself.

"You were right about her," she later told him, acutely aware the admission felt like betraying the daughter she so loved. But her husband needed to hear the words. When he turned and put his arms around her, she felt more secure. Counting on his sense of humor, she let out an animated growl. "But I need to know you care about me and my feelings more than being right, you big dope." Proving that she knew him well, her husband laughed, and hugged her tight.

Three years have passed. Leilani says her husband still always thinks he's right. Leilani knows that's not so, but rather than a point of conflict, it has become their private joke. Although born from the pain of estrangement, their ability to laugh at themselves and their relationship's dynamics has brought them closer. Leilani feels closer to her sister-in-law too. Occasionally, at family gatherings where their husbands and all the brothers are together, her sister-in-law looks over at her and winks, sharing a secret laugh over the tough, imperfect husbands they so love.

Hopefully, some of these examples provide insight into your own relationships. Get professional counseling if you feel the need, whether individually or as a couple. Talk to other successful couples, or read about how they have weathered life's storms. As Marla believes, perhaps the estrangement highlights existing problems. With effort, the two of you can take notice, and strengthen your bond. You face choices. Make ones that benefit you and your relationship.

You and Your Other Children

Many women expressed concerns about relating to their other children. Some of the mothers had been given confusing advice. Others wanted to protect the estranged child's reputation. Many feared their remaining children might also desert them.

Virgie saw a therapist a few months after the estrangement began. In weekly appointments over the course of three months, Virgie's therapist validated her feelings, and advised her not to poison her relationship with her younger son by talking with him about his brother's estrangement. The therapist's thoughts made sense to Virgie, but over time, following his advice backfired.

"When I was having a bad day, I'd avoid my son," she says. "I didn't want him to see me cry. I didn't want him to feel bad about his brother. And in the beginning, I had a lot of bad days." It wasn't until her younger son's high school girlfriend telephoned that she realized how distant their relationship had become. "She told me my son didn't think I cared about him," Virgie explains. "He'd gotten the idea that I cared more about our older son than him."

Virgie immediately explained to her son why she'd avoided him: out of fear he'd be burdened by her sadness and her belief that if she talked about his brother, he'd feel like she loved his brother more. "They were the fears my therapist had instilled in me," says Virgie. "And I told my son that at the time, they made sense."

Virgie had taken her therapists' advice not to "poison" the relationship to an extreme, but perhaps her therapist could have done a better job in explaining his intent. Burdening your children with your pain is not wise or kind. However, to *never* talk about the estranged son or daughter to their siblings is unrealistic, and could have negative consequences. If you never mention their estranged sibling, your children may feel they can't discuss him or her either, and may keep their feelings bottled up. An estranged family member can already be like the elephant in the room at family events, where it's impossible not to notice the absence, but people may pretend they don't. Why create an atmosphere that magnifies the effect?

Don't make talk of the estranged child taboo. Depending on the age and maturity of your other children, it may be appropriate to bring up the estranged brother or sister yourself. As you're fixing the green bean casserole your estranged son always liked, you might tell a child that it feels sad their brother won't be there to enjoy it. Or perhaps you make a more direct statement about how much you miss their sister.

And be prepared for the response. Your children may express anger or tell you they're sad. It's okay to admit that you're sad or angry, too. You might also express confusion or hope. Try letting your child lead. Be empathetic. Be kind. But also be honest. Parents don't always have all the answers. It's reasonable for your children to know that you miss the estranged child, that you don't understand the situation, that you feel the action is unfair, and that you wish things were different.

On the other hand, if you act as if you're not bothered at all, might your children deduce that you don't care? If they think you don't care about their estranged sibling, maybe they will wonder if you'd care if *they* walked out and never came back. Or, as in Virgie's case, if you avoid your children to spare them your grief, they might get the idea, as her son did, that you're not interested in them anymore.

Hold onto your motherly sensibilities. Share your feelings enough that you're honest, yet maintain a safe space for your children to also share their feelings.

Also, don't let your sons and daughters become your emotional dumping grounds. In the first several months after Dan's estrangement, I believe I erred too far in that direction at times—particularly with my adult daughters. If you can relate, don't be too hard on yourself. You're only human.

When I failed in this area, I apologized, and then worked to improve.

The estrangement affected us each individually, and as a family unit. We experienced the loss—and healed from it—together. In those rough months, we all saw vulnerable sides of one another that I now believe have drawn us even closer.

My other children were already all young adults at the time of Dan's estrangement. You may have younger children. The unique dynamics of your relationships must be taken into account when it comes to interacting with your children of any age. Consider the following questions and examples as you create a strategy:

How can I support my other children, and let them know they're important to me? Carve out time. Make a decision to show your children how much they mean to you. Laugh together often. Don't let one child's bad behavior overshadow your affection for another. Be present with them.

Mother of four, Char, tells about her youngest daughter from a second marriage: "Olivia was four when the big brother she loved so much left our little family. She missed him terribly." Char describes Olivia's pain as easier to care for than her older daughter's, who at 17 no longer climbed into her lap for reassurance. "I could snuggle up with Olivia on the sofa, and she'd feel safe," says Char. "But her sister needed me to spend more time with her. Sometimes we'd go a whole day on some outing, and it would take her that long just to open up about how much she missed her brother, too."

Char's daughter, now in her early twenties, has told her mother how much she appreciated the time Char spent. "It was so difficult," says Char, recalling her own emotional trauma. "I would struggle not to think of my son, and not to bring him up. But I willfully set aside my feelings, and opened myself to experiencing the present with my daughters. I used to tell myself to hold on, that I could collapse later, and cry alone if I needed to."

As Char concedes, it may be difficult, but making a decision and following through with setting aside your grief enough to share good times with your other children allows all of you to move forward, make new memories, and grow closer as a family.

My feelings are similar to Char's. Once I realized how my response to

Dan's actions was stealing precious family time, I made what sometimes felt like gargantuan efforts to focus my attention on those who were close. The sense of shoring up those relationships became central to moving on.

How can I be honest without hurting my estranged son's reputation with his siblings? In some cases, siblings have witnessed bad behavior or abuse, and may have developed their own opinions. They may judge their sibling, harbor anger or ill-will, or feel as if they need to protect you. Many mothers say that hearing their children talk badly of the estranged child requires patience and restraint, but allowing their children to express themselves provides insight. This prepares them to respond sensibly, and from an informed place of wisdom.

Many parents want to protect the estranged child's reputation, in the hopes their siblings will forgive, and accept the child back into the fold. Hope for reconciliation may be at the root, but it's important to recognize you can't predict the future or force your children to reconnect even if you eventually do. Don't jeopardize one relationship for another that's uncertain.

Char recognized her older daughter's anger, and allowed her to express it whenever she felt safe. "Her anger wasn't wrong," says Char. "I was angry, too." Char validated her daughter's feelings by agreeing that she shared them, but she also kept her own temper in check. "I didn't want to fuel her bad feelings against him. For all I knew, one day, he would grow up emotionally, and we'd be faced with trying to put the family together again."

Char came to a forgiveness point before her daughter did. "Probably because she didn't want to see me hurt," explains Char. "She knew how her brother acted, and how much he'd hurt me. She was very protective." Since then, her daughter has worked through her feelings, and has also forgiven him. "It's wise to forgive but maybe not to instantly forget," explains Char. "He would have to prove himself."

How does my behavior affect my other children's sense of security? Obviously, a mother's emotional availability, and her continuing of routine tasks and family activities goes a long way in creating an atmosphere of security. It's the sense of normalcy that Kathleen from the Great Lakes area sought when she insisted the family take their annual ski trip despite the sudden estrangement of her oldest daughter. And it's what motivated me and my family to make our daily jaunts to the county fair during its run, despite what was going on with Dan.

It's important to note that many of the mothers felt that once they expressed their desire to get on with life, and were determined not to allow the pain to cripple them, their families felt freer to express their own pain, fears, and vulnerability. As I stepped away from the emotional despair, my children felt they could safely share their own sadness.

To illustrate, the spring following Dan's rejection, my daughter, Hilary, sat in the corner chair in our living room. Tears wet her long lashes rimming her big brown eyes as she related one night when she'd been outside the back of the store where she worked. She had seen Dan heading towards the pizza place across the lot. He'd seen her, too, and she'd waved. A few minutes later, he had sauntered back across the asphalt, and asked her if she was working. She'd only nodded, stunned to see him there. They stood looking at each other, and after a moment, he'd stammered something about calling her later, and then walked away.

"I started to cry," Hilary said, fresh tears falling on her cheeks. Such a brief exchange, yet she recalled every detail. He wore diamond studs in his ears and Vans shoes that his wife had picked for him. "I was with her when she bought them," Hilary said, remembering the Christmas before we lost Dan. She described his jeans with fancy stitching and pocket flaps with ornate trim—all so unlike the Dan we knew. "But he wore a plaid flannel shirt," Hilary said. "He still had that one thing that tied him to our family."

Her statements held meaning beyond the words. I understood that she spoke of the difference in the family he chose over our own. My husband and sons have always worn plaid flannel shirts, a symbol of the "working man."

As if to emphasize, my daughter added, "Who knows? Maybe the shirt wasn't even one of ours. Maybe it was one of those knockoffs."

I knew the shirts she meant, the flannel plaid in trendy colors, the fashion industry's nod to the working man. She referred to the changes she saw in her brother, in the man she figured his wife was molding him to be.

"Is that how it will be?" Hilary wiped the tears from her cheeks. "He can just pop up somewhere and still upset me?"

I understood those feelings. The pain in her question tore at me. "No," I said, unwilling to accept what she said as true. "Not always."

Beyond the window, birds flitted in and out of the vines climbing the copper rain chains. The heavy wind chimes clanged gently in the soft spring breeze. Life marched on.

"I'm sorry you're hurt." I knelt on the floor and hugged Hilary, my gaze fixing on the on the greenery and bit of sky framed beyond the window. In the forever home that Brian and I worked so hard to create, our family was going on, but we also waited.

You and your family may juggle feelings of hope with those of letting go. Be a safe place for your children to share their pain. Be a resilient mother who cares and remains loving, honest, and present for your family. Your patience, calm wisdom, and willingness to remain open, provides needed security for those you love.

Is fear getting in the way of parenting? It's common to worry that other children will also leave. As a result, mothers worry about disciplining younger children, or find themselves forever apologizing or over-explaining. The fear is understandable—and awful. Some experts make adult children's estrangement sound as contagious as the common cold. However, among the more than 9,000 parents who had answered my survey as of this writing, less than 15% reported that more than one child was estranged. And a third of these parents said an ex-spouse negatively influenced their children against them. We talked earlier about parental alienation syndrome (PAS), and its effects on the family.

Within the small percentage of families where more than one child is estranged, one sibling sometimes persuades another. It's slightly more common for sisters to unite in estrangement than brothers. Often, an older sibling influences a younger one. Sometimes drug abuse is involved, or mental illness is a factor. Keeping the lines of communication open with the important people in your life is always advisable.

For me, in the months following Dan's estrangement, worry that my other children would also leave me loomed, a gloomy specter of an uncertain future. At times, I over-explained, worried I would hurt someone's feelings or come across as meddling, and push them away.

My other children seemed aware of my worries, too. In the beginning, one of my other sons would patiently reassure me. "Don't worry, Mom," he would say. Or, "I didn't think that." But after a few months, his responses became more dismissive. "I knew you were going to say that," he'd tell me. Or, "You don't have to explain." He was tired of me doubting him—and I understood.

Try imagining your son or daughter's feelings. Your fears of them also leaving make sense to you, but your child may feel unjustly accused. How would you feel if someone didn't trust you, just because someone you're related to had treated them badly?

Let this sort of insight help you. Just as supportive friends who will remind you of your strengths are helpful, your relationships with your remaining children can help you recover your old self.

Revisit the affirmative statements you created in Chapter Two's *Power a Positive Outlook* exercise. Mine went like this: *I am a strong woman, and a good mother. My value isn't tied up with or diminished by Dan's rejection. His decision has more to do with him than me, even if I don't understand it. Neither does his behavior predict my other children's.*

Can you come to similar conclusions? Use the ones you came up with earlier, or write down some positive thoughts about yourself now.

_____

_____

_____

_____

_____

For your own benefit, and to support the relationships you cherish, work at moving forward. Make a decision to do so. Don't stay forever wounded, stalled by decisions that are out of your control.

What if your other children stay in touch with their estranged sibling?
Kathleen refused to worry about her estranged oldest daughter turning her brothers and sister against her. Because her daughter was away at college, she was physically remote. She didn't reach out to the younger children, who were then aged 11 and 15. However, Kathleen's oldest son had just moved out, and Kathleen knew he stayed in touch with his sister.

Although Kathleen was curious, she didn't want her son caught in the middle. She told him outright that she didn't want to intrude on his and his sister's relationship. Her son respected his sister's wishes not to talk about her to his mom.

Now, seven years later, Kathleen's estranged daughter has recently been in contact with her other siblings. Her sons agreed to meet their sister for a hike in a nearby national park. When they returned, they told her their sister looked healthy and seemed well. "They talked to me," says Kathleen, of her sons, now aged 18 and 25. "But I tried not to grill them with questions."

After the outing, her estranged daughter also contacted her little sister, and then unexpectedly stopped by her sister's place of work. "She wasn't prepared for the meeting, and was upset," says Kathleen. The two went to dinner, and Kathleen's younger daughter told her mom she ended up letting her sister have it. "They were in a cozy little restaurant, and she just broke down," Kathleen says. Her younger daughter explained how much her sister had hurt her, and said she seemed receptive and expressed a desire to get together again. "I was really proud of her for being honest," says Kathleen. "They didn't make definite plans, but I respect the sibling relationship. I hope they're able to move forward."

I feel similarly. Although my children aren't in direct contact with Dan, one of my daughters recently told me she'd been contacted on social media by Dan's wife. She was quick to assure me she didn't accept the connection. Not long after that, one of my sons asked how I'd feel if he did accept her invitation. "It's up to you," I told him, and meant it. I'm not afraid Dan or his wife will turn any of my children against me. In all honesty though, as I write this, questions come to mind: *What if he did? What if they all left?*

With a spirit of acceptance, and awareness that coping mindfully helps, I note the worry, observe it, and then let it go. It won't help to let the feeling take root. My reaction is simply that: *an automatic response that doesn't serve me.* Physical feedback tied up with a thought. After all the dashed hopes, the longing, and the fear, I can accept the reaction as normal. I can be kind to myself, nurturing and compassionate as I observe the feeling, but also lovingly firm as I choose a better response.

The truth is, no matter how much I might worry, if my children choose to walk away, they will. All I can do is cherish my time with them now, make sure they know how much I care, and respect them as the lovely, creative, kind, intelligent beings they are. With respect comes trust—that they will make wise decisions they can live with and be proud of later. It's all any of us can do or hope for.

With younger children, protecting them may dictate your response. After three years of estrangement, Char's son stopped by and asked to see his little sister, who is now just eight.

"She was four when he moved out," says Char. "And very sad her brother left. She'd also heard his yelling and verbal abuse." Char left her son sitting in the porch shade, and then went to tell his little sister he'd come to see her. "She got wide-eyed and shook her head," says Char. "Then she climbed into bed and pulled the covers over her head." Char hugged her daughter, but didn't try to persuade her to come out. "I just told her he might be here for a little while, in case she changed her mind. Then I went back out and told her brother that his visit came as a surprise. His sister wasn't ready to see him." He stayed for a few more minutes. Char got him a soda. "Thankfully, my neighbor was in the yard. He did most of the talking with my son," she says. "I learned what he was up to in his life by listening in."

After Char's son left, she went to check on her little girl. "She hugged me tight," says Char. "And said she wasn't sure how she felt. That she figured he'd probably just leave again."

Occasionally during the last few years, Char has had to counsel herself when it comes to discipline of her little girl. "Not that she has behavioral problems," says Char. "She's a good kid, but I've had to remind myself not to give in to her all the time. Things like an extra cookie or staying up late might be okay sometimes, but it can't be a habit that comes from my fear. Being more of a friend than a mother wouldn't be good parenting."

While Char is obviously a smart mother who cares, she tearfully admits, "Occasionally, I'll find myself wondering if all my efforts are in vain. She could grow up and hate me like her brother."

The emotional struggle Char calls "shameful," is shared by many mothers. Especially in the toughest parenting moments, when a child is difficult or in some way causes stress, these mothers wonder if their investment of time, energy, and love will leave them heartbroken. In those instances Char reminds herself what we all must: one child is not another. She owes her little girl the best and most loving mother she can be—no matter the possible outcome.

In moments like these, remember who you are. For coaching clients whose forward momentum is stalled due to worry or fear, I've suggested a short saying with a familiar ring. It's a helpful tool to access our own motherly wisdom for ourselves. When shadowed by past relationships, disappointments, or unhappy situations over which you had little control, use "MOM" as an acronym to help you break free, live in the present, and do your best: *Mind Over Memories.*

You can quiet the fear or dread. Mother yourself with MOM. Turn your thinking around. Be compassionate and kind as you take yourself by the hand, and offer gentle reminders that you're strong, and wise. You're a good mother.

As Char expressed, allowing one son or daughter's hurtful actions to negatively influence your parenting isn't fair to you or your children. The vast majority of parents who have watched one child walk away in estrangement never see another follow.

Don't let the child who is missing be forever present and getting in the way. Remember: *mind over memories.*

The best advice comes from an estranged child's sibling. Kathleen's younger daughter told her, "Focus on the people who want you in their lives."

Extended Family

After two years of increasing emotional distance, Denise's only daughter completely cut her off. "I'm a cancer survivor," says Denise. "But this rejection is worse than all that. It's broken me down physically and mentally." Though very close to her own mother who is 91, Denise shields her from the truth. "Mother doesn't know we have *zero* contact," says Denise. "Whenever she asks about her, I make excuses. You know, like she's just so busy. Mother's weak heart doesn't need this pain."

In my own situation, my husband and I felt compelled to tell close relatives the basic facts early on, mainly because we wouldn't be at Dan's wedding. They had planned to go, and would have been shocked not to see us there. But I can relate to Denise's feelings. My husband and I feel a bit protective of the family elders—especially my husband's aunt and uncle, since their only child lives so far away. That's why during the holidays after Dan's estrangement, we decided ahead that if they had questions about him, we would keep the conversation light. At that point, we were still confused and hurting, but there was no news to tell. Dan was living on the outskirts of town with his wife, and working. Brian's octogenarian uncle and aunt had recently been through a harrowing health scare. Why burden them with our pain?

Outside a steakhouse where we'd taken them to eat, Brian's Uncle Chuck bowed his grayed head toward me. "Go on," he had said, his blue-green eyes twinkling. "Feel my scars."

Gingerly, I slid my fingertips into the soft depressions atop his head. A couple of months earlier, he'd been in a hospital bed with tubes dangling from those spots, draining a brain bleed. We hadn't been sure he'd recover. Yet here he was teasing me.

"Your head's like a bowling ball now," I joked, jerking my fingers back from the squishy spots where the skin had knit over the drill holes.

He'd spent a month in a rehab center, but was now home with his wife and doing well. After the stressful few months they'd been through, they didn't need to hear our troubles. But as we sat in a booth waiting for our lunch orders, questions about Dan soon came up.

"No," my husband replied. "We haven't seen him."

Uncle Chuck pinned me with his intense eyes. "Do you mind if I ask what happened?"

I shrugged. "We don't really know." It was difficult to field questions when we didn't have answers.

Aunt Carolyn, always cheerful, filled the silence. "Maybe his new wife wants him all to herself," she said. "Some women are like that." The lilt in her voice was merrier than the Christmas music playing in the background, and I was grateful.

"Maybe," I agreed. "And she is his wife." Aunt Carolyn had previously shared with me how hurt she'd been when her daughter had moved nearly 4,000 miles away at age 19. In the last 30 years, she'd been far from her daughter and granddaughters. I knew she understood, at least on some level. "I appreciate your concern," I said. "But we don't have any news. We do know he's working, and he's fine." I shrugged again, ready to move on to other topics. "Please don't worry. I'm sure we'll figure it out eventually." Then I patted my belly, adding a little too emphatically, "I'm *so* hungry! I hope they hurry with the food."

Brian then steered his uncle onto the subject of diesel engines. Perhaps it was the social etiquette of their generation that kept them from further probing the subject, but nothing more was said. Since then, they have occasionally asked about him. And each time, we've replied honestly, but without much elaboration. We don't intend to worry them over something none of us can control. Besides, we're fine. We've moved forward, and so has Dan. That's the truth, and the message we try to convey.

How much you tell or don't tell will depend on your relationships. Getting back to Denise's family, they have very few gatherings. Denise doesn't worry about her mother accidentally finding out the truth. But the possibility is worth considering. Finding out about the estrangement along with your protective deception could come as a sort of double shock. Also, is it possible that the person from whom you keep the truth will sense something is wrong? If that's the case, the person may worry anyway—perhaps about imaginings that are worse than estrangement.

While each of us must come to our own decisions, we owe it to ourselves to honestly assess our situation, examine our feelings, and identify our motivations. Consider the questions in the shaded box below. If you feel like it, use paper to elaborate on any thoughts that come to mind surrounding the questions.

Fully exploring your thoughts and feelings can provide insights and sagacity that help you make decisions you can feel good about later. Perhaps you will discover you require other family members' input or assistance. Or, like my husband and me, you will plan on easy responses that, while telling the truth, minimize pain or emotional upset, and focus on the fact that we are hopeful, but also getting on with our lives.

Pause And Reflect: Should I Share?

- Am I fearful of the possible reaction? If so, how/why?
- Do I feel ashamed, or believe I will be ridiculed or blamed?
- Am I seeking to avoid conflict? If so, why?
- If I don't tell, will I worry the truth will accidentally come out?
- Will other people tell my relative?
- Would this person feel lied to and excluded?
- Will my relative sense that I'm keeping something from him?
- If I hide the estrangement, will I avoid my relative?
- Will it negatively impact our relationship?

Some of us have only occasional gatherings of relatives who don't know the gritty details of our loss. And we may be reluctant to share. Elaborate as fully as you feel is appropriate, or are comfortable telling.

Rather than dread the event, or fear the questions, create a plan that helps you feel in control. As much as you can, prepare ahead for possible questions, and your responses. Keep in mind the family dynamics. In certain situations, patterns from childhood in your family of origin may influence you even now.

Denise is glad her brother, 16 years her senior, doesn't live close. "We only occasionally talk by phone," says Denise. "And I haven't said much about my daughter. He would just play the role he's been dealt. You know, to him I'll always be the kid sister he counsels. I couldn't take his so-called *advice* on this issue. His two kids are so successful. It's all la-la and wonderful in my big brother's world."

We can appreciate Denise's honesty, but it's helpful to be aware that especially when we're experiencing troubles, others' lives can seem ideal. We see a public face. Even families that seem perfect likely have some issues that remain private.

Childhood patterns and sibling rivalry come in many forms, and may take hold when least expected. One mother shared, "My estranged daughter became fodder for my sister to go on about her son's bad choices. The next thing I knew we were embroiled in a one-up match about all the bad shit our kids have put us through."

Perhaps this woman's sister intended to convey a sense of solidarity in sharing her own problems, but this mom left the party feeling worse than when she'd arrived. "Misery loves company," she says. "I thought I was past all the childhood competition, but my sister pulled me in. Trying to out-do each other, we were both slinging the mud. Next time, I won't let that happen. I'd rather pull her up than let her pull me down."

In Chapter Three, we explored planned answers, put-offs, and ways to change the subject. Those examples can help you in family situations, too. Also keep in mind the suggestions about examining and/or discussing your feelings before social events, and using planned exit strategies (covered in this chapter under *Leaning On One Another).*

Finally, if your estranged son or daughter is friendly with extended family members who seem insensitive, consider calmly expressing your feelings to them. You may be happy they're in touch, and glad to hear some news. But if you feel as if they side with your child or are taking your place, things can get touchy. Some parents have shared with me that a calm, candid discussion helped. If the involved relatives have children, you might ask them how they would feel if they were in your shoes. Before any discussion, it's best to fully consider your intentions. If you're glad your child is in contact with family, make that clear. Then, offer ideas to help. Maybe you don't want to hear every detail of their interaction, but appreciate an occasional update.

Some parents ask relatives who remains in contact with their child to intervene for them, and discuss the estrangement. Be aware that making someone else your advocate can backfire. The son or daughter may then disengage from other family members. Or even persuade relatives they were right to reject you.

Every family is different, so weigh decisions carefully. Don't be hasty, but do take action that supports you. You'll find more about extended family in the social media section that follows.

The Social Media Conundrum

Do you look at your son's Facebook page just to know he's okay? Then find yourself crying, tempted to send yet another message into what's become a black hole? Perhaps your daughter is still "friends" with other family members who are also in your friends list, so you see them interacting with her. All their "likes" and "shares" call attention to what you're missing.

Some parents see their child's comments, and feel like there's a message in them—one meant to upset or offend them. When animosity and verbal abuse have been a part of the estrangement, or often when a third-party figures into the break, parents frequently report that anger plays out on social media. It can all be so embarrassing, yet many seem fine with public strife.

Let's examine the challenges social media presents—and find some answers to help.

"Are we really *connected*?" one mother asks. She describes the bits of Facebook contact her daughter tosses her like this: "It feels like crumbs to a starving woman." Although her daughter remains a "friend," she never answers messages. In real life, she's fully estranged. "But I can see my grandchildren's pictures," this mother says. She clears her throat, and her voice drops lower. "I can see all the fun they're having without me."

That's the conundrum so often expressed. Parents are grateful to maintain friend status but repeatedly suffer the sting of rejection. Nowadays, smart phone apps with social media notifications switched on may be the emotional equivalent to reaching into a hornet's nest. Yet, as this mother so aptly explains, "As long as she keeps me as a friend, there's hope."

You may feel similarly, but do consider the cost. You know from an earlier chapter that I defriended my son and his fiancée on social media almost immediately. I later regretted that hasty act of self-preservation. It was done too soon, and without clear deliberation that, as I explained, might have led me to take less permanent action. However, after many months or even years of estrangement, a mother's decision to defriend can be an informed, level-headed choice. Deciding purposefully and with forethought, the action can be empowering.

Defriending is not your only option. Some of you can't imagine giving up your only window into your children or grandchildren's lives. I can empathize. These are sons and daughters we've loved. Children and grandchildren that may carry our family name as well as our genes. Many of us hope to one day enjoy relationships with them again, or even meet grandchildren for the first time. There are other options to protect your emotions and keep you safe. But before exploring those possibilities, fully consider your situation.

Ask yourself:

- *What is my intention for staying Facebook friends?*

Or, if you're not directly connected, but log in through one of their "friend's" accounts to get access:

- *Why do I keep peering in on my son or daughter's life?*

Many mothers feel that social media adds to their pain. If you agree, consider these questions:

- *Is staying connected hurting me more than letting go?*

- *Can I move forward in my life if I'm repeatedly stepping back toward my pain?*

There's a wise saying about not being able to embrace the future unless you let go of the past. Take time to think these questions through. Your answers can help you make decisions that benefit you. Consider dividing a sheet of paper into two columns, and list the pros for remaining connected on one side, and the cons on the other. Reflect upon your emotions as you create your lists. This isn't about which list is longest. Decide which list holds more weight. Only you can choose what's best for you. And there's no need to hurry your decision. Read on for practical information and settings in social media to limit your connections. Then come back to your answers and/or list feeling more empowered.

When it comes to the digital world, choices are almost limitless. A few clicks to select social media settings allow us to choose how we'll interact. You can use selective settings to limit your exposure. Below, I've focused on Facebook, and included a few specific instructions. But in the world of technology, things change quickly. On any social media site, explore the "help" or "FAQ" areas, and search for the functions that enable filtering of what you see. If you can't find what you need in a site's help files, then try searching the Internet as a whole. You might be surprised how many blogs include helpful tutorials. In any search engine, try enclosing specific phrases in quotation marks. Use phrases such as, "How to block Facebook posts," or "How can I limit a Facebook friend's posts," or "Filtering on Facebook."

You don't have to defriend your son or daughter to protect yourself from a steady stream of postings that make you feel left out. By using the site's filtering functions, you can create a boundary, but still have access to photographs and posts.

If you have a smartphone and are using social media apps, stop the bombardment of photos and posts that arrive at all hours. Delete social media apps entirely. Or, go to the app's management settings and turn off the app's notifications so it isn't forever beckoning you. You can always look at posts and pictures later, but not having a steady stream of updates or instantaneous access can limit the negative effects on you.

I'll stand by my statements in Chapter Four: *Honor your adult child's wishes to separate from you. Stop lurking in his or her life.*

Still, I recognize this may be difficult. Some of you aren't ready to let the access go. Others don't want to, or don't feel the need. Be aware that access can be a two-edged sword. Although not related directly to estrangement, a study published in 2015 demonstrated the pressure on social media users to stay connected for fear they will miss out.[3] The term, FOMO, which stands for "fear of missing out," was added to the Oxford English Dictionary in 2013. For some people, the pressure to avoid missing out results in compulsion.

It's also important to recognize that social media isn't always a reflection of the real world. Did you know that in 2012, Facebook conducted a controversial study, and manipulated nearly 700,000 users' newsfeeds to control what sort of postings they saw? For one week, targeted users consistently saw either negative or positive posts in their Facebook feeds. And then those users' posts were analyzed. As you might expect, those who saw more negative postings were affected negatively by the manipulation. Their own postings became more sad and depressing.[4]

Reflect upon the next set of questions and their discussions. Doing so may help as you consider how social media impacts your life.

Am I "out of control"? That's how some parents describe their impulse to lurk in their sons' or daughters' online lives. Relegated to the sidelines, the Internet provides a window—its view like an addictive drug. "I feel driven to look at my daughter and my grandchildren," says one mother, who describes the longing, the withdrawal, and the pressure that builds until she races to the screen. Then she sees their smiling faces, and is hit again with the stark reality that they're moving on without her, seemingly happy in their lives. Then there's the letdown. She explains, "The abandonment crushes me all over again."

Her experience is like many who are hurt and then hurt again by the effects of behavior that has become a compulsion. If this describes you, defriending your son or daughter might be a more self-respecting choice. At the very least, create limits—and stick to them. Revisit the goal-setting techniques in Chapter Three. Remember Geneva, who set specific goals for how often she texted? She kept sight of the overall goal behind her behavior (to let her child know she was open to reconciliation but not become obsessed with hearing back). If you must *snoop*, at least limit yourself. The word may seem harsh, but I use it deliberately. With the Internet making so much of people's personal lives public, we've become a world of snoopers—perhaps to our detriment. We're now privy to so many thoughts and images that would have once been private. When you get the urge to snoop, try telling yourself: *None of my business; none of my concern.* Those thoughts can be freeing.

Get tough with yourself if you need to. You deserve to break free.

It may be important to note that some parents are compelled to periodically check social media pages because of special circumstances. They do so to put their minds at ease.

Liz, a mother in the U.K., believes her controlling son-in-law is to blame for her daughter's estrangement. "To my knowledge, he's never physically abused her," says Liz. "But he's always been in emotional control." In the five years since she was last in contact, Liz has come to accept that, at least on some level, her daughter is a willing participant. She's the one who signed an order barring all contact by her mother. "But I know he's to blame, and I still worry," says Liz, who checks her daughter's page from time to time.

In the U.K., as in the U.S., you may be surprised to learn that restraining orders are not all that difficult to get. Liz isn't the only mother who shared the experience of this humiliation. Liz will continue to look at her daughter's page as long as it's not made private. "I suppose that makes me a stalker," she says. "Right. I still have to look."

How can I prevent my child from seeing everything I do? Some parents complain that posted interactions with their estranged child's siblings who remain close spur hateful comments online. Others mention public ridicule from their child's fingertips. To better control who sees what *you* post, Facebook allows you to choose which friends see different updates or shares. You can also filter what content you see. Be sure to investigate and adjust your privacy settings, too. Otherwise, if a friend hits the "like" button on one of your posts, your original posting may be visible or shared. Ditto the visibility of your profile.

What if my son or daughter slanders me in posts? Earlier in the book, we heard from mothers whose children posted lies on social media. If this happens to you, consider reporting the abusive posts. You can do so by clicking on the arrow that appears at the upper right of the posting itself. You'll see "Report post" as an option in the menu that pops up. Clicking on that choice brings up more selections. You can choose the one that best fits your situation, and follow through.

What if family members remain connected to my estranged child? Many describe ambivalence over their child's social media connections to others in the family. You may be thankful your child remains connected. Maybe it helps you hope. On the other hand, seeing others invited to events when you're not can hurt. Not to mention seeing the slough of subsequent photos. Plastered across mutual friends' pages, your absence in the lovey-dovey group shots they're all commenting on with insider jokes can feel like public humiliation. Maybe you get angry. Feelings of disloyalty can then damage your other relationships. The sister, the brother, the aunt, and the cousin you used to share secrets with or revere seem oblivious to your feelings. *Doesn't anybody care?*

In these situations, you can try the limiting and selectivity features described above. You can also set and stick to goals about the time you spend on social media. Or, you can try using Facebook's blocking features to completely deny access to certain individuals. Blocking keeps you from seeing all of their posts, likes, or shares, too (even in mutual friends' conversation threads).

For some parents, the best solution is to sign off Facebook or other social media entirely. If you do, consider telling people who are important to you, and asking them to stay in touch in other ways. Social media is convenient, but others in your circles may also find the medium perplexing and be troubled by the public arguments, ballsy opinions, and negative jokes that sometimes take place. They may appreciate some actual face time with you.

Several recent studies and surveys reveal that average time spent on social media networks per day is more than an hour. Only you know whether that average is correct for you, but perhaps digital socializing steals time from more personal interactions.

What action can I take to help myself now? No matter what your particular situation or problem is within the social media realm, don't continue in the same old misery. Remember RA-RA? *R*ecognize, *a*nalyze, *r*egroup, and *a*dapt. By examining your feelings surrounding the questions placed earlier in this section, and perhaps making a pros and cons list, you can analyze your situation. By exploring your options, making some decisions, and taking action, you adapt. Give yourself a *Rah-Rah!*

Whether you make an informed decision to do nothing, use selectivity functions, create audience lists, defriend, block, or delete your Facebook account entirely, make your decision empowering. Visualize your action in a way that enables your forward momentum and strength. If you did the *Visualize Your Life* exercise at the end of Chapter Five, recall those optimistic images. Get out your collage or computer graphics if you made them. Then close your eyes, and imagine yourself at peace with your decisions.

It's also wise to replace the habit of social media with other activities. Remember how Julia filled the mornings she used to spend on the phone with her son? You can change your routines too.

A Better Experience

The special people we hold dear and close are along with us on this journey. With forethought, empathy, and much reflection, we can act with integrity, communicate openly, provide assistance, and show our love.

Don't let bitterness or worry cast hurtful shadows on your family life. Remember: *M-O-M (Mind Over Memories).* Nurture yourself and those you love in the here and now. Do your best to continue forward in graceful optimism. Aware and caring, you can set the tone for a meaningful and fun experience in the family. Be fully present, appreciating every moment as it unfolds.

✈ The Shape of Your Family

Refer to the opening of this chapter where we talked of the family as a shape or form. Maybe your estranged child made up a family of three, forming a triangle as in Pauline and her husband's case. Remove one, and your triangle breaks. Two lines connect at a single point. Pauline has grown stronger through all of this. She's straightened her shoulders and stood up tall. Instead of broken triangle parts, maybe now she thinks of herself and her husband as two pillars, side-by-side, but each complete.

If you think of your family as a square, when one section walks away the others can bend and curve to make a circle instead. A family that joins hands in a circle, but now has an estranged and missing piece, can choose to draw in closer—or perhaps open wide for new relationships.

In your mind, or with paper and pen, play with ideas to fix your triangle, join your circle, become a new and even stronger shape. Don't settle for a broken triangle. You *can* close the gap, assess and reshape, and develop into a new and even better form.

In the alternative, conjure up an imaginative symbol for your family. In a creative writing class years ago, students were required to choose and write about a metaphor to represent their families. I chose a forest, where trees stand uniquely strong, yet together form a safe, inviting place. Sunlight penetrates for swaths of warmth, yet restful shade persists. Even without Dan, I see my family as a lovely forest. The image still comforts me.

Come up with positive imagery for your post-estrangement family. Draw a picture, paint one with words, paste magazine cut-outs, or simply let your imagination soar. Use the space on the next page if you'd like to.

Remember, it's only an idea, a snapshot in time. If your child some-day returns in a way that suits you, the picture can be changed. If the idea doesn't feel right to you tomorrow, you can flex and bend. It's *your* imagination. Make it work for you.

CHAPTER SEVEN

What Does It Mean To Reconcile?

Most parents hope for reconciliation. Particularly in the early days, we fully believe that a reunion will occur. We imagine an apology, a discussion, and an examination of what went wrong. We expect an admission of wrongdoing perhaps, from a child who has come to his senses, and is working to make amends. We imagine hugs, and tears . . . and then what? Do things go back to the way they were? Do we take the blame? Forgive and forget? Or will there always be a little part we hold back? At some point, as an estrangement endures, most of us begin to wonder if the reconciliation we imagined is realistic, or even possible.

Is "reconciliation" even what we think? The idea of mending the relationship may not mean the same thing to your son or daughter as it does to you. In fact, you may end up reconciling *without* your child. How is this possible? Below, we'll look in on my own and several parents' experiences, explore many facets of what it means to reconcile, and examine the situation from an honest perspective.

Hurtful Hope and Boundaries

On a pleasant day late in summer, my husband and I sat on the sofa together in comfortable silence. Outside the window, our massive fig tree was alive with birds, feasting on the fruity spoils. My husband's mobile phone rang, startling us from our reverie.

Brian glanced at the screen, and then he answered, his voice immediately strained. He spoke in a clipped cadence that wasn't like him. His tension reverberated, a current of distress that rippled through the air, shattering the serenity of our peaceful afternoon.

In dread, I waited, filled with curiosity, yet knowing not to interrupt. *Who was on the line?*

Beyond the window, the mockingbirds pecked at the yellow-green figs. They tore at the pink-brown flesh inside, and then wiped their beaks on branches to rid themselves of the stickiness.

"Yeah, she's here," Brian said to whoever was on the phone. Then he held it out to me.

"Who...?"

"Dan," he said softly, his mouth settling into a stiff line.

Panic flared, the wreckage of our last few exchanges coursing through me. In an instant, I relived the utter disbelief of that first midnight call, and the embarrassment and shock that had followed. Just two months earlier, after the death of his high school friend, I'd sent Dan a text. He had replied to me in anger.

I hesitated, fearful and alarmed by this sudden call, just 10 days shy of a full year since the last time I had laid eyes on my son. The date he moved out of the alley cottage he'd left in disarray, the day he walked away to his car without a good-bye. Those moments were burned into my memory like a tattoo. I took the phone. "Hello."

Long awkward pauses fell between clips of fast conversation. Dan told me he'd lost weight, that he had a really good camera, and that he'd been hiking. We have the love of picture-taking and hiking in common.

Perhaps he was struggling as much as me. Maybe he had rehearsed this conversation, and thought of ways we could connect. Although I wanted to feel close, to have the time fall away like it does with cousins even after many years, the distance gaped. He sounded a bit like a stranger, a small distant figure, someone I barely knew.

Dan's voice cracked, and I assumed he spoke through tears. He told me it hurt him to say that he hadn't seen me, his own mother, in a whole year. "I know everything was my fault," he said.

"Yes, it was, Dan," I agreed, immediately aware of how harsh I must sound. It was good to hear him say the words, but his hurt still sliced at me. *My son.*

He went on. "I want us to have a relationship."

"Well, why can't we?" I blurted, immediately letting down my guard. Even after all the hurt, and having reached the point that I could go for more than a few days without thinking of him, I realized I'd been waiting, and ready. My heart was open.

"Well, it's hard." He paused, the silence stretching out for half a minute. "With my wife. She thinks you owe her an apology."

I bristled at his statement, old irritation stirring. That, too, had been ready and waiting." That would be generous," I replied, clamping my mouth shut on additional words. Empathy tried to niggle up, and open me to hurt. There was nothing more to say. Not in that moment, not when he'd called out of the blue, admitted everything that had happened was his fault. He wanted a relationship. I let that thought anchor me.

Dan explained that he was calling from a work event in a nearby town. He was alone. He prattled on about trips him and his wife had taken, and places they had hiked. We had those trails in common. He talked about cooking, another thing we both like to do, and for a few brief moments in the otherwise awkward call, the passage of time did drop away. The distance disintegrated. The son I had always loved returned to me, our bond still tight.

He went on to talk more about recently getting into shape. "I think my weight gain had to do with all that happened," he said.

I remembered seeing him in the grocery store months ago. He had sauntered past me without a word. I had noticed the extra weight on him then, and had worried.

"I've lost weight, too," I told him. "It's been hard this past year, but I'm doing better now. I'm moving on, especially since your friend's death."

He began to cry again then, and I felt my own tears fall. I swallowed against a sob, and sounded raspy as I spoke. "I was really torn up, but I'm getting back on track."

Dan let out a little laugh, maybe to relieve the tension. I wished things were different, and hoped we could continue to connect. But my energy waned. I was suddenly drained by the effort required to try and find more to talk about with this son who had become a stranger. My ear burned, hot from the mobile phone I'd been pressing so close. And part of me doubted the connection was even real.

"I'm not used to being on the phone this long," I finally said, the tee-ter-totter of hanging on his every word finally crushed by my need to break away, crawl off, and protect myself. I was scared to trust him.

"I'll call you again, Mom," he said.

"I hope you will," I said. "I'd call you, but wouldn't know when might be a good time."

"I'll call you," he assured me. "*Soon.*"

Did we say we loved each other? I can't remember for sure. I only know that when I handed the phone back to my husband, his expression matched what I felt. Not something easily described; a torn feeling, a rip-ping open, and a need to close off, to reestablish guard.

Brian and I didn't speak. Companionable silence once again filled the space between us. We watched the birds in the fig tree outside, feasting.

What happened in the days and months that followed that call is echoed in the stories of other parents' lives. They tell of similar calls, flir-tations with reunion that spur their hope, and then leave them even more devastated.

Dan had seemed so sincere when he told me he wanted a relation-ship, and I believed him when he assured me he would call again soon. But afterward, the days stretched out like a rubber band you know you're pulling too far. You know it will break. Through fall and into winter, I waited for Dan to call. I rejoined an educational program I'd opted out of when the estrangement began, and busied myself. But even as I bustled about, I was waiting.

We celebrated Halloween with our grandchildren, marveling at how fast the youngest had grown; the one that Dan had never met. As always this time of year, the raucous crows flocked to eat the ripened pecans, and then they left again. November brought cooler weather, wind that shook loose the trees' colored leaves, and foggy mornings when spider webs dripped with pearly dew. I cried on those mornings. I stopped cooking healthy meals or exercising. I inched forward on a course of study that kept me attuned to the changing of the seasons, to growth and life and time passing all around. Yet I stood still. I was sluggish and sad. The phone always rang, but it was never Dan.

Thanksgiving came and went. A smile here, a burst of laughter there, food cooked with years of experience that made it tasty, but missing the present joy of creation and family connection I usually love. I hid my despair.

Finally, plagued with scary visual disturbances caused by what I learned were ocular migraines, and feeling sluggish and sad, I saw a doctor. She confirmed what I already knew: I needed to take better care of myself, and get a handle on my stress. Otherwise, I'd be a prime candidate for a heart attack.

When I told my family, everyone was openly upset. I assured them all I'd be fine, confessed that I'd been waiting for Dan to call again, and that I now realized waiting around wasn't wise. I needed to take control, and call Dan myself.

A few days later, I had my son on the line. "I've been waiting on pins and needles," I said. "I was so excited after we talked, and you said you'd call, but it's been three months."

"Oh," he said. "Sorry." His words came quickly, and were halted by off-line greetings to people near him, in his life I knew so little about.

"I had been doing so well," I told him, explaining how I'd been to the doctor for the visual problems, the weight I'd regained, and generally just not feeling well. "It's related to stress. I've been so emotional since you called that day, and—"

He cut me off. "Okay then, Mom," he said, sounding agitated. "I just won't call."

"Well, I don't mean that," I replied, surprised by his quick response.

"If it's better we don't talk," he said.

The swift ease of his dismissal hurt. "But you said you wanted a relationship."

"Okay then, you can call me whenever you want, Mom, how about that?" His words were hurried, his voice a sharp edge.

"Well, I guess.…" I stammered. Where did we go from here? He was clearly busy, perhaps didn't want to hear, or didn't care. Looking back, I wonder if he thought I was trying to give him a guilt trip by telling him I hadn't been well. That hadn't been my intention.

Later, when I shared the conversation with my family, the consensus among them was clear: Dan had placed sole responsibility for any relationship on me. He wouldn't be troubled to call, but he would answer the phone if I called him.

There was my family, my other adult children all worried about me, plainly stating they wanted me well, wanted me around for years to come. And then there was Dan, outside the circle of people who embraced me. His surprise phone call had been momentous, setting me on a track of waiting and hoping. But to Dan, apparently the call hadn't been momentous at all.

With that realization, I set upon resuming my life. I accepted what was. I pushed forward, celebrated Christmas, and started the New Year fresh and looking forward.

Several weeks later, when some of our family was together, we decided to text family greetings to Dan. And late in the evening, at a time we guessed he might be alone, he replied his thanks.

Maybe there was hope, but I wouldn't count on it. My happiness wouldn't depend on any reunion that may or may not occur. I made a decision to accept the facts, deal with what was rather than what I wished for, and move ahead.

The months passed happily, all of us busy with our lives—and Dan in his. My ocular migraines were a thing of the past. I had regained my health, my confidence, and my optimism for a bright future, even without my son.

In the summer, Dan contacted me again. How ironic that one of the olive trees at the front of our property had dropped a branch. Busy, we had left it lying at the edge of the driveway for at least a week. Then Dan called, asking if he could come by.

That day in my living room, as he sat there in cuffed fashion shorts, a trendy shirt and shoes, I remember thinking he was sadly beautiful, like a butterfly with broken wings. Maybe that's how all mothers feel coming face-to-face with an estranged child's change. Although he was jovial, he talked and smiled, he was also different, changed in a way that his newly refined manner of dress didn't explain.

He was apologetic and tearful as his father, me, and two of our other children gathered round. My daughter, Mimi, sat in the corner chair, quietly crying. At one point Dan turned to her and said, "I missed you, too."

That visit had all the earmarks of a successful reunion. We were together, and wanting to connect. But when I broached the subject of all that had gone on, Dan refused to talk. With a firm shake of his head, he replied, "I won't discuss that without my wife." Not wanting to ruin the moment, I let the matter go. Besides, there was something noble in his words. I couldn't fault him.

He didn't stay long that afternoon, but a few days later, he sent a text, asking for us to go to lunch. He said his wife would come along. Immediately, I agreed, and several in the family said they would also go. My family was adamant that I was not to meet with Dan and his wife alone. (If you face the prospect of a meeting, see the box, *Precautions For Meetings*, which follows this section.)

Hopeful, excited, and a little bit wary, for the next several days, the upcoming lunch date was all our family talked about. *Finally, we would reconcile.* But the day before the meeting, Dan sent a text. They couldn't make it after all.

In the confusion of my emotional letdown, I accidentally texted to Dan a message I meant for one of my daughters: *They cancelled the lunch.*

I immediately noticed my mistake. Embarrassed, I nonetheless realized that it didn't hurt for Dan to know how much our meeting had meant to me. I texted to explain: *That was meant for your sister. This was a big deal.*

Several days later, Dan sent another text. He suggested a lunch date the following week, but I was working. I suggested another day, and they weren't free. I remember putting down my cell phone, thinking that might be it. We might not hear from Dan again. But on a Sunday morning a few days later, the pair showed up unexpectedly at the house.

Unlike on his last visit, this time Dan was less apologetic. Although he brought me a gift, explaining with exuberance how he'd purchased the curio item at an antique shop he remembered us visiting when he was a kid, the meeting didn't go so smoothly. He used the F-word as he spoke, and was clearly back to taking the "sides" he had so painfully spoke of when our estrangement first began.

There were clarifications, too, about what it would take for us to rekindle a relationship. I needed to discuss what had happened, and come to some understanding in order to move on. All of us did. Dan's wife refused. She wanted to forget the past. She made it clear that she expected us to act as if nothing bad had ever happened. And Dan emphatically agreed.

I remember feeling frustrated and not quite sure what to do. Here was an olive branch, extended by people with whom I no longer felt a sense of trust. When they had arrived that morning, I was still in my robe, about to get dressed and go out. My daughter and I had made plans. Yet here I was, forced into an impromptu visit, a conversation that didn't feel good, and being told we'd have to forget the past if we wanted to be friends.

They also spoke of moving soon, of joining her parents who had recently relocated to a faraway state. Her siblings had already moved there to be with them. In my heart, I knew that this reunion was more of a good-bye.

We did share some happy moments. I showed Dan my new pizza peel and stone, and he tasted some of my homemade bread. But the meeting dragged on, and the tension increased. Our whole family had been affected by the break, and some of Dan's siblings hovered nearby, uncertain and remaining somewhat emotionally cool.

I did apologize that morning, hoping to bridge the horrible gap. But I wasn't sure why I was apologizing, or what it really meant. To her credit,

Dan's wife replied that she was sorry too. They were words from both sides. Genuine, yes, but also tokens. The apologies didn't feel right or real.

In the end, my family wasn't comfortable moving forward without some visitation on the past. How could we move forward without understanding what had gone so wrong? How can you put a bandage on a wound that hasn't been cleaned? It would only fester. But it wasn't me who pressed the issue that day. It was my daughter, Hilary, who held them accountable. In a tense moment, as the five of us stood outside near our little lily-filled pond, she calmly recounted the facts. "Can you at least be honest?" she asked.

Dan quietly conceded. "I can understand your feelings."

But his wife argued. Hilary argued back, insisting she admit to the pain they had caused us all. Both said ugly words. Then Dan's wife burst into tears, and ran away to their car, mascara running down her face.

Dan hesitated for a moment before speaking. "I need to go be with my wife." And then he followed.

As they drove off, Hilary's big liquid-brown eyes filled with tears. "I guess I ruined everything," she said.

Instantly empathetic, I took hold of my daughter's arm. "Are you kidding? All you did was tell the truth." In some ways, Hilary had been the closest to Dan. Sometimes, their friends had overlapped. Of all his siblings, her brother's actions may have hurt her the most.

"You're not mad at me?" Her voice quavered, the fear in her eyes cutting at me.

My husband looked stricken. A hurting sound I'd never heard before escaped his lips. He pulled us into a three-way hug, his strong arms safe.

"No," I said into my daughter's soft hair. "You've been a loyal daughter. How could we be mad at you?"

Over the next few days, our family discussed the tense relations. On his earlier visit, Dan had said he wouldn't talk about the past without his wife. But now we knew that she refused to discuss the past at all. When Dan had come alone, he'd seemed remorseful and sincere. In her presence, his attitude took a turn.

With the well-being of our entire family in mind, my husband and I concluded that if we were ever to successfully reconcile, Dan would first need to work at reconnecting with us all on his own. Then, to forge a bond between us and his wife, Dan could be the bridge. Days later, when Dan texted inviting me to lunch with him and his wife, I replied to that effect. I told him we loved him. I asked him to call to talk.

Oh, OK, he replied.

But he never called.

 Some may question our motives, judge us, or wonder why we didn't bend. Parents new to estrangement, yearning for the child they so miss, may long to reconnect on any terms, and believe we threw our chance with our son away. Those who have walked on the proverbial eggshells to stay in touch no matter what, and have been hurt again, will understand. One-sided relationships never work.

In essence, our proposed condition for moving forward formed a boundary in which to work. Parents have a right to negotiate terms as they navigate relations with adult children, estranged or not. When our children are young, their needs most often come first. As adults who call the shots in their own lives, the field levels. In functioning families, at least most of the time, all parties show courtesy, respect, and care. We're there for one another. We're a family. But we also have lives apart.

As you can imagine, at times we have second-guessed our decision that put the ball firmly in our son's court. Maybe I should have called to say the words aloud rather than text him in reply. Maybe we should have gone to lunch, and presented our thoughts in person. But we have also contemplated the history. The shock of the midnight call, the wedding disinvite, our dashed hopes at the rental home he left in disarray, his tearful plea for a relationship after a year of silence, and the slow period of subsequent waiting that affected my health. Add in the tense frustration on the day he came with his wife, and we always conclude that for the sake of our family and our well-being, our decision was sound.

Precautions for Meetings

Particularly when a third party has been instrumental in the estrangement, parents often look back on an unsuccessful meeting as a set-up. You're wise not to go alone. This is especially true if there is a history of lies, competition, or animosity. Parents who have gone alone have seen their good intentions twisted—and have no witness to dispute claims about what transpired. You may hear your own words return to you in ways they were not intended, and used to further an unflattering tale and hurt you. Don't provide the opportunity.

Don't second guess yourself. That's what the subtlest manipulations are intended to cause. Some parents doubt their judgment, or have experienced machinations so subtle they're reluctant to believe what's happening to them. Manipulative people may have spent many years honing behavior that is used to disorient, confuse, or intimidate. It may not always even be a conscious choice, but part of a relationship pattern. Regardless, it isn't healthy for you.

Learn more. Do some research about manipulative people, and even the term "gaslighting." The behavior is named for the 1944 movie, *Gaslight*, in which a husband manipulates his wife into believing she's crazy (but the behavior can happen in other relationships).

Trust yourself. Most of all, I implore you to trust your intuition. If you feel uneasy, ensure your physical and emotional safety. Have family members or trusted friends present. Meet in a public place. Or don't go at all. Don't allow your desire to connect to cloud your better judgment. Trust your gut.

Protect yourself. Any contact with a person you don't trust, suspect is manipulative, or gossips, could be used against you. Don't put yourself at risk. Hearing so many stories of estrangement leads me to advise you that when it comes to a manipulator, even what seems like the nicest gesture may be a trick. Don't engage. Protect yourself. Keep responses short and sweet. Often, "thank you," is enough.

Trust your gut.

Below, I've listed a few questions to help you decide whether you're dealing with manipulation. Ponder these questions with your own experiences in mind.

- *Have you heard your words return to you subtly twisted, or in a way that makes you uncomfortable?*

- *Have you had conversations the other person later denied?*

- *Have you felt strangely odd about a circumstance, a conversation, or some situation, but couldn't put your finger on why?*

- *Have you had suspicions you're afraid to voice for fear they will sound farfetched, or are too complex or confusing to even explain?*

As a parent whose child is estranged, you may already be emotionally vulnerable. Take care to take care of yourself.

A couple of months later, our son did pay a short visit alone before moving cross-country to be with his in-laws. The meeting was a little strained and awkward, but at least he came. He brought beer that night—perhaps it was liquid encouragement—and sat at the end of our living room sofa, drinking it as we talked.

Feeling as if this was our last chance, the conversation quickly wound round to the estrangement. At one point, Hilary told Dan that we'd often thought of sending him a note or letter, but weren't sure he would ever get them. Referring to his wife, Hilary said, "We thought she might intercept."

Dan chuckled. "No."

"So you weren't staying away because of her," she asked. "We thought maybe—"

He cut her off. "It was never her."

The room was still for a moment. His words contradicted what he'd told me on that first phone call, a year after his estrangement began. And then my husband somehow filled the gap. Dan and his dad talked about TV—*American Pickers, Fast And Loud, Pawn Stars, American Restoration*, and *Storage Wars*. As the conversation circled the surface, I sat in silence, aching to connect, but not sure how. My son wore a plaid flannel shirt. And as he sat near the lamp, I noticed the lines on his face. He looked so tired.

A short while later, he said he thought he'd go. Outside, I asked him if he was sure he was okay to drive. He only laughed. "I'm fine, Mom."

Tears streaming, I hugged him hard. He stood there, rooted, motionless as I embraced him. In some ways, it was like hugging a stranger, but it also hurt. He is my precious son, the baby I rocked, the boy who brought me joy, the teen who had grown so handsome and strong. . . .

When the phone rang the next morning, the last person I expected was Dan. He said that he'd intended to get his passport while at the house. "Did you want to come get it," I asked. "Or . . . I could mail it if you'd prefer."

"I'd rather come over," he replied.

My heart soared at his words, a firecracker of hope. I would see him again. He wanted to come. For the rest of that day, I paced the house. Going from window to window, I watched for him, a crazy joy leaping inside me at an opportunity to see him one more time.

But that afternoon, the phone rang. "Could just mail that?" Dan said.

"I'll need an address." My words sounded hollow, each one a weightier stone.

"I'll text it," he said, explaining that they would be staying with his in-laws for a while. "Thanks, Mom."

And then he was gone, the reality so final it sucked the air from my lungs.

I set the phone on the bench beneath the pecan tree. My vision narrowed, seeing only the rough folds of bark as I bent toward the tree. I couldn't breathe. My chest was tight, my throat so dry it closed in on itself. My heart constricted in a fist of pain.

I'm going to die.

The thought enraged me. *Breathe.* I wouldn't let him do this to me. I refused to die of a broken heart. "Breathe, Sheri," I whispered, willing myself calm. "You're okay." I pressed my forehead to the scratchy bark. "You'll be okay." I drew in a shallow breath, and then another longer one. From the tree branches above me, doves cooed. I would be all right.

A Broken Heart

If you have felt so emotionally raw that you couldn't breathe, accompanied by chest pain, you may know what a broken heart feels like. The term, "brokenhearted," has been around for ages, but only recently have doctors confirmed that emotional upheaval really can affect the heart.

"Broken heart syndrome," or "stress cardiomyopathy," is a temporary condition that disrupts normal heart function and severely weakens the heart. Believed to arise due to stress hormones brought on by a sudden shock, loss, acute anger, or other emotional (or physical) stress, the syndrome occurs more often in women than men. Symptoms can mimic a heart attack.

According to the sources listed below, most people recover well, and don't suffer the condition again. However, it's wise to seek medical care for any symptoms that could be indicative of heart trouble.

Johns Hopkins Heart and Vascular Institute (search "stress cardiomyopathy"): www.hopkinsmedicine.org/heart vascular institute/

- Mayo Clinic (at the website, search for "broken heart syndrome"): http://www.mayoclinic.org/

Coming To Terms with Reality

The facts are that my son spent an hour with us before he moved away to another state. We sat and talked. We didn't argue that night, and I hugged him when he left. So, are we reconciled? Not in the sense I'd hoped for. Not in terms of the restoration so many parents imagine: our child returns, we mend the relationship, and then we move forward in harmony.

Yet despite the false hope, and visits that served as doses of reality about how much distance between Dan and the rest of us exists, I do feel a sense of reconciliation. As in another meaning of the word: *I am reconciled to the facts.* In the same way someone might accept a hardship, learn to live with a disease, or consent to a less than desirable circumstance, *I am reconciled to the reality of our estrangement.*

Sure, there might be an occasional birthday or holiday text. And I sometimes wonder if my son might one day share a picture of a child I wonder if I'll never know. Nearly two years ago, his wife texted me their new address, and wrote that when the time is right, she is sure we will reconnect. She included a photo of my son in the snow, and a short report that they have both settled into jobs and a church they like. Grateful for the news, I replied a simple, *thank you.*

I hope for their continued happiness. I wish them the best. But texts don't make a relationship. That sort of distant contact isn't restoration, not reconciliation in the sense that most of us would like. While we might not see a cousin for ages, but then the years and time seem to fall away, it's different when someone as close as our own child tears so brutally at our heart. There is still the past with its hurt and puzzlement.

My family has come to terms with the distance. The more time that passes, the more Dan makes himself a stranger. And I've accepted that. Those are the terms. I'm reconciled to the facts.

Other parents tell similar stories. Their child sends an annual gift basket or card. Perhaps they even see their child at a wedding, a funeral, or some other family event. Some of these parents have come to accept the quick clasp of a hand, or even a hug. But they have no illusions. Does that mean they never cry? That they never lie awake after seeing their child, and wish things were different? Not always. In the same way we might miss a deceased relative during holidays, or long for a second chance at some other life choice, the ghosts of hope, love, and pain may come to visit. But we don't have to let them stay. When you have truly released the probing question of why, given yourself credit for doing your best, and assigned your child the full responsibility for choosing to turn away, you're free to accept the tiny hiccups of sadness and longing as part of being human. Notice those feelings with self-compassion, accept them for what they are, and then let them go.

Remember Pam, whose estranged daughter, Martha, mistook her mother's text as coming from someone else? Then when Pam let her daughter know it was her, Martha didn't reply. Her silence spoke volumes. Yet even after many years, her daughter still sends a yearly Mother's Day bouquet. Like me, Pam is reconciled to the facts. For reasons Pam still doesn't comprehend, her daughter doesn't want her in her life. At this point, Pam has let go of trying. "It takes time to build trust," she says. "And I'm in my seventies now." Pam speaks of the fleeting quality to life. Wasting her precious days trying to mend the relationship, when Martha is happy with things as they are, would indeed be a waste.

Other mothers have a son or daughter who calls out of the blue every few years, or even stops in to see them as if nothing has happened. Constance has a 39-year-old son who lives in another state. "He comes over, will hug me, and tell me he loves me," she says. "He'll snap selfies of us together, which I'll see on Facebook later. But then he'll go stay with family members who took my husband's side when we divorced fifteen years ago." Constance has long since gotten over the pain. "Of course I wish it was different," she says. "But I live my life, and he lives his. I truly believe my son does love me, but he's stuck in some warped dysfunction that started at the time of our divorce. Since I'm powerless to change it, why not accept the tiny visits, and then get back to my life?"

Her acceptance didn't happen overnight. "It took me a good five or six years to let it all go," Constance says. "It's just healthier for me not to fight what is. Not being sad all the time allowed me to build a life. I'm in charge of myself, and I agree to see him on his terms when he comes to town."

Coming to terms with reality can also mean seeing your adult child for who he or she really is. We have our touching memories. A soft cheek we loved to kiss. Fluttery eyelashes so long they reminded us of Sesame Street's Snuffleupagus. A kid who played sports, got good grades, and made us proud. A son who was always dirty or a little daughter who brought us socks when our feet were cold. Maybe you had an accident-prone kid whose knees were always scabbed, or a child who melted hearts with his smile. Our memories are uniquely our own, and special. But that person we were once so close to may no longer exist. If you're pining for a child who has changed, you're pining for a memory.

Other mothers have arrived at similar conclusions, coming to terms with the reality, so they can move on.

Listen in on three mothers' thoughts below.

Elaine: *"I give up. That's what I told myself after nine months of no response. To keep doing the same things over and over and over, and expect the same results, really is the •efinition of insanity."*

Krista: *"What's that prayer about letting something go? Well, after two years of sending gifts, cards, and letters, I did. So far, my son hasn't come back to me. I'll still love him forever, but maybe only from afar. Like the prayer says, I really have let him go."*

Camilla: *"Giving myself some credit for shaping my son toward the successful man he is today has helped. He's not in my life, but his work is integral to the lives of many others. It may sound self-serving or even like denial, but I've put my son in the realm of other great men in history. Their families ma•e sacrifices for a son's public service or other greatness. They would have appreciated any bit of distant news. That's how I choose to think of my son. Like one of the greats who left his family for a greater good. So if I receive a bouquet on my birthday once every few years, or he happens to attend a family function, I can be grateful. He's cordial enough, and I can be proud."*

Reconciling yourself to the facts, and coming to an acceptance point that allows you a helpful perspective can take some time, but it's a progressive transformation. Months or years of distance allow perspective that doesn't usually appear overnight. In retrospect, most mothers whose estrangements have endured wish they'd have gotten on with their own lives sooner. If giving in to free yourself as these mothers did appeals to you, begin to shift your thinking now.

You may need to "give up," as Elaine put it. Or as we've discussed in other chapters, think of accepting the situation less as giving up and more like giving *in*. Doing so then allows you to work with what *is*, rather than what you wish would be. With that perspective, you can find a way to let go. Like Krista, you can decide to love from afar. Perhaps that means seeing your son or daughter like a wild bird you were entrusted to raise. You fed her, kept her warm and safe, and watched with delight as her fluffy baby feathers were replaced with graceful wings. You helped him grow strong, taught him what you knew, and encouraged independence.

As your fledgling took flight, your heart soared with him. Now, you can release your expectations. Give them wings. See them flutter away beyond the clouds. As the sun sets in a rosy sky, fix your sights on accepting tomorrow as a brand new day *for yourself.*

As Camilla did, give yourself credit for the time you spent, the sacrifices you made, and the love you shared. Even if your son or daughter is not currently a great person of history as Camilla chooses to view her son, the future may hold wonders. You've set free a unique individual, one-of-a-kind. Now set yourself free.

See your provisions and love as a launching pad. You did your best. Even if you believe you made mistakes—which all parents do—you can choose to view them in a positive light. Perhaps your real or so-called mistakes provided nuggets of wisdom and opportunities for your child's growth. As your own life circumstances may have taught you, even scars, once they have knitted over, can make you stronger.

Change how you see yourself. When you look in the mirror, do you see a victim? As Camilla has, can you instead see a giver? Can you see yourself as a nurturer with a unique and lovely gift? Then open yourself to also receive—your own love, your own freedom, your own happiness.

If your son or daughter sends a bouquet or the occasional holiday or birthday text, can you think of these as Camilla's "distant news"? Those bits of contact may be your child's way of showing his or her appreciation for all you've done, and all the love you gave. Those gifts or gestures may, in fact, feel as one mother said, like "crumbs to a starving woman." But for whatever reason, that may be all your child will give. Does that make the behavior fair or right? *No.* Am I validating those actions? *No.* But this isn't about your child. This is about you. As Elaine has decided, continuing to *do-do-do* and *try-try-try* in a flurry of raging emotions that keeps you victimized, might feel as she says, like "the definition of insanity." See yourself as a mother who did her best, and then set her child—and herself—free.

That's in line with Pam's decision to give away the most recent annual Mother's Day bouquet. She used to set the flowers in a prominent place, and look at them longingly. She would care for the stems, change the water, and prolong their life and beauty as long as possible. She now knows that doing so only helped her to deny the truth of her daughter's distance, and perhaps even kept the loss she felt alive. This past Mother's Day, she accepted the delivery, and then immediately removed the card. She gave the flowers to a young neighbor woman to enjoy.

Pam no longer views the yearly bouquet as evidence that her daughter may be having a change of heart. She knows that was only wishful thinking. The small gesture is not a reason for Pam to believe her daughter may be coming around. Pam has chosen to accept what is. Acceptance has helped her to get on with her life.

You may not feel Pam's sense of finality, but you can learn from her choice not to waste precious time trying to mend what another person seems fine to keep broken. You can decide to give in, let go, give yourself credit, and see yourself in a new and freeing light. And remember, setting aside the trying for the moment, does not mean you cannot pick up the baton of hope and attempt to reconnect later. A decision made now to free yourself, does not mean you are required to forever and always halt all acts toward reconciliation.

While you may have seen advice on the Internet or in books and magazines from experts that say you'll be damaging your adult child if you stop reaching out, you're wise to challenge the advice. There is no one-size-fits-all solution. In my opinion, having experienced estrangement, and with insight from more than 9,000 parents, such a blanket statement is wrong, and may only prolong your hurt.

However, you may feel as many parents do, and what may actually be at the heart of such advice: that until you feel you have done everything in your power to reconcile, you cannot feel right about giving in or letting go.

Without feeling satisfied that we've done all we can, we may be haunted by the worry that if our son or daughter died tomorrow, we'd regret our inaction. We'll get to the matter of exhausting all efforts later in the chapter. For now, use the next exercise to take an honest look at the relationship you shared with your adult child.

✈ Examine Your Relationship

Healthy adult relationships require boundaries and mutual respect. Is that the sort of relationship you have shared with your estranged child? Often, estranged mothers find themselves pining for the sweet child they once knew, or getting caught up in old expectations. Let's take a realistic look. Reflect on the questions. In your answers, elaborate in order to think the questions through.

- Was the relationship one-sided? *How?* Did I allow my adult child to manipulate or take advantage of me? *How?*

_____

_____

_____

- Did my child cut me off when I drew boundaries, stood up for myself, required her to contribute, or to pay his own way? How?

_____

_____

_____

- Was my child physically or emotionally abusive, or disrespectful to me? How? When?

_____

_____

_____

- Did I dread visits? Was I often inconvenienced, or feel used? When?

_____

_____

_____

- Was I reminded of "mistakes," or made to feel guilty? List examples.

_____

_____

_____

- Did our interactions often make me angry or resentful? How/Why?

_____

_____

_____

- Did I feel the need to be careful what I said or did? If so, how?

_____

_____

_____

Look back on what you've written. For a few minutes, allow yourself to reflect on the relationship. Remember incidents, recall your feelings, and take notice of how the memories manifest in your physical body.

- Do I want to go back to that same sort of relationship? Write down your thoughts/emotions.

_____

_____

_____

Sharing with a counselor, a trusted friend, or in a support group might be helpful, but that's for you to decide—later. Don't censor yourself here. Your thoughts and feelings are valid, and worthy of your attention.

If an inequitable, unkind, or hurtful relationship feels necessary, or appeals to you more than honoring your values and what you know is healthy for you, take an honest look at what's behind that notion. When you ask yourself *why* you are willing to dishonor yourself—your health, your happiness, your financial wellbeing, or in any other way—what thoughts and feelings occur to you?

_____

_____

_____

_____

If, after doing the exercise, you feel that *any* relationship with an adult son or daughter, even one in which you feel used or abused, is more desirable than *no* relationship or perhaps a very limited one, it's important that you consider what might be behind those feelings. As an example, co-dependency could be a factor. It's equally possible that you suffer low self-esteem, or perhaps your natural temperament is one that avoids conflict (even to your own peril).

The thrust of this book is reclaiming your life. Self-reflection can be a part of that.

Suggested Reading

Co-Dependency:

*Co-Dependent No More: How To Stop Controlling Others And Start
Caring For Yourself,* by Melody Beattie

The New Co-Dependency: Help and Guidance For Today's Generation,
by Melody Beattie

Self-Esteem:

Breaking The Chain Of Low Self-Esteem, by Marilyn Sorenson

*Self-Esteem: A Proven Program Of Cognitive Techniques For Assessing,
Improving, And Maintaining Your Self-Esteem,* by Matthew
McKay and Patrick Fanning

The Self-Esteem Workbook, by Glenn R. Schiraldi

Temperaments:

Personality Plus: How To Understand Others By Understanding Yourself,
by Florence Littauer

Please Understand Me II: Temperament, Character, Intelligence,
by David Keirsey

*The Temperament God Gave You: The Classic Key to Knowing Yourself, Getting
Along With Others, And Growing Closer,* by Art & Laraine Bennett

An Apology Letter: Should You Write One?

You may have been advised to write a letter in which you tell your estranged
adult child that you're sorry. Called an "Amends Letter," or a "Letter of
Apology," the concept is often sold by experts in the field of estrangement
as a step toward reconciling. As a result, parents' may get their hopes up,
only to have their expectations dashed. Should *you* write a letter of apology? And if you do, what should you say? Let's take a closer look.

From time to time, the idea of sending apology letters is brought up
in the support forum or in comments at my website. The voices of mothers who have tried them often then ring out in unison: *"Don't do it!"* That's
because the letters can backfire. Words can be twisted, come across as

desperate, or perhaps even seem insincere. Instead of opening the door to reconciliation, mothers often report more silence and anger—or as some put it, more "venom."

Here are several excerpts from mothers who have shared their letter results with me:

- *"As my therapist advised, I sent a letter apologizing and asking my daughter's forgiveness for her list of accusations about how much I'd hurt her. I asked to meet with her and any counselor or pastor so we could work things out. No response. I have never heard from her again. I've since reached out, but she never responds."*

- *"I wrote a long letter asking for forgiveness. My son sent me hate mails that only hurt me further."*

- *"I wrote expressing how sorry I was for any pain I ever caused, and told her I love her. She eventually replied with a 20-page letter criticizing my entire life. I wrote back, and said I loved her. Since then there's silence. I feel worse than ever, and don't know what else I can do."*

- *"I don't agree with my daughter's childhood memories, but wrote an 'amends' letter anyway. I wanted her to know her feelings were heard. She texted that the letter was 'nice,' but has ignored overtures since."*

- *"I know from a friend who's still in contact with my daughter that she showed my amends letter to the police, and tried to have me arrested for harassment. The officer rea• my letter, an• tol• her it wasn't groun•s for arrest. Of course he did! I had apologized for all of her complaints. I look back at photos of our happy times together and don't see her 'truth,' but I wanted to understand, so wrote the letter apologizing, and telling her that. Now, knowing she took it as harassment, how can I contact her at all?"*

- *"After I sent a letter of apology and a thousand dollars as a wedding gift, my son calle• me. I was so flabbergaste• an• happy, that I apologized again. I was thrilled to hear from him, and told him that. Then he blocked me from his phone and Facebook."*

Obviously, these parents were disappointed. Does that mean the letters *never* work? I can't honestly answer the question since I don't hear success stories. That doesn't mean those stories aren't out there. However, if you do an Internet search that links "estranged adult children" to "letter of apology," "amends letter," or a variation, what you're likely to see are angry adult children on estranged adult children forums picking the letters apart. Adult children often have snarkier names for their parents' apology letters:

- Emotional Forgery
- Lies, Lies, Lies
- Narcissist (or "Nmom")
- Robotic

To be fair, you'll also find tired parents who, in discussing these letters, have slipped into a bit of snarky sarcasm themselves. They're letting off steam, sometimes lamenting the act of apologizing for things they didn't do, and may be angry with experts who recommend the letters.

The truth is, no matter how sincere an apologetic letter may be, your estranged adult child may not receive it as intended. If you decide that an apologetic letter is right for you, it's my opinion that you should keep it short. Don't apologize for things you didn't do. Keep your apology general. *I'm sorry you have felt hurt. I'm sorry we're estranged. I'd like to make things right between us.* If you send a letter addressing all that your son or daughter says you did wrong, you provide written words for an angry "child" to pore over, pick at, and twist. You may only add fuel to the fire.

If you're considering writing an apology letter, please turn back to the exercise in this chapter where you examined your feelings about your relationship with your adult child prior to the estrangement. Is sending an apology letter motivated by desperation or low self-esteem? Are you groveling? Is an amends letter an attempt to hang onto *any* relationship, even one that hurts you?

While you may have high hopes and the best of intentions, if you write one of these letters, please be prepared for possible negative consequences.

As one mother said, expecting a letter to repair the problem is "delusional."

An apologetic letter's success or failure may also come down to timing. If you know your son or daughter is angry, in a haze of substance abuse, or otherwise non-receptive to you, sending a letter at this time may not be wise.

In a 2015 study, researchers found that "most respondents who were estranged from a parent" strongly agreed with the statement, "We could *never* have a functional relationship again."[1] While that may sound disheartening, keep in mind that study respondents were voluntary. It's highly likely that those motivated to respond were in the throes of an active estrangement, and struggling with the intensity of emotions that accompany one.

Again, consider whether the timing is right for any sort of letter. As most of us know from life experience, what looks impossible at one point, with emotional healing and the gift of perspective may later not seem so inconceivable. Later in this chapter, we'll talk more about how the passage of time may sometimes play a role in reconciliation. For now, let's get back to rebuilding personal strength.

Boundaries: Setting Your Own Terms

Much of this book has focused on recapturing self-worth and building your autonomy apart from your child. This is necessary if you're ever to reconcile on terms that are fair and just, based on equity that respects all parties. We must have a sense of self that understands and honors our values if we're to reconcile from a place of wholeness rather than one of need.[2]

Marti and her husband were surprised when their son called after three years of silence. "He told me he had a daughter now, and asked if he could bring his wife and toddler by." Marti was hopeful and agreed. Then she received an email from her son. "In it was a list of rules," she says. "We were not allowed to talk about the past. We could talk to him, but not to his wife. We could only touch the baby if she came to us, and we weren't allowed to encourage her in any way."

Marti and her husband discussed the rules, and although they didn't expressly agree, they emailed back for their son and his family to come.

"The meeting was awful," says Marti. "Our son chatted on about how great his job was, how much he loved their little girl, and how he was going for a promotion. Meanwhile, our daughter-in-law sat stone-faced in the corner. And every time our sweet little granddaughter ambled near us, she'd lure her back with a cookie or a toy."

The cruel experience became too much for Marti to bear. "I finally offered my granddaughter a cookie myself. She was such a little cutie, and so much like the way I remember my son at that age. But then his wife scooped her up, and left the house in a huff. Our son told us we should have followed the rules."

Marti says that a few months after the visit with her son and his family ended so badly, he sent them an email saying he'd like to try again. "But he reminded us of his rules," says Marti. "It's clear that he wants a different relationship with us than we do with him. This isn't reconciling. I emailed him back that we'd be willing to go to counseling with him and his family, but he didn't reply."

Although Marti and her husband were sick over their decision, they weighed it against their feelings about going along with their son's one-sided rules. Having their granddaughter in the room, but not being able to interact with her, was torturous. Requiring that they not discuss the past wouldn't allow them to explore what had gone so wrong. "How could we ever develop trust if we didn't understand what had caused the estrangement to begin with," Marti asks. "To suggest counseling was our only choice." Marti and her husband now believe what a friend of their son's recently told them: that their son was abusing prescription pain killers at the time of the estrangement. "Counseling might have brought that out," says Marti. "Maybe he's ashamed."

Parents may, at times, view even their healthy relationships with adult children as not *always* on equal footing. For instance, you might recognize and accept a younger person's inability to see a particular matter from your more experienced standpoint. Motivated by love, mutual respect and care, you may at times choose to help an adult son or daughter financially or in other ways—and be appreciated for those kindnesses.

However, this sort of help, forgiveness, or excusing is different than a relationship that enables bad behavior, fosters dependency, and makes you feel invisible, unimportant, or as if you are not valued in your child's eyes (other than what you can do for or give to them).

Let's talk for a moment about episodic estrangements. It's not uncommon for estranged adult children to reconcile for a time, and then estrange themselves again. Sometimes, friendly periods alternate with intervals of separation over many years. Parents look back on a period of connection and come to believe their child allowed them into their life again only due to financial (or other) needs.

Physical therapist Sondra's estranged son reconnected suddenly after many years. He came back into her life when he was married, with two very young daughters. Soon afterward, he divorced. He asked for his mother's help, and Sondra stepped in to assist with her grandchildren. Her participation helped facilitate a joint custody arrangement without expensive daycare. Looking back, Sondra believes her son reconnected because he knew his marriage was coming to an end, and he needed her to help with his children.

Portrait-artist Barb experienced a similar reconnection. Her daughter got in touch when she was pregnant for the first time. Once her grandson was born, Barb babysat. Two other children were born soon after, and she developed bonds with them all—only to see the children ripped away from her a few years later when she was no longer needed to watch them. She misses those children dearly.

Even Evelyn, whose son and his wife bring their three sons at Christmastime but remain coldly removed from her for the rest of the year, suffers a sort of episodic estrangement. In her case, the reunions themselves aren't warm or lasting. Evelyn no longer believes her son wants a genuine relationship with her. She can only speculate as to why he returns each holiday.

Jerri and her husband experience reunions when their son shows up unexpectedly and sometimes stays with them for days or even a few weeks. They have come to accept the letdown that always follows. When their son arrives, they open their doors and hearts. But they also don't overspend or pamper him. They do worry about his young son, who they're now raising, getting attached to him. While there is no animosity or arguing, these parents eventually steer their son to take more responsibility—college, occupational training, or simply work. And when they do, he leaves again.

Jean, a single mother of one adult son, suffered periodic estrangements for more than a decade. "He always came back eventually," says Jean. "We would have some satisfying weeks, but he usually wanted me to give him money. I see that now. I suppose I saw it all along, but didn't admit it to myself."

Their latest reconciliation ended when she would not pay for his car insurance, and he charged off in a fit of anger. At 67, Jean's arthritis required she stop working. She had no pension. Faced with a limited income, Jean realized that helping him financially over the years hadn't been wise. Torn, she still agreed to pay for three months' worth of car insurance. At age 29, this was her son's first car. He had moved outside the city, so required transportation.

Jean's son wasn't satisfied with her plan to pay for only the first three months. He took her check, left in a huff, and returned after three months. "He apologized, and sweet-talked me," says Jean. "He helped me at the grocery store. Then he asked for money." Jean found herself wavering, contemplating how long she might live, whether a few bucks would really make a difference, and if she should just buy her way into her son's life. "But I won't be around to bail him out of debt forever," she says. Jean explained that his decision to move had consequences. Pushing him to take responsibility was in his best interests. Her son told her he would probably have to give up his car, and then he might even lose his job. Feeling tortured, Jean began to cry, but did not give in.

Two years have passed. She has reached out repeatedly to try and mend the relationship on equitable terms, but has been unsuccessful. Jean won't capitulate. "The parenting role has its pain," she says. "But even if I had lots of money to spare, what would giving in teach him?"

Now, let's look at another set of circumstances.

Abbey was disappointed by her 18-year-old daughter's decision to leave college and move in with a new boyfriend. She tried to reason with her daughter, but was told to "bug off." Her daughter stopped taking her calls. Abbey worried for her daughter's safety, and feared she was throwing away her future. But her daughter refused to talk. She even moved to another city, which Abbey learned from a relative. After six months, her daughter called. She had landed a decent job, and needed money to buy clothing appropriate for the office. She also asked to use a spare car—a 10-year-old model she had used when she was in college.

Wanting her daughter to succeed, Abbey and her husband agreed to the clothes. Rather than send money, Abbey insisted on shopping with her, and they bought a few simple suits. "She looked healthy and well," says Abbey, who felt better after seeing her daughter. That's when these parents also gave in about the car. "We didn't want to worry about her on public transportation," Abbey explains. "So we just gave it to her. It's what we would have done before she left college anyway."

Abbey hopes her daughter will eventually fully reconnect, but for now, she's thankful for an occasional call. Her daughter chats about her job, and things going on in her life. If Abbey ever offers advice, her daughter hurries off the phone. Abbey is disappointed that her daughter rarely asks how she and her father are doing, but for now, Abbey has accepted the imbalanced relationship. She is taking into account her daughter's age, and hopes the behavior is temporary.

So far, she hasn't asked for money again, and her occasional calls seem genuine enough. Abbey isn't certain what sort of relationship their future holds. Time will tell.

Agreeing To Disagree

Sometimes, estranged parties can agree to disagree, and let bygones be bygones, in order to forge ahead. One mother whose son and his wife recently reconnected after 16 years explained it this way: "He called and asked if they could come over. My husband and I were surprised, but hopeful. When they arrived, we offered them refreshments. None of us talked about the past. They told us what was new in their lives, and we listened, feeling relieved to know they're successful in life. And they're even nice. We then told them the things we're interested in. My husband's fishing, and my work the last six years as a hospice nurse. It was pleasant, and interesting to stare our son in the face and kind of see ourselves in him. That was three months ago. Since then we've talked on the phone, and made plans to meet their children, who are now teenagers."

Maybe these parents missed out on many years with their son, but the time is gone. Why waste more time with regrets? This mother no longer feels the need to hold her son or his wife accountable for the hurt they caused. She's long since over that pain anyway. By accepting reality, and letting her son and his wife go when they estranged themselves so long ago, she was able to get on with living. She believes her son has had a change of heart. There is no overnight restoration of what might have been had they remained close, but perhaps these small advances will lead to something more meaningful. It will be a new relationship, of course.

Despite their openness, these parents admit to reservations. If not a change of heart, what might be behind their son's sudden contact? Or put more bluntly, what are his motives? Could he be hoping for an inheritance?

While they see no reason to discuss these reservations with their son at this time, they're also smart not to beat themselves up for having the thoughts. Remaining guarded is a natural response, and in light of their long estrangement history, is sound. These parents are hopeful, but cautious. They recognize that to rebuild trust takes time.

Exhausting All Efforts: Consider Yourself Toxic

Some parents worry they haven't done enough to try to reconcile. That worry keeps them from moving on. Each parent must determine for themselves what exhausting all efforts means, and how much they will try. In this section, I've included some thoughts on how to make an effort. Please note that I'm in no way advocating that you should do whatever it takes to have some semblance of a relationship, or that the efforts described later in this section will even work—especially in the long-term. Before we get to those, let's examine recent research that allows parents to step into estranged adult children's shoes.

Research from 2015 that examined 898 unrelated parents and adult children reported that the reasons parents give for estrangement is very different than those that estranged adult children provide. In the study, the average age of the children was 40, and they typically became estranged at age 31. Parents tended to blame estrangement on situational factors and external circumstances. Children more frequently blamed a parent's character or personality, which they often categorized as toxic. Parents more routinely cited children's sense of entitlement—while children believed their parents only *perceived* them as feeling entitled. Similarly, children who said they felt unloved blamed their parents. However, parents weren't certain of any role they might have played in their child's *perceived* feelings of not being loved. When parents mentioned a third-party such as a significant other or spouse, they often believed the person was instrumental to the changes in their child that then contributed to estrangement. Children, however, saw their parents as unaccepting of the person or the relationship.[3]

In my own research, parents often come up with a variety of possible reasons and multiple factors that may have contributed to the break. Obviously, this speculation reflects the fact that in many instances no clear-cut reasoning is provided by the child. Parents are left to soul search. In the 2015 study, researchers viewed this sort of soul searching as evidence of parents' willingness to take on their child's perspective. By contrast, children were less likely to try on parents' perspectives. And it's important to note that the ability to step into another's shoes helps family members to have empathy and to remain close, as was discussed in Chapter Six.

So, what can we do? You may have heard the expression, "walking on eggshells." Many parents use the term to describe how they felt even before the estrangement. Taken literally, it's virtually impossible to walk on eggshells without breaking them. Nevertheless, many parents say they've been willing to do so in an attempt to maintain peace. Reconciling may very well entail such tip-toeing. Are you willing? Is this really reconciliation? Tuck those questions away. For now, let's try to see things from the adult children's point of view.

Are you seen as toxic? Use of the word "toxic" has changed in our society. Most of us would agree that a toxin is seen as a poison. In the financial world, toxic refers to something that has no value, as in "toxic debt." When it comes to how estranged children use the word, perhaps both definitions apply.

In the 2015 research mentioned earlier, toxicity is defined as ongoing disrespect, continuing hurtful situations, anger and cruelty. The study lists a quote provided from an adult child who referred to "the past," which was never talked about or resolved, and memories of the past that were triggered by being near the family.[3]

If you use the keyword "toxic" to search at Amazon.com for self-help books with publication dates prior to the mid-1990s, only a few books come up. After that time, however, the word "toxic" increasingly refers to relationships. Now, there are hundreds of self-help books on toxic people and relationships, including many on parents. This demonstrates a shift in thinking about the word's application. While parents might immediately think of poison, our children may instantly associate the word with relationships and people. You may not know there's a Britney Spears video by the name, but your adult child probably does. Perhaps the proliferation of self-help books about toxic relationships is a product of our throwaway society. If a relationship is toxic, then what's the point of preserving it? No one is expected to ingest poison.

As you read the information below, consider how your actions might be seen as toxic by your adult child. Settle into his or her shoes, and take a critical look at yourself as you make any efforts to reach out.

Are you reaching out too often? First, consider your child's responses to your efforts so far. Does your child send your gifts back to you? Does he or she ignore cards, letters, emails, texts or other messages? If so, then will one more card or letter make a positive impact? Or will it make you seem pushy instead. Your child's indifference may clue you in to take a break. Perhaps set a date in the future, six months or a year from now, and then reach out again. After an interval of time, you can tactfully and non-obtrusively let your child know that you still care, and that you'd still like to reconcile. In the interim, do healthy things that please you, develop your skills, and promote your own wellness.

Has your child obtained legal orders or protection papers? Don't go against them. In the eyes of the law, and in your child's eyes, your contact is harassment. In the future, you may be surprised that your child reaches out to you. For now, get on with your life. Do something fun, enjoy friends, learn something new, and take care of yourself. You may feel as if it's an endless wait, but remember, wait without the A is wit. Keep your wits about you, and think of something to do while you're waiting.

When reaching out to your child does makes sense, put the perspective-taking that parents are so good at into practice. Consider every potential contact from your child's point of view.

Do you inconvenience or annoy your child? Consider what form of contact will be best received. A call, a text, a card. . . ? Think this through thoroughly. For example, do you call just so you can hear your child's voice (even if it's only a recording)? Any message you leave takes up virtual space. Will your child have to hear your voice when he retrieves other, perhaps more desired, messages? Maybe your behavior will be seen as domineering, or bothersome.

If you mail a package, will receiving it create an inconvenience? A gift sent in love could potentially be viewed as inconvenient if the package is brought for delivery when no one is at home—and a trip to the post office is required to collect it.

Will your gifts be seen as bribes? Some children say their parents use material things and money to try and control them. Though you intend kindness and to convey love, could your gift be seen as a sort of bribe? Will your child feel a sort of obligation to you in accepting it?

Think before you speak. How does your son or daughter usually respond to contact? If your texts often result in short texting exchanges, then reach out when you have the time. Don't make contact when you're too busy to spend a few minutes reading return texts and replying.

Think before you speak (or write). What would your child be glad to hear? If your child considers you "toxic," words you intend as supportive and kind may be received as critical or nosy. Your concern may be seen as questioning your child's judgment. Sharing news of a family member's ill health might be viewed as an attempt to trigger guilt. Your intended jokes may be viewed as criticism. You may intend to soothe, convey patience, love, understanding, and regret. But your child may believe you're being negative (or toxic). Consider running your words by someone you trust, allowing them to play the role of devil's advocate. Parents in a supportive group may have insights from their own experiences that can help.

Don't make contact when you're under the influence, feeling down, upset, or tired. Once, when nobody in my family was well enough or available to attend a Mopar event with my husband, his car won "Best in Show." I was at home with a virus when my husband called to share his news. Immediately upset that he was there all alone, it crossed my mind to me to send Dan a text: "Bet your dad misses you tonight. ..."

Of course, I caught myself, and deleted it without sending. To Dan, my words would have sounded like critical sarcasm or a guilt trip (and he'd have been right). Besides, in reality, even if Dan was still emotionally and physically close, he might have been working or otherwise unavailable—as were all of his siblings and I on that night. When you're stressed, ill, or tired, postpone reaching out. We're only human. Words spoken when we're vulnerable may not be helpful—and could qualify as toxic.

Keep your goals in mind. Geneva's overarching goal was to make sure her daughter knew she still cared. Because that goal is so common, let's assume it's yours, and see how the other considerations presented here can be taken into account.

Consider how often to reach out. In your child's eyes, how often is reasonable? While a text on your child's birthday, other holiday, or perhaps every couple of months might be tolerated, or in some cases welcomed, would a weekly text be as well-received? Turn the tables. If you received a call every week from someone you considered toxic, how would you feel? Give your child some space. In essence, estranging themselves is a very dramatic way of expressing a need to get away. If someone else very plainly removed themselves from your life, would you feel as justified in giving chase?

In terms of toxicity, dosage is a factor. Even water can be considered "toxic" if too much is consumed. While a once-in-a-while call might be a welcome sip, forcing your reluctant son or daughter to drink isn't possible. Consider your own well-being, too. How does a steady *drip-drip-drip* of negativity or non-response affect *you*?

What are you willing to endure in order to reconcile? Once you've reached out, what else can you do? Hoping to reunite, would you be willing to tolerate your child's negativity and anger in order to better understand it?

Two mothers shared unusual circumstances when they were called in long distance as part of an adult child's therapy. In both instances, the adult children were in their mid-thirties, and had been in therapy for more than a year. The mothers were asked to participate by reading their adult child's emails and taking their phone calls. Both mothers were instructed to listen to or read the accusations, blame, and anger, and not to defend themselves or explain their intentions. Hoping to reconcile, the mothers agreed. Their children's intentions were not as clear.

In one of these arrangements, the psychiatrist explained that the daughter's feelings were her "reality." In the other family, with a different doctor, the mother was instructed to hear out her son's complaints and empathize, even when she didn't agree with his accusations. Any defensive feelings she might have, this psychiatrist told her, were likely caused by her own shame, or a need for recognition. He explained that this part of the therapy was about her son being heard.

If I was in the second situation, I might have questioned the mental health professional's evaluation of my potential feelings and their cause. How do *you* feel about these scenarios? The approach wouldn't be acceptable to all parents. One of the mothers said her son brought up things she'd said many years ago, telling her how much she'd hurt him. To her, the words were just things she shared like anyone might in a normal conversation. She tried to understand her son's perspective, but the situation seemed unfair. The other mother quickly grew distraught. To her, the hurtful phone calls condoned her daughter's verbal abuse.

If you find yourself called into your child's therapy, don't be afraid to negotiate the terms. And ask questions. In both of these situations, the adult child had already been in therapy for an extended period. Ask how long this new phase is supposed to last. What is the goal? What comes next? Does the adult child want to reconcile? Has the mental health professional had prior success with this sort of interaction? Do you get a turn to speak? Do your goals align with those of your son or daughter?

Your feelings about whether you would be willing to endure this sort of emotional pain to better understand your child's feelings, and their "reality," are yours to decide.

Bridging the Gap

If you're among the parents able to bridge the gap of estrangement, and you and your child successfully reconcile, I hope you will reach out to me and share your story. As I gathered information and people's stories, it is obviously parents who had *not* reconciled that contacted me. A few people in the forum community at my website have had promising contact, but are wary of potential problems in the future. Time will tell if the reunions will last. Maybe in the future I can share success stories.

✈ Reconciling: What It Means, What It Takes

With the above examples and your own situation, in mind, ponder the questions. Write down your thoughts, feelings, and answers. Don't censor yourself.

- What does reconciliation mean to me?

_____

_____

_____

- Is my view of reconciliation currently possible? Why/Why not?

_____

_____

- Am I willing to compromise or alter my thoughts about what it means to reconcile? How?

_____

_____

_____

- Realistically, what would I have to do to reconcile at this time? Would the reconciliation be real?

_____

_____

_____

- How would I have to adjust my thinking, actions, and beliefs?

_____

_____

_____

- What am I willing to do to reconcile?

_____

_____

_____

- What would my child have to do for me to believe the reconciliation was genuine?

_____

_____

- Knowing that a decision I make today does not have to forever bind me, can I "reconcile to the facts," as was discussed earlier in this chapter?

_____

_____

Notes

CHAPTER EIGHT

Life Goes On

Many parents confided what can be considered phase-of-life struggles and decisions, which are made more difficult by a son or daughter's rejection. This chapter is designed to help. Sections deal with grandparents' rights, end-of-life decisions and estate planning, physical changes, helping a spouse during serious illness, and coping with your own health crises. Whether or not any of the issues apply to you now, we all face various life trials. Reading what other parents have done and why can help you find solutions in your own unique situations.

Many of the tips, suggestions, and techniques shared here apply to overall wellness, stress reduction, and recovery. So they will be of benefit as you cope with estrangement.

What Rights Do Grandparents Have?

All states have grandparent visitation laws. But that doesn't mean you'll get to see your grandchildren. Each state has its own statutes for considering a child's "best interests," although the term is not always well-defined. Most state courts allow parents with an intact family to decide what's in their children's best interests. If the parents don't want you to see your grandchild, the court may not interfere. States have varying ways to define the term "intact family" too. So, if your child is divorced, or for some other reason one parent is not living in the household, grandparents are not automatically awarded visitation.

With its year-2000 Troxel v. Granville ruling, the U.S. Supreme Court strengthened the right of parents to decide what is in their minor children's best interests. Parents in the state of Washington had appealed a judge's decision allowing the grandparents visitation, and the Washington Supreme Court overturned the judge's decision. The U.S. Supreme Court also sided with the parents, and held that the state statute unconstitutionally infringed on the parents' right to make decisions for their children.[1] However, the U.S. Supreme Court did not identify a clear constitutional standard for deciding children's best interests when parents and grandparents disagree.[1]

More recently, in a 2012 Alabama state case, parents had cut off the grandparents' contact with their children. The grandparents put up signs along the school bus route that declared their love, and also attended their granddaughters' ball games and other public activities. Eventually, they sued for, and were awarded, daily telephone calls and unsupervised weekly visits. Birthday and holiday arrangements were also ordered. But when the parents appealed, the visitation was reversed. The Alabama Supreme Court also struck down the state's Grandparent Visitation Act, holding that a judge may not interfere with parents' rights unless the parents have been determined unfit.[2] The grandparents attempted further appeal, but the U.S. Supreme Court declined to hear the case.

There is still no clear-cut standard of constitutionality for states to apply. Nevertheless, when grandparents seek visitation rights, they must often provide evidence that parents are not fit, or that harm will occur if the children are not allowed to see them.

To find out more about grandparents' rights, start at www.Grandparents.com. The site has a guide to the rights of grandparents that lists state-by-state facts, as well as many informative links. Consult with a family law attorney to explore your specific rights, but proceed with caution. It would be better to come to a solution without the law. A letter from an attorney as a first step toward gaining visitation is almost sure to cause opposition. An informal letter from you may be a more sensible first effort.

It goes without saying that if you take legal action to try and force your estranged child to allow you to see your grandchildren, your estranged son or daughter will be angry. They have cut you out of their lives. Weigh the circumstances and your and your grandchildren's needs, against the possibility of further eroding relationships. Would a bitter fight between the adults further confuse and hurt the innocent children?

Some grandparents have persisted in asking to see their grandchildren, and their estranged children have at some point, on some level, relented. Some routinely see and/or care for their grandchildren despite the situation with their adult children. Others are allowed occasional visits, for which they're grateful.

The examples I have heard often involve situations where children are dropped off or picked up without any direct interaction between the estranged parties. A grandchild may relay messages about details of dates or timing. Often, the expressed or unspoken rule is that Grandma doesn't talk with the grandkids about their parents.

Some tell of more supervised visits, during which the estranged son or daughter waits in another room, or leaves a spouse to oversee. In some instances, grandparents quietly endure as estranged adults murmur rude remarks during their visits. These grandparents hope to preserve the relationship with their grandchildren, so continue the visits despite the strain.

As grandchildren grow older, they will become more independent. A few people have shared their joy at having received an unexpected call or visit from a grandchild they have so missed. Some grandparents reach out on social media and get a favorable response. Many continue to send cards or gifts for years, into what seems like a black hole. However, eventually as the children mature, they may take the initiative to contact their grandparents—either with their parents' permission, or on the sly. Obviously, these situations are tricky. If you communicate with a grandchild, your actions may anger the parent. Again, weigh your unique circumstances against possible repercussions. Ponder worst- and best-case scenarios. Act or don't act from a place of deliberated wisdom rather than in emotional haste.

It may be heartening to know that sometimes an ex-spouse facilitates grandparent visits. You'll recall Sondra, whose ex-daughter-in-law facilitates her continued relationship with her granddaughters. If your child has divorced, perhaps communicating with the ex will help in your plight. Obviously, you'll weigh your individual circumstances carefully, and decide what action, if any, to take.

While there is hope, in many instances, grandchildren do remain lost to estranged grandparents. One agony is the worry that the grandchildren they have been so close to will be told, or conclude on their own, that Grandma no longer loves them. Some, however, have worked to overcome the pain in the ways outlined later in this section. And they feel successful at doing so.

Losing contact with the grandchildren adds another layer of frustration and grief. My grandchildren are not from Dan. And I'm fortunate to know them. Still, I can relate to the sense of loss that goes with losing contact. When some of my grandchildren who lived close to me relocated to a distant city, my world turned upside down. It was as if the future shifted. Activities that connected us, and made me *Grandma*, seemed to fade away. No more impromptu after-school visits and picking oranges from our trees. No more juicy smiles and sticky-fingered hugs. A simple trip to the grocery store became an emotional mine field. No more need for raisins in the little boxes, or cereal with prizes inside. If I was no longer the grandma who was always close, always ready for them, then who was I in their lives?

I don't pretend to know the lonely prospect of *never* hearing those sweet little voices, or not watching those lovely children grow into mature adults. But in my sadness over my grandchildren's move, and from the heartbreaking stories shared by thousands of grandparents whose relationships have been cut short, I can imagine. I can empathize. And I can tell you this: Within reason, do *what it takes to feel as if you've done your best to in some way convey your love for them.*

Below, I've listed a few ideas for dealing with the emotional pain and separation from grandchildren.

Keep a scrapbook or memory box. Some grandmothers find that maintaining a designated book or box for their grandchild helps. They insert photos from previous times together, and write about how much they enjoyed them. They update the pages with notes about what they wonder about their grandchild, perhaps relating to a special memory. If a grandmother has foot surgery, she might make a note about the time she and a granddaughter got a pedicure together, and add a picture of her own foot now, covered in clumsy bandages. To commemorate birthdays, add a card and a handwritten note. Believing their grandchildren will one day be given these items provides a modicum of peace.

Keep a journal or write letters to your grandchildren. Even if you mail your letters, keep a copy that could be given to them later in case their mail is intercepted. Correspondence, or even a journal you keep, could later be shown to grandchildren who grow up, come to see you, and ask, "Why didn't you come to visit us?"

If you do write letters or keep a journal to be shown to grandchildren someday, practice self-restraint. While expressing the facts as you understand them or sharing your dismay over what caused the break could help, badmouthing grandchildren's parents won't likely endear you to them. This isn't about blame. Your thoughtful words can convey love, and demonstrate kindness, which won't support a foul tale that may have been told about you.

Find surrogate grandchildren. One mother describes getting involved with her sister's seven grandchildren as taking "positive steps" that helped her recover. In her sister's grandchildren, she found renewed joy. In today's reality of two-career families, having her as an extra grandmother has been a blessing to the family. Her close relationship with the kids allows her sister more one-on-one grandma time with each grandchild, which they all value. Maybe a younger friend has children that you can be a surrogate grandmother to. Maybe you know a family that lives far from grandparents. They might welcome a grandmotherly figure.

Consider public greetings. Some grandparents who don't enjoy direct contact with their grandchildren post greetings to their own Facebook timelines, or write a blog. They wish their grandchildren a happy birthday, Halloween, or some other holiday, believing their grandchild may one day look them up—and discover they weren't forgotten. Of course, their parents may also see any public postings.

Make children part of your life. Are you missing the joy of having children, with their innocence and zest for living, in your life? Evelyn's work at the nearby elementary school lets her enjoy children, and they keep her up on what's relevant to today's kids' lives. The schoolchildren bring her joy, and she cherishes her interaction with them.

If you want to be involved with children, consider joining a foster grandparents program. You may even be eligible for a stipend. Perhaps your place of worship needs help in its nursery or Sunday school classes. Teen groups may also value help. Search for volunteer opportunities with children in your city. Depending on your circumstances, perhaps becoming a foster parent, or even beginning a second career with children, is in your future. Enjoying other children doesn't substitute for your own grandchildren, but being involved with people we enjoy helps. Finding meaningful purpose is part of healing, which we'll discuss more fully in Chapter Nine.

Foster Grandparents Programs

- *Corporation for National & Community Service*: www.nationalservice.gov/programs/senior-corps/foster-grandparents

- *Senior Corps*: www.seniorcorps.org/rsvp

End Of Life Decisions: Who Is Your Next Of Kin?

Do you have an advanced directive authorizing a specific person to make decisions on your behalf if you become incapacitated? In the U.S., the absence of such a document most often puts first your spouse, and then your adult children in charge. Would you want your estranged child to have that authority? Decide in advance who will make health-related decisions if you're unable to do so for yourself, and take steps to make that decision known.

You don't require an attorney to prepare an advance directive, but each state has specific criteria to make one legal. Having your advance directive notarized will protect your decision. Learn more at www.CaringInfo.org, which is the website for the National Hospice and Palliative Care Organization program. Advance directives for each state are available for download (free), along with related information.

Once you have created an advance directive, be sure your family and anyone you've named is aware of your wishes. Providing copies may be helpful, should it become necessary for them to assert your wishes.

While informing the important people in your life about your advance directive, also let them know whether to contact your estranged child in the case of severe illness. Will your child be called to your death bed? You may not want to think about the question, but it is important.

Some mothers feel that the prospect of the finality of death can bring people together for reconciliation and a time of forgiveness. Believing their child *must* be given the chance to make amends while there's still time, they give explicit instructions to inform their son or daughter.

Pam says, "No." Although her estranged daughter interacts with family members, Pam has given them instructions: "They know *not* to call her."

Mothers who share Pam's feelings have often had experiences that sway them. Many have already faced a serious illness, and were disappointed when their child was informed but never bothered to call. Why open themselves to the prospect of more disappointment? Others figure any last chance visit would only be an attempt on their child's part to assuage guilt. Some don't want the added drama of any long lost progeny showing up. Often, they are thinking of family whom they know will already be stressed. Why ask them to contact their estranged brother or sister, and add further grief?

Have you considered end of life scenarios as they pertain to your estranged child? In the mid-chapter exercise, you'll find questions to help you more fully explore your situation and your feelings, as well as make some decisions. But first, let's discuss other matters that pertain to your child's potential rights, and how you can make choices about those rights now for some peace of mind.

Your Estate: Who Benefits?

Strife often occurs when someone dies leaving an inheritance to be divided. A whiff of money can turn a seemingly mild-mannered relative into Mr. Hyde. And the situation grows more complicated when there is an estranged child in the family. Providing detailed information about who gets what specific personal property, and how other assets will be divided, will assist your executor or trustee in carrying out your wishes. Also consider giving things away to the important people in your life now, while you're still alive. Perhaps especially in situations of estrangement, you'll want to make things as simple as possible. If you leave no instructions, even your estranged next-of-kin may benefit from your death. Depending on where you live, your outstanding debts may also affect them.

To examine the complexity that estate decisions can involve, let's look at Cynthia's experience. It took Cynthia and her husband six years to come to any decision and take action about their trust. Their estranged son, Jonathan, is the middle child of their three. He still occasionally sends a holiday or birthday text, but other than that, they have no relationship. He never answers if any family member contacts him. At first they blamed his wife, who has a history of picking fights with their two daughters and their spouses. Now, they've come to terms with the fact that their son is complicit. "He's also got a passive aggressive bent," says Cynthia.

For the first three years, Cynthia remained her son's Facebook friend, but seeing his lovey-dovey postings to his mother-in-law became too painful. She defriended him, and purposefully let him go.

After much deliberation, Cynthia approached her husband about changing their trust. "I worried that he would rock the boat," says Cynthia. "I imagined my daughters, distraught with grief. And then I imagined Jonathan showing up, and making things even harder for them."

Among their assets, Cynthia and her husband own their primary residence outright. They also own a duplex nearby that has a mortgage covered by the lessees' monthly rent, plus provides some income. "We wouldn't want Jonathan trying to force them to sell, so they could split the money," she says. "If our daughters want to keep and lease out the properties, I want them to have that option. And I'm confident they could agree. But Jonathan might become a bully."

Cynthia's husband couldn't bring himself to completely disinherit his only son, but he also didn't want their daughters to face a hassle. In the end, he and Cynthia specified in the trust that Jonathan should receive the contents of his father's utility garage. "My husband and I took photos and listed every single item. There are welders and equipment, two classic Harley Davidson cycles, and various tools. We also made an exhaustive list. That way, if my husband sells any item before his death, he can cross it off, make a notation of the sale date, and sign. There will be no question that the girls or their husbands took anything."

In the trust documents, Cynthia and her husband specifically named their two daughters as joint heirs for everything else, and stated outright that their son was to receive only the contents of the garage. The trust also mentioned their son's possible "issue," which is a legal term used to refer to any children he might have. No provision was made for them. Cynthia and her husband concluded they weren't likely to ever know his children, and because of other unknowns, didn't feel comfortable providing for them.

The thought of their son's potential children, their grandchildren, was a sticking point that required careful deliberation. If their son died prior to one or both of them, they considered leaving the garage contents or the proceeds from the sale of those contents to any children he might have. However, they decided that since they no longer even know their son, they couldn't be sure he wouldn't have children outside his marriage—children that maybe even he didn't know about. Not wanting to open a complicated can of worms, they decided that if their son died before either or both of them, the contents of the garage would be made a part of the estate as a whole, and their daughters would benefit.

Later, troubled by the emotional stress of making all those decisions, Cynthia and her husband added a handwritten letter to the trust file. In it, they included the date of estrangement, how puzzled and hurt they had been by their son's departure from the family, some words about having forgiven him, and an explanation about their making decisions about the trust in order to make things simpler for their daughters.

"Nobody knows when their hour will come," Cynthia says. "I don't want my daughters in a mess with their brother because we didn't spell things out. I also didn't want our son to feel guilty for the rest of his life."

Although their actions gave Cynthia peace of mind, if their attorney had known about the handwritten letter, he might have helped them with its wording. In cases of disinheritance, simple language that an heir is known to you, but has been purposely left out, is often recommended. Estrangement adds complexity, so extra care is necessary. Before writing a letter intended for an estranged child after your death, and before adding anything to a legal will or trust document, consult your attorney.

A will is not the same as a trust but has similar intentions. For some, crafting a will makes more sense than a trust (which can contain your will). Here again, consult with an estate planning attorney. If contested by an estranged child (or anyone), a verbal bequest or handwritten will without witnesses and notarized signatures might not hold up. For your peace of mind, and to make the situation easy for your intended heirs, legal assistance is prudent. In some states, wills can be registered with the county at the time they're made, which protects your decisions.

In Minnesota, Melissa hired an attorney, and registered her will. "That makes it enforceable," says the mother of three, whose middle child is estranged. "If a will isn't registered, a will can be conveniently *lost.*"

Having a will written and registered was a last step for Melissa. Her father had left her all sorts of antiques, and she'd amassed her own items over several decades in the same home. She didn't want her children fighting over all the items.

She contacted her estranged daughter twice to provide her with the same opportunity as her siblings had. With Melissa's approval, they had begun to look through things, and take what they wanted. Her estranged daughter never responded.

In the will, Melissa had an attorney help with language that leaves money designated for her estranged daughter in the possession of her oldest son, but provides a caveat. "If my estranged daughter is sick or in dire need, he's to give it to her," says Melissa, of the decision that took four years to make. "Otherwise, the money will be his."

Melissa feels good knowing her estate is settled. But she can change her mind. A will can be altered, and then re-registered at any time.

People have varying beliefs about what it means to be an heir. Although Pam doesn't want her estranged daughter present if she's seriously ill or dying, she wouldn't dream of disinheriting her. "Why would I do that?" she asks. "She's my rightful heir. Her actions don't change that."

Pam's comment demonstrates that she has thought this through. Take some time to examine your own feelings and beliefs. Then, make decisions that best represent you, your life, and your beliefs. Anger and emotional pain can cloud judgment. Examine your motivations. A well-planned decision to disinherit or make changes that serve the best interests of beneficiaries after your death is wise. A vindictive response is not.

Widowed Maggie, who has come to believe that her only child, a son, is mentally ill, hasn't seen her three grandchildren in several years. Now in her nineties, traveling the long distance to her son's community had become difficult. Also, on past visits, Maggie felt ostracized and picked on. In the past two years, her son and his wife have made it clear that they want nothing to do with Maggie. However, they allow Maggie to talk to the children on the telephone. The weekly calls occur with their father listening in.

Recently, Maggie made some new decisions regarding her estate. She left a valuable piece of property to her grandchildren, which will be sold on their behalf when the oldest, who is now thirteen, comes of age. Each child will inherit equally. The remaining monies will be held in trust for the younger two, and distributed to each as they reach legal age. Maggie hopes the money from the sale will afford her grandchildren opportunities she believes would not otherwise be available to them. "I know I won't be around to see it," she says. "But the money will provide them with choices."

Laws vary. Your best bet is to find an estate attorney who will take the time to understand your unique situation, answer your questions, and plan carefully so that your wishes are carried out. You won't be around to answer questions or testify if an estranged child takes the matter to court.

In many countries, children have the right to inherit barring any unusual circumstances. Commonwealth countries preserve children's rights to inherit due to Family Maintenance statutes. In the U.S., what's considered "testamentary freedom," allows parents to disinherit. However, children can sometimes get disinheritance overruled by a jury.[3] That's why it is so important to get legal assistance in your area.

Making what seems like such final decisions can be difficult, but is important. You need documents in place now. Regardless of what may or may not happen in the relationship, you can change your mind, and the documents, later.

One mother who had disinherited her son later included him again. They remain estranged, and her son has been very cruel. She doesn't understand his anger, saying that she raised him with love. She explained her change of heart like this: "Providing for him after my death will be my final act of unconditional love."

This mother also considered leaving a letter that expressed her forgiveness, and how much she had loved the son she adopted as a toddler and raised. She wrote the letter, but later discarded it, believing her son wouldn't care what she said. "Writing the letter felt good," she says. "But those words were more for me than him. They helped me clarify my feelings for myself, and know my decisions were right for me."

If it makes you feel good to express your forgiveness and love despite the estrangement, a letter you leave (perhaps most wisely with your attorney's approval) could be a beautiful illustration of love and grace. However, you have no control over how it's received.

After fully deliberating your own situation, consult legal counsel experienced in your area's probate laws. With specific documentation in place that reflects your decisions and protects your estate for those you choose, you can rest in peace that your wishes will be honored.

Decisions for My Estate: Questions to Help

- Do I want my estranged child to benefit from my estate?

- Will I provide for my estranged child's children?

- How will my other beneficiaries be impacted by including my estranged child?

- Are my other children/beneficiaries in contact with my estranged child?

- Is my estranged child likely to cause issues for other beneficiaries?

✈ Nearing the End of Life: Will Your Adult Child Be Informed?

We all know that at some point our physical lives here on Earth will end. While you may have always assumed your children would be near, a child's estrangement adds uncertainty. This can be an uncomfortable topic, but it's something you need to think about. Contemplating your final days can help you make important decisions.

The visualization and questions below are designed to help you clarify your feelings, anticipate potential problems, and make a plan that provides you with peace of mind. Start with this question:

If you faced a terminal condition, would you want someone else deciding whether or not your estranged child should be informed?

Imagine lying in a hospital bed, knowing you are soon to die. Imagine the people you *know* will be at your side. See them there with you. Reflect upon their feelings and your own. Then imagine your estranged adult child entering the room.

- *How does the scene unfold?*

- *Who else is present? How do they react?*

- *Does arguing occur? Do people hug?*

Picture the scene. Fully imagine how you will feel as the interactions take place. As you contemplate the situation, reflect on any thoughts that come to mind: possible problems, whether or not you can control what's happening, and worries over how you and anyone else present will feel or respond.

Now, with all of this in mind, ask yourself: *Do I want my estranged child present?*

If so, or if you're still uncertain, consider these questions:

- *How can you work* now *to minimize potential problems?*

- *What can you do to prepare loved ones in advance?*

You could talk to your loved ones in advance, and maybe even ask for their input. Then, with a clear picture formed by your own desires and others' responses, you can make a plan.

If you decide that you want your estranged son or daughter informed, you'll need to choose someone to perform the task. Also choose an alternate person as a backup. *Who do you feel can best handle the task?*

If another of your children may be angry at the estranged child, he or she may not be the right choice. Sometimes, the first person who comes to mind pops into your head for a reason. If my estranged son was to be called, I immediately think of one of my sons as the person to make contact. I know he would be level-headed and able to keep his emotions in check. I would choose his brother as an alternate, for the same reasons. My daughters could also perform this task. But I imagine them being torn up emotionally in facing my death—and I prefer to protect them as much as possible. I'm very fortunate to have so many from whom to choose.

- *In your own life, who is best suited?*

Really consider who might best handle the task. Be sure to talk with these people about the role you'd like to assign them. Your plan won't work if someone is taken by surprise and refuses to make the call.

Also, consider parameters. A variety of scenarios might occur, so consider in what situations your estranged child should be informed.

- *Do you want your estranged son called only in the event you are placed in hospice care and your remaining time is limited?*

- *Shall your estranged daughter be informed if you are terminally ill, but are still at home living independently?*

- *What if injury causes a coma or you're on life support? Then should your estranged child be called?*

You might also imagine how the conversation will go.

- *What might your estranged son or daughter ask or say?*

- *What if she asks whether you want her to come? How do you want your representative to respond?*

Taking account of all of your thoughts and responses, write out a plan. Provide specific instructions. The more you have reflected on your feelings, the more direction you'll be prepared to give. Thus, the person you've chosen to make the contact will feel secure and confident in completing the task. Perhaps you will write a short script, so your designated caller can rely upon it—even telling your estranged son or daughter they are reading a script provided by you.

No matter what you decide, no one will know your requests unless you tell them. Apprise the people who will be charged with the task of honoring your wishes.

Other Considerations

Other time-of-life circumstances that collide with the upheaval of a child's abandonment can make it seem as if your world has spun out of control. Earlier we met Meg, who realized that because her life had changed, she needed to adapt. Meg used the technique that sounds like a cheer: RA-RA. Just as Meg did, you'll need to recognize what needs your attention, take time to analyze, regroup, and then create a plan to adapt.

You, too, may suffer a whirling tornado of issues beyond estrangement. While you may not be able to stop the spinning, you can slow up long enough to take control. Turn back to those pages in Chapter Five now if you need to, then cheer yourself on as we look at some of the time-of-life situations many mothers have shared.

Changes Related To Menopause: This Is *Your* Time

Symptoms related to the change of life can make a difficult situation such as estrangement even more of a struggle. Some mothers tell me that an adult child's departure adds ammunition to their already woeful thoughts about losing fertility, growing old, and a general sense that, for many things, it's now too late. Those feelings of loss have striking parallels to the emotional trauma of an adult child's estrangement.

So, how can you navigate the "change" amid the stress? The same way you deal with estrangement. *Start with the way you think about it.*

We're in an era where older women are increasingly recognized for their achievements and wisdom, yet much of society is youth-centric. Just as a mother who is suddenly rejected can feel as if she's no longer seen as useful, wanted, or loved, mature women can feel invisible. Changes, within and without, can challenge confidence. Those feelings can be even worse with an estrangement, which can make us more vulnerable to low self-esteem.

Some cultures hold the aging woman and associated changes in a positive light. The Japanese, who have fewer physical complaints related to menopause, call this phase of life "konenki," a word meaning renewal and regeneration—a beginning rather than an end.[4] Seen in this way, you're discovering a new you and a new place to fit in the world. The changes associated with menopause can be valued, and embraced. If symptoms arise because of the physical shifts occurring inside you, take heart. They're usually temporary, and proof that you're changing, regenerating into a new and more powerful you. We can adopt this attitude toward estrangement as well—so this new beginning in a new phase of life can be extra powerful.

If you're drawn to the idea of a stage of renewal, then count yourself among the wise. Ancient societies venerated the aging woman as healer, teacher, and sage. Honor that positive energy within yourself.

By moving beyond the loss and pain, an adult child's breaking away provides you the freedom to spend time and energy on yourself. How about trying a hobby you've been putting off? Is there something you've always wanted to do but never previously had the time for? The excitement of trying something new can enliven feelings of renewal. Evolve. Reinvent yourself. Give yourself permission to enjoy your life.

For me, reclaiming the long held dream of keeping bees was a part of my own renewal and reinvention. The insects' rhythm and order calmed me, much like the smoke I puffed into the hive before removing the box lid calmed the bees. The low, contented hum of their buzzing rose in pitch as I tugged out a waxy frame crawling with the winged the creatures. As I handled the bees, I was engrossed, aware of my breath and my heartbeat. Conscious of the need to make my presence serene, I kept my movements slow and deliberate. And their buzzing would again throttle down to a peaceful hum. Seeing these amazing insects up close provided me with a window to an ordered realm, a glimpse into something rare and precious that fueled my own peace, and increased my sense of balance in my tilting world.

Bees have always fascinated me, but if Dan hadn't left, I might never have leapt into beekeeping. Captivated, I experienced a sense of marvel reminiscent of childhood. My self-esteem soared. I had moved on and changed, flowed with the river of my life, its joys *and* its sorrows. As a Rejected Parents Facebook Page (facebook.com/rejectedparents) follower recently said, "I beat estrangement, and it didn't beat me." You, too, can have this sort of victory.

Besides the positive spin we can put on this life phase, recent research shows that the bothersome symptoms of menopause can be minimized in a number of ways. Whether you're pre- or post-menopausal, amid the stress of estrangement, you can benefit from the techniques for well-being that are discussed over the next few pages.

Take Action To Help Yourself

Tai Chi and Quigong. These ancient Chinese practices blend meditation, breathing, and slow, fluid movements that mimic nature. Tai Chi and Quigong promote physical balance, so decrease the risk of falls, help with bone density, aid flexibility, increase muscle strength, and improve sleep. Tai Chi and Quigong have also been associated with decreased pain, lowered blood pressure, and psychological benefits including improved confidence and mood.[6, 7] That's good news since so many women have related complaints, worry about bone loss, experience insomnia, joint pain and stiffness, and suffer the blues.

Find an in-person class through community education resources. Or turn to DVDs, and fit short sessions into your busy schedule. With calming music, inspiring scenery, and practitioners who go through the movements at varied fitness levels, DVDs are a sensible choice. Lee Holden's *Quigong for Seniors* offers a gentle, thorough introduction. The deliberate breathing combined with the flowing actions of Quigong movements such as the one known as "Pulling Down the Heavens" is fun, and enhances well-being. I have found Quigong grounding. It settles my mind and emotions, gives me an appreciation for my physical and spiritual self, and improves my focus. Amid the chaotic thoughts that come with estrangement, the tranquility of Quigong becomes an oasis. I hope it will help you, too.

Paced Breathing. In recent studies, a twice-daily practice of rhythmic, slowed breathing decreased the incidence of hot flashes by half.[8] Paced breathing also helps when a hot flash occurs. If you're otherwise healthy, according to the Mayo Clinic, it's safe to practice this diaphragmatic breathing.[9] Respiration is longer and more purposeful, reducing the typical 12 to 14 breaths per minute 5 to 7. In times of stress, our breathing can become shallow. A practice of paced breathing can promote an awareness of the present moment and help with mindfulness. Use an internet search for "paced breathing" to learn the technique. Or ask your physician, a yoga instructor, or other wellness practitioner.

Reduce stress. This directive can irk me. I know how impossible the task can feel in a full life. The thought of trying to reduce stress can create more. Still, it's important to try. Take a deep breath and relax. You're about to get some practical help.

Stress and anxiety can worsen menopausal symptoms, so an estrangement doesn't help. In a study of 400 women over a six-year period, those with the highest anxiety levels endured as much as five times as many hot flashes.[10] Lifestyle changes and relaxation techniques can help. Try calming activities that soothe and relax you the way beekeeping did me. Read on for more ways to reduce stress, and effectively deal with the stress of estrangement.

Get active. In a 2008 study of 401 women over a span of eight years, those with the highest levels of activity reported less stress. Not only traditional exercise was counted, but other activities from climbing stairs to walking a few blocks in the course of a normal day were included. As little as 38 minutes of walking, five times a week reduced stress.[11]

No need to start running marathons. With your doctor's approval, make some basic changes that add activity to your life: park far from the entrance, walk the dog a little farther, take the stairs, use your lunch break to stroll the block, sweep the porch more often, "pump" full shopping bags like weights as you leave the store, or wash your car the old fashioned way. Even small changes add up. You could stand up during your coffee break, or walk to the corner when you get the mail.

Reclaim old activities or try new ones that get you moving: ping pong, bowling, tennis, badminton, horseback riding, dance, hiking, swimming, or skating to name a few. Exercise helps with your emotions.

Even my beekeeping added physical activity. The hive boxes were kept atop a hill so it required walking to get to them. And caring for them required lifting the heavy, honey-filled frames. Can you use an existing hobby to add activity? Where can you add movement to your life? Make changes for the better.

Guided Imagery. Whether you come up with your own fantasy escapes or let purchased sessions whisk you away, a few minutes of mental vacation time can reduce stress. Find a comfortable, quiet space such as your bedroom or while you're in the tub. Close your eyes, and imagine yourself in a restful setting. Is it a beach? Fully engage your senses. Hear the roar of waves as they roll in and out again. Imagine the call of a gull overhead. Feel the powdery sand beneath your feet, and the kiss of the breeze on your sun-warmed shoulders. Fully immerse yourself. See the deep blue sky, the sparkle of sunlight glinting on the sea, and smell the salty air. Are you there yet? Do you feel more relaxed?

Use your smartphone or another recording device for do-it-yourself guided imagery soundtracks. Look up examples on YouTube.com. Or, purchase professional recordings. I once wrote an article about using visualization for weight loss, and was delighted to meet guided imagery expert Belleruth Naparstek of HealthJourneys.com. Her recordings cover specific needs such as better sleep, as well as general wellness and reducing stress.

Improve your diet. Stress triggers release of the hormone cortisol, which contributes to food cravings. But when you reach for options high in simple sugar and unhealthy fat, which "blunt" the hormone, you train your body to see those foods as a solution—so the cravings get worse.[12] Instead, reach for foods that are rich in Vitamin B complex, Vitamin C, and Omega 3s. Research has shown these assist the body when under stress. The website for the magazine, *Eating Well,* has a good guide for foods that help with stress, but it's not the only one. Do some research, or consult with a dietician, wellness coach, or your physician. You can make a start by minimizing processed foods and drinks.

Rest. You need it. Women are notorious for doing too much, and putting themselves last on their own to-do lists. Don't make that mistake now. Herbalist and author Susun Weed sees menopausal symptoms as signals for a woman to draw inward and concentrate on the self. Hot flashes, insomnia, and other change-of-life indicators are natural internal urgings to spend time alone, take physical and emotional care, and focus on transformation.[5] As a caterpillar spins its cocoon, you, too, must find rest. Nurture your body as well as your spirit. From the tranquil depths of self-care, you will emerge anew.

Suggested Reading

New Menopausal Years: The Wise Woman Way, Alternative Approaches For Women 30-90, by Susun S. Weed. This book covers herbs and foods that assist with wellness, as well as seeing the change in an empowering light. Women's cultural wisdom provides new perspectives.

The Wisdom of Menopause (Revised Edition, 2012): Creating Physical And Emotional Health During the Change, by Christiane Northrup, M.D. The details of modern science are woven with threads of the author's life as she helps women to recognize and honor their internal compass.

Sickness and In Health

Among the saddest stories are those of parents who face cancer or other serious illnesses without their children's support. Some have already been estranged. Others tell a son or daughter the diagnosis, and are met with harsh words and abandonment.

Whether personally going through a time of sickness, or watching a critically ill partner agonize over the rejection, the reality can be cruel. You'll need to make a decision to muster up required strength.

First, we'll look at couples. Then, we'll address mothers who are on their own.

A 2011 AARP Public Policy Institute/United Hospital Fund survey on family caregivers provided some valuable insights. If you're helping a life partner manage a serious health condition, you may already be aware of the complexity caregiving can entail. There's more to it than helping a person bathe, eat, and move from the bed to a chair. Spouses manage demanding medication regimens and tasks for which they're not trained or prepared. Caregiving spouses can feel stressed and isolated, suffer their own poor health, and feel depressed. Yet they are charged with the task of providing emotional support for a partner. The illness, and how it has altered their lives, becomes a constant.[13]

Let's start with the caregiver's perspective. You long for your mate's strength and companionship as you face the emotional train wreck of your child's estrangement. You may even have feelings that are painful to admit. You may be angry at the sudden demands on you, and then feel guilty for them. You may long to resume your life and activities, and then judge yourself as selfish. *Don't.* According to Hugh Marriott, who authored a humorous book for caregivers, those sorts of feelings are the norm.[14] So don't berate yourself. Accept the fact that you're human, and proceed with kindness—to your spouse and to yourself.

Resilient couples can overcome the negativity an illness forces upon them. If possible, make dealing with the situation a joint endeavor, because couples who do, find the situation easier.[15] Rely on old habits and communication formats that have been successful throughout your marriage. Have you typically discussed important decisions over a long dinner before proceeding? Perhaps making time to analyze needs, and then creating a routine together, supports normalcy in your relationship and allows the ill partner to maintain some control. Discuss things over a long lunch or on a Sunday drive. Or, take dinner trays to your bed together, and talk in comfort. You know what works for you and your mate.

Soon after my son's estrangement began, my husband was run off the road by a hurried driver on a rainy morning. Knocked unconscious, he woke up smashed into a telephone pole. He suffered head and neck injuries. Following the existing patterns in our marriage, it was natural for me to take the lead in medical matters, and make sure he followed up with a neurologist. I accompanied him to the exam, asked questions about related symptoms, and then monitored my husband's behavior to make sure those symptoms faded over the next several months as was expected. I also arranged ongoing care for his other injuries, and made sure he kept appointments.

Meanwhile, my husband assumed his typical stance when it comes to his health: He's fine, and he doesn't need any help. As always, he eventually gave in—taking the tone of humoring me that's become familiar. In essence, we paired up for the dance we've always shared—and which works for us.

What is your "dance"? How can you honor that pairing now?

Bea, whose youngest son is estranged, cares for her husband who has Parkinson's disease. "He was always a strong, independent man," says

Bea. "I know our son's estrangement has made his health struggle more difficult, but the last thing he wants is me feeling sorry for him."

Before her husband's illness, they were avid peak baggers, making special trips just to climb certain mountains. Her husband's increasing weakness changed things. Now, he doesn't have the strength, but he still likes to talk about the outdoors. "We have always loved nature," says Bea. They owned a home with a lake view. From the deck, they watched ospreys fish from the air, and delighted in the waterfowl and their fluffy babies that floated along. Because of her husband's illness, they moved closer to the city a year ago. "But we still have a patio," says Bea. "Sparrows nest in the flower baskets I've hung all around."

For their wedding anniversary, Bea stocked up on birdwatcher books and feeders. At times, the couple sits for hours chatting like excited children about all the birds they've lured into their tiny yard. In those moments, they forget all about her husband's Parkinson's, and the sadness that their son wants nothing to do with them. "As amazing as it might sound," says Bea, "I think our son's neglect, and my husband's illness, have made us closer than ever."

Bea and her husband's long talks helped them foster good communication, which is especially needed when one requires help. Asking for assistance doesn't come easily for everyone, and can be loaded with all sorts of negative feelings related to self-esteem, relationship dynamics, and autonomy.[16]

If you're the one who is not well, help your partner help you. Make your needs known. This is no time to expect mind reading. Yet research shows that hinting and complaining, as well as nonverbal cues such as sighing and fidgeting, are common. People often expect their partners to interpret ambiguous signals of their needs despite not expressly stating them.[16, 17, 18]

Even in times of stress due to illness, it's helpful to keep the situation in perspective and nourish times of joy. Try setting aside times when you agree not to focus on the illness, and talk about non-related things instead. This may help you maintain the strong relationship with the partner you love and enjoy.[19] The same is true of discussing the estrangement. Don't let the illness, or the estrangement, become your only connecting point. Bea believes their birdwatching has helped. They also watch a steady stream of comedy movies to keep the mood light.

On Your Own: Taking Care Of Yourself

For those who can't turn to a spouse or partner for support and care, facing a tough illness requires a strong will, ingenuity, and adaptation. The realization that the people you have loved the most don't seem to care, can be overwhelming. And now you'll have treatments and medication to manage, as well as other commitments. You'll need to get organized, and make a plan.

In Chapter Five, we met Rowena who, among a long list of disasters, was diagnosed with serious illness. As Rowena did, decide what's most important right now, divide big tasks into smaller steps, and let some things go. In other words, *P, B, & J*: prioritize, break into manageable pieces, and just leave some things alone.

You'll also need to ask for help. No matter how difficult for you, this is crucial. Chapter Five also includes examples of tasks you can delegate, or let go. At the very least, surgeries and other treatments, such as chemotherapy, require a driver. Make a list of friends, neighbors, family members, or co-workers who could possibly help.

Check with local churches as well. Some have support programs with volunteer drivers, and don't require church membership. Check with hospitals and health organizations for community resources. The American Cancer Society's Road to Recovery program connects volunteer drivers with patients needing transport to and from treatments.

To find more resources, speak with your local hospital's social worker, or check with a senior center in your area. Beneficial patient support groups allow you space to share feelings, and understand that you're not alone (even if you feel that way). The United Way, as well as Area Agencies on Aging, can also help. Your region may have support for meals, shopping, housekeeping, and companionship.

Resources

- *American Cancer Society, Road to Recovery Program*: http://www.cancer.org/treatment/supportprogramsservices/ road-to-recovery

- *Area Agencies On Aging*—use the pull-down menu to find your state, and then find your county, which will bring up local services: http://www.aoa.gov/AoA_programs/OAA/How_To_ Find/Agencies/find_agencies.aspx

- *United Way*: http://www.unitedway.org

Leslie, an independent-minded widow whose son is estranged, has never been one to ask for help. Faced with Stage 3 cancer, she was determined to survive. Swallowing her pride, she composed an email explaining her situation, and sent it to a few acquaintances: the real estate agent she'd used when she sold the family home, her tax man, the Avon lady, and her chiropractor's office. Leslie's real estate agent phoned the next day, putting Leslie in touch with a wellness assistance group in the senior community where she'd recently moved.

Having new friends to talk with on the car rides to and from her treatments proved pleasant. Leslie discovered she enjoyed having friends, and began seeing people in a whole new light. She has since recovered, and now volunteers for the wellness group that assisted her. Although Leslie remembers feeling inconsequential, as if no one cared if she lived or died, she now sees the illness as a blessing. "I saw the value of living fully," she says. "I stopped beating my head against the wall my son built between us, and accepted reality. Even if we never have a relationship again, I have a good life to live."

Ask for help. You may be surprised how many others have found themselves in need, and will network for you. Who knows? As it did for Leslie, a whole new world may open.

The Golden Years

Many of us believed that as our children grew into responsible adults and settled into their own lives, our lives would become simpler. Maybe we'd retire, explore the country in an RV or travel the world by jet and cruise ship. Or we'd engage in meaningful work, a cause, or even a hobby we'd previously put off. Among the thousands of parents of estranged adults who have contacted me, many have referred to their golden years with a tinge of sarcasm or disappointment. The years they assumed would be so restful and bright arrived instead with shock and despair.

Be gracious and generous with yourself as you navigate this unexpected turn, and move in a new direction. Sometimes, the problems we encounter shed valuable light on our journey, and lead us to new and satisfying places.

As I write the last few paragraphs of this chapter, my husband and I are the very ages that my mother and father died—far younger than the norm. In facing our own mortality, we recognize that time is fleeting. Our lives wind ever forward, underlining the fact that, no matter how many, our days are precious few. As I said earlier, knowledge isn't power unless we use well what we have learned. Keep that thought in mind as you turn the page, and begin this book's final chapter. Let loose the past you cannot change. Unfold the future like a precious gift. And hold the present dear.

CHAPTER NINE

Walk Forward

In becoming a parent, you took a leap of faith. I bet every mother reading this book at one time or another worried during her pregnancy. Even eating nutritious foods and practicing good habits, something still could have gone wrong—and you knew that. If you adopted, it was also a leap of faith. You stepped out. You took a chance. There were no guarantees. You knew there could be obstacles, even if you put them out of your mind.

As your child grew, you thought of choking hazards, accidents, strangers, and driving too fast. You kept watch, informed your child of dangers, and lectured your teen about safety behind the wheel. But you still knew, deep down, that something could go wrong. And there were tragic reminders every day in the news.

When you cradled your baby, the fragrance of sweet milk and powder swirling all around, you never dreamed this beautiful little soul would one day abandon you. We don't usually put estrangement, rejection, abandonment, or abuse in the same category as health issues, stranger abduction, or accidents. But when it comes to the possibility, they're not entirely different. No matter how much we showed our love, were kind and supportive, and did our best to form a bond, a desirable outcome wasn't absolutely certain.

Some people go whole-souled into marriage—only to have a spouse they trusted do them wrong. Others have a business relationship that goes terribly sour. And in some families, estates and inheritances ruin relationships.

During our children's formative years, we didn't imagine them ever rejecting us. Who warned us of that? And if anyone did, we weren't listening. But the truth is that no matter how much we romanticize any relationship, let alone motherhood with its idealized dream of a future filled with connection and joy, there are no guarantees. Sometimes the people we love hurt us. Sometimes, even our own children do.

As it turns out, parenting is a gamble. That's true even for well-intentioned parents who work at shaping their children into empathetic adults, good workers, and team players who care about life and the people around them. *Parents like you.* Even if you were the best role model ever, your success was a crap shoot. It's the sad truth. And for whatever reason, at this time in history, the odds are higher this will occur.

This may sound harsh, but ask a person in leadership whether anyone they ever believed in disappointed them, or abandoned the plan and went off on their own. There will always be a few. Parenting may be so much more, but it's certainly a form of leadership. And even the best leaders aren't always revered or respected.

You've already gone back over your mothering and mentally (or even literally) chronicled the events of your child's life, and the part you played in them. You weren't perfect. You admit you made some mistakes. But you had good intentions. You were a good mother whose love shined through.

Now, turn your attention to what's ahead. Lead yourself into a future that's painted as you like. Pull out the image you created in the *Make it Tangible* part of the *Visualize Your Life* exercise from Chapter Five. See yourself in that light. Moving forward is what this chapter is about.

Play The Hand You're Dealt

In his hit song, country music artist Kenny Rogers croons, "You've got to know when to hold 'em, know when to fold 'em, know when to walk away, know when to run."

Thousands of parents have arrived at my blogsite in "hold 'em" mode, not sure what to do or how to change things. They're bewildered, and at a standstill. In shock, or emotionally fatigued from abuse or neglect, they're clinging to the idea of a relationship they always planned on and perhaps once shared with the child who has rejected them. The idea of "folding," laying the metaphorical cards down, and walking away may not have occurred to them. In fact, they may have been told that walking away isn't an option for parents of estranged children, and that they should persist until they get results. And so these parents exist in a *perpetual* holding pattern, waiting, wondering, preoccupied, and sad. The results aren't in their hands.

Then they happen upon a message that appeals to their logic. They come to realize that it's not in their best interests to play a game in which their adult child makes all the rules. With a shift in perspective from victimization, loss, and powerlessness over what they cannot control (their estranged child), to what they can control (themselves), they adopt a better outlook. For many, if not most, to "fold" becomes the only sensible option. It may also be the only healthy one.

In the last several decades, research has connected psychological stress to impaired immune function.[1] Specific biological properties, such as the inflammatory molecule, C-reactive protein (CRP), accompany such impairment. Recently, scientists have discovered that people who have trouble letting go of a desired outcome have increased inflammation, as shown by CRP levels.[2] In sharp contrast, the ability to stop reaching for unattainable goals is associated with better health, as well as more normal patterns of the stress hormone, cortisol.[3]

Parents of estranged adult children know all about emotional distress and adverse physical effects. The situation can feel overwhelming and hopeless. Health and well-being suffer. Don't aggravate the problem by clinging to an ideal that's beyond your control. Don't make things worse for yourself by continuing to reach for the unattainable. And don't keep the pain alive with negative thinking and broken-record questioning. Remaining a victim in your own mind, and adopting extreme beliefs—*I'll never give up; I'll never get past the pain*—is like handing control of your future health and happiness to your estranged child. Be honest, and answer the questions below.

- Are you allowing your estranged child to control you?

- Are you allowing your thoughts and feelings about the situation to control you?

- Are idealistic views of motherhood and unconditional love interfering with your ability to accept your child's decision to let you go?

- Are you letting those same ideals, or perhaps ones about never giving up or not being a quitter, prevent *you* from letting go?

- When it comes to trying to connect with your child, does it feel as if you've been spinning your wheels?

- Do endless thoughts and unanswered questions torment you?

At this point, those questions must have a familiar ring. I'm mentioning these ideas once again because negative thinking and fruitless actions can become habitual. Breaking away from thoughts and actions that dig you into a rut of victimhood that zaps your energy, relinquishes your power, and sets you up for more disappointment, requires commitment—and work. Review earlier chapters if you need to. Read up on coping mindfully, and do the exercises. Now is as good a time as any to take yourself by the hand, and take charge.

I often hear parents say they're *supposed* to love their children unconditionally. They say society expects that sort of love, particularly from mothers. Some even say we're designed to love our children unconditionally.

But even the best of ideals, when entrenched, can become unhealthy. Unconditional love shouldn't keep you stuck in despair, or enable your grown child to hurt you. Besides, letting go for your own good doesn't mean your love is conditional. The decision to move forward is about recognizing your own worth. You have a right to take care of yourself. Most of you set boundaries for your child's health and safety as he or she grew. Set them now, for your own health and safety.

Remind yourself that continuing to strive for what's beyond your control negatively affects you.

Try viewing the estrangement and how you interact with it like walking with a rock in your shoe. You're always aware the stone is there, digging in with every step. Eventually, the friction will cause a tender blister, wear a hole, and prevent you from walking any further. This book has been all about setting the stone aside, so you can continue forward unimpeded.

Walking Forward

In order to feel comfortable "folding," you may be like some parents who feel the need to take a final action that clarifies your position to your son or daughter. If so, you may want to reach out and clearly state your wishes to reconcile. Say that you're willing, available, and hope that one day you can reconnect on agreeable terms.

Consider carefully how you'll communicate that message. Recall the discussions in Chapter Seven about how your contact may be received, or seen as proof that you're toxic, and then imagine how a potential scenario might go. My advice is to avoid drama. Don't show up at your child's workplace. Don't make a surprise visit at home. If you telephone, will you be allowed to speak?

Let go of expectations, too. This is about helping *you* move forward, not about changing your child's mind.

Be prepared for backlash. You may receive a response that begs you not to give up. Usually from an involved third party, it's a scenario I've heard often. Blame may be attached. Or even guilt. You may be told that a "good" mother would never give up on her child. Or, how it must be nice to be able to walk away from the mess you made. Words like "please" and "I beg you" might be thrown in alongside insults.

You'll need to determine for yourself whether the plea is sincere. While that's a possibility, the situation I often hear is one of ensnarement. With guilt or hope as the lure, the parent is reeled right back in to a web of twists and turns, with more hurt and confusion.

Think through thoroughly the idea of some final effort before folding. The ideas in this book are about supporting you. Your decision to accept the hand you've been dealt, and to move on in your own life doesn't necessarily need relaying to your son or daughter. Your silence will likely speak for itself.

Once you've worked all of that out, the question then remains: *What's next?* For me, there's my continued work in facilitating parents' support. Bringing parents together and knowing I have helped them feel supported gives me a sense of satisfaction and meaning. What's required for anyone to truly get past the pain of estrangement and move forward with a happy heart is to find meaning in their life. Engaging in an activity or cause you value, will help you disengage from what you can't control. That will shield you from some of the adverse effects that go with the difficulty in letting go.[3]

In Chapter Two, Georgia described her two daughters' pre-estrangement sibling rivalry like a game of tug-of-war, with her caught in the middle. After their estrangement, Georgia found meaning by helping young single mothers. Two of them have become like daughters to her. Although Georgia had successfully moved on, she admitted to still resenting the fact that her daughters were close to their mothers-in-law. "I wasn't just rejected," Georgia says. "I was replaced." During one of our discussions, it dawned on Georgia that her daughters might feel the same about the young mothers she had grown so close to. Shifting perspective allowed Georgia to release the final dregs of lingering hurt. It was like two sides of an equation: balanced out.

Other mothers we've met in earlier chapters have found meaning in a variety of ways. Julia's work with seniors brings her joy. Her experiences have made her especially attuned to any sadness they share. She lends a supportive shoulder and an empathetic ear when any of them talk of their children who, busy in their lives, rarely visit. Julia believes her attentive presence helps. Her work gives her life more meaning.

Similarly, Kathleen works for an organization that makes a difference in the lives of families impacted by disorders such as depression and schizophrenia. In helping them, she helps herself.

Meg always considered time in the kitchen a sort of meditative outlet. Recently, when Meg realized that in light of the estrangement, her family recipes might end with her, she decided to take action. She spearheaded a cookbook project with her own recipes and those contributed by other businesswomen. Proceeds from the sales go to a charity that helps local children in need.

One mother is making a quilt based on the message from a popular children's book that reminds her of the estranged parents she has met in the support forum at RejectedParents.NET. She plans to enter the finished quilt in a competition and use her creation to bring more attention to the sad plight of rejected parents.

In response to my lighthearted poetry challenge in the support forum, one mother felt a new door had been opened in her life. She had never considered herself a poet, but the rhyming words flowed out and brought her joy. The poems give her a place to leave her thoughts, and then she can walk away feeling free. She now plans to publish her poems in a two-part book. One part will hold sorrowful poems about the biting pain of estrangement. The second will express her regained joy.

Other parents embraced the poetry challenge for a few hours or a few days. They found help within the thoughts and emotions they let flow. Among parents like them, they expressed themselves without fear of judgment. They even poked fun at their situations, and felt lighter for it. Those who only read others' poems found them meaningful, funny, or representative of their own pain. Try a silly poem or two of your own. You might be surprised how joyful it makes you feel.

Whether they realize it or not, parents who routinely share information and offer advice in the forum are engaged in meaningful work.

One kind mother makes a point of welcoming new members, because she wishes she'd have known she wasn't alone when her child's episodic estrangements began. Another mother gracefully encourages others toward acceptance. She knows from experience it's the way to peace.

Despite their pain, all of the women discussed here have used the experience of estrangement in positive ways—and so can you. Like it or not, your child's rejection is now a part of your story. Make it a good one.

A poem, a quilt, a drawing, or some other creation acts as a vessel, a place to collect or make purpose of your thoughts and feelings. That may be why people across the spectrum in terms of age, condition, and distress, experience positive outcomes via art therapies.[4] The practice of drawing, writing, or other creative pursuits sometimes uses verbal or visual metaphors to derive more meaning. A patient diagnosed with a terminal illness might be asked to draw the disease. Painting a picture of something strong, a tree or a mountain perhaps, might be likened to building one's own sense of strength.

While formalized art therapy might be a wonderful experience, individuals express themselves through art of all sorts, and find doing so therapeutic on their own. In creative work, people find satisfaction, and even healing. Losing yourself in an activity you enjoy or feel good about may bring blasts of insight when you least expect them. Discernment that can help you shift your perspective, look more deeply at a particular memory, or find another way to see or explain what's happened—if only for yourself.

If you set your mind in the right direction, you can apply your pain to the simplest tasks, and create meaning in almost anything. Search for healing metaphors in your everyday life. In the tactile motion of sweeping the floor, imagine clearing the emotional muck, and opening an unobstructed path forward. As you wipe the mirror clean, discern a clearer view of yourself and your future, no longer clouded by the fog of pain. Shift your furnishings for a different view, and imagine gaining a new perspective on your life.

Caring for plants can be representative of nurturing yourself. As you nurture a scraggly seedling into a lush specimen that scents the air, attracting butterflies and birds, feel yourself blooming ever stronger. Even a single specimen in a pot indoors or on the patio can be beneficial.

As leaves reach for the sun, imagine turning yourself toward the warmth of what supports you. As fruits or vegetables ripen, see your own life as fruitful. Studies galore demonstrate reduced stress from spending time in gardens. Gardening helps people acknowledge their own growth as they witness it in a plant they nurture.

The earth has healing properties, too. Gardening enthusiasts who get a little dirt under their fingernails know how good they feel after a day of planting. As it turns out, there's a friendly bacteria in the dirt that cheers us up. "M. vaccae," as it is known, enhances mood and vitality with properties that act similarly to serotonin when we come in contact with it.

One mother tore out old landscaping, and redid her front yard in sandy soil for drought-tolerant bushes with silver-gray foliage. On her busy suburban street that serves as a thoroughfare for locals heading into town, neighbors admired the fruits of her labor that quickly became her passion. People offered her compliments, and asked for her advice. What started as a distraction from the hurt became restorative art, and a path to mastery and social connection that helped her heal.

If getting out into a garden doesn't fit your lifestyle or abilities, try an easy-care indoor plant, or perhaps set up a terrarium. Studies have shown that having plants in a room can heighten mood, reduce anxiety, increase optimism, and even improve memory and cognition.

Today, "fairy gardens," are becoming popular, with tiny buildings and statues artfully arranged in a pot or jar. Some use dried moss and no living plants, so don't require care. As you create a tranquil, diminutive setting, imagine your immediate world just as magical or serene.

In times of pain, creativity can blossom. Find a creative outlet you can immerse yourself in and enjoy. Start a hobby to distract yourself, and then be surprised how far it takes you. Discover meaning in almost anything you choose. No need to seek world peace or some sort of global change. Finding meaning can be as simple as waking up each day and remembering who you are: *I'm a kind person who cares about and nurtures myself and others.* Then set out each day with that purpose in mind. A thoughtful gesture that may seem insignificant to you can make another person's day. Even in the tiniest of ways, our lives can be meaningful. Aligning our actions with who we know ourselves to be is the very essence of authenticity. Don't allow your estranged child to steal you away—from yourself and all the others whose lives you touch.

✈Who Are You Really? What's Your Mission?

Who are you? What's in your heart? Compose a statement for yourself, a mission of sorts, in its simplest, truest form. Don't overthink or struggle with this idea. This isn't about creating a "mission statement" as the term is known in business. There's no requirement to answer specific questions as they apply to specific goals. It's more about your essence as a human being, as in the example: *I'm a kind person who cares about and nurtures myself and others.* It's a statement of belief that provides focus. Something you can remind yourself of as you wake each morning, or at times when you're feeling stressed, frustrated, or even defeated. Here are a few more examples:

- I live a life of prayer, which helps me demonstrate grace to myself and others.

- I notice what others miss or what doesn't get done, so I often pick up the slack. It feels good to help.

- I am a good listener, and because of that, have insights to share.

- Even in the tensest moments, I find what's funny. I make people laugh.

Your answers in Chapter Three's *At Your Best* exercise can help you identify what invigorates you, or where your passions lie. If you need to, remember what you were like pre-estrangement. Search your heart for positive answers. Would you call yourself ordered? Do you thrive on routine? Do you defer to a higher power? Are you innovative? Are you at your best when you're helping other people? Maybe you look for and find the good in every situation. Perhaps your highest value is inner peace, and you make a point of conducting yourself to foster that feeling. Have people always gravitated to your high energy, your sense of humor, or your natural ability to lead? Perhaps they come to you when they're feeling low because your presence is naturally calming.

How do you define yourself? Phrasing such as, "I lift people's spirits," and "I'm an encourager," can boost self-esteem. Or, something like, "I provide a calming presence," can help make your own mood serene. "I make people laugh," can help you find the humor in day-to-day life—and share it. Your unique sensibilities, shared, might make someone's day (or your own!).

Think of and write out a statement or two that reinforce these ideas. Transfer your words about yourself to the bulletin board, or write them on pretty note paper and put them in a convenient spot. Read them each morning, and then set about your simple mission every day.

_____

_____

_____

_____

_____

_____

Be Resilient

Loosely defined as thriving despite adversity, resilience is enhanced by context, outlook, mastery, and enjoyment. The mother whose neighbors flocked to her garden found mastery doing something she enjoyed. This raised her dwindling self-esteem. Helping others with their gardens provided satisfaction, and a feeling that she belonged. This took up the void left by her estranged child, and refocused her purpose. Now, she looks back on the estrangement as "just another twist in a life that's been full of them."

How can you enhance your own resilience, despite the loss? In our gardening example, mastery and enjoyment are evident. Let's talk more about outlook, and context. Our gardening mother eventually minimized her child's rejection as "just another twist." Search your memory for adversity you've overcome. Resilient people draw on past experiences as far back as childhood to help them deal with current hardship.[5] They have been through difficulties before, and are confident they will again prevail.

In a 2008 study, the most resilient older adults discussed sorrows and misfortunes in a whole-life context, and in the past tense. At first, as participants recounted tragic events, researchers believed they were just reliving old hurts, and even adding their current despair to convey a pattern of woe that marked their overall lives. But what was happening was quite the opposite. Talking about all of the things they'd been through actually helped the participants to see themselves as surviving those stressors, and going on to thrive.[6] The patterns they found centered on how they had coped and continued on. We can learn from their resilience.

Recall some traumatic events of your life. The death of a parent, a loved one's illness, an embarrassing moment, a car crash—you name them. Reach back as far as you'd like, or choose more recent events. This is personal to you. It's not necessary to choose your absolute worst traumas. Think or write about a remembered event or two in the past tense. How did you cope? If you can, identify patterns in how you managed the stress and moved beyond it. Did you turn to close friends or family to encourage you? Did you use your sorrow to spur you forward, pursue education, or a dream? Perhaps you learned to ask for help, grew closer to God, or learned how strong you could be.

_____

_____

_____

_____

_____

Now that you've identified past experiences you can you draw strength and learn from, apply the knowledge to your current situation. You have successfully moved forward before. Be confident in the reality that you're even wiser now.

One way I have always coped has been to connect with nature. Watching a pale blue dragonfly hover above water, or noticing the way the wind ripples through the trees, focuses me in the moment and provides me with peace. Thankfully, I've learned that pausing to watch milky clouds drift across the blue sky or a hummingbird going from flower to flower directs me to the present and calms me. Nature connects me to something much bigger than my own life, which provides perspective. And then I take charge where I can. It's how I cope—and thrive.

In Chapter Eight, we met Maggie, who shared her decision to leave property to her grandchildren. She characterized the decision as a "creative" solution. Maggie realized that using creativity to make decisions and be pro-active is how she has always coped. Knowing this, and acting on it when she felt powerless over her daughter's estrangement, has helped her feel more like herself.

What's your story? How have you coped in the past? How can you apply your own unique sensibilities to moving past your current pain?

Let's talk for a moment about optimism. As I did, lying in the dark on that first Christmas night after my son's estrangement, you may think up all sorts of scenarios in which you end up alone and sad. The feelings are understandable, but are not helpful. Let's address that uncertainty, or perhaps more accurately, *dread*. In short: drop it. *How?* That's where optimism comes in. You may be more optimistic than you think you are—as we'll discuss below. Be aware that I use the word "faith" almost interchangeably with "optimism." Here, faith doesn't necessarily refer to a spiritual belief.

Optimism is faith in practice. It's a belief that "everything will be okay," as one of my sons recently reminded me I often say. But it can also be much more. Optimism is based on a faith in your own ability, or in the ability of those you admire, to figure out solutions and a way forward. Or, it's a simple faith in life.

America's history is full of optimists, starting with people who piled into a boat and sailed across a vast ocean, arrived in a rugged, foreign land, and began the pursuit of happiness by facing unknowns. Sure, some of them probably lamented the difficulties. Some shed tears as they navigated darkness to find a new life. But their action demonstrates faith, an optimistic belief in their own abilities. Their beautiful idea, freedom for themselves and generations to follow, made their load light.

Adopt a similar attitude. Be determined as you escape the tyranny of sadness and pain. Trust in yourself as you chart a new course. You're at the helm.

In modern life, ponder the faith it takes to get in a car and drive. Where I live, traffic is everywhere. One SUV cuts you off, and then for no apparent reason, another stops abruptly ahead. A few calming breaths later, a tiny hybrid swerves into your lane. Driving is optimism in practice, faith in your ability and reflexes. If you're like me, that faith exists despite past close calls and crashes. Do you have an accident story but still drive? Then you know about faith—or, as some might quibble, you're aware of the risks, but choose to believe you'll be fine.

What activities in *your* everyday life demonstrate optimism or faith? People sign off on years-long loan terms, trusting in their ability to pay. We post a letter, believing it will arrive at its destination. We walk out into the snow, and are optimistic we won't slip and fall. The very act of living, of carrying on our lives, requires a measure of optimism. Use the faith you surely practice to help you move forward now. Looking at the strength you've previously displayed, tell yourself: *Everything will be okay.* Believe it.

Another factor that helps people bounce back and thrive is maintaining a sense of identity. But that can pose a problem for mothers feeling as if their identity has been shattered. Here again, how you interpret events shapes how well you cope.

In Chapter Five, you'll recall that on the day Rowena received a diagnosis of cancer, her daughter wished her dead. Then her house flooded, the neighbor sued her, and her dear old dog died. Rowena pulled herself out of the doldrums by remembering her mother's strength.

"I cried for weeks," she says. "People do cry when bad things happen. But eventually, I dried my tears and got on with life. Getting on with life is what we strong women do."

Connecting her predicament to her mother's strength, and the strength of *all* women, reminded Rowena of her own strength. As always, she would "get on with life." That sort of coping is a resilient pattern in her life.

How can your life experiences help you to reclaim your identity or devise a stronger one?

Recall the simple mission statement(s) you created in the last exercise. In the next set of lines, try formulating a phrase or two that propel you forward, such as Rowena's belief that she always gets on with her life. Or my frequent saying, based on past struggles I've survived: *Everything will be okay.* Do that now.

Social routines also aid resilience. In the early days when suffering shock, you may not feel like socializing. Later, you may need to force yourself. Loneliness hampers resiliency. I know it's hard to see all the hunky-dory families having fun, and feel like the freak show. That's why identity is so important. Remind yourself what sort of person you are, and what your core mission is. Go back and read through the earlier passages on shame, envy, and bitterness (Chapter Five). Then venture out. In the study, the most resilient people had activities they looked forward to, with people they enjoy.[6]

Lila isolated herself for two years. She felt bitter and sad as sat at the window, watching the whole world go on without her. When she finally remembered who she was, she got back to her hiking trips, quilting club, senior center outings, and charity work. Lila had always been an involved person. Reclaiming her identity provided her life with structure and routine. She was too busy having fun to mope.

Finally, let's talk about flexibility. Some mothers will admit to having been a little *too* flexible, bending like contortionists to put everyone else's needs and wants ahead of their own. But bend too much and you snap. If this reminds you of yourself, it's time for some serious self-care. Be patient as you move toward a personally meaningful focus that honors who you are. Aim for healthy flexibility that enables you to accept change, and moves you to honor your core being as you bounce back or toward an even better place.

Suggested Reading

The Survivors Club: The Secrets And Science That Could Save Your Life, by Ben Sherwood. This engaging study of crises, and how people beat the odds, shows readers what survival requires. Real-life stories inspire the required gumption to take action in current adversity, and prepare for uncertainty ahead.

Take Notice, And Savor

The best things in life may be free, but not unless we take notice and appreciate them. In a recent study, older adults who had the ability to notice and savor positive experiences were happier and more satisfied with life. Older adults who were generally considered less resilient derived the most benefit from learning to notice and savor.[7]

Many of us have suffered the looping negative thoughts known as rumination. We have vividly recalled the cutting horror of our child's words, and relived the devastation. Repeatedly reviving the negativity can have dark, rippling effects that injure health and well-being. The converse is also true. So, breaking a negativity cycle with a positive habit is wise. Let's take a closer look at savoring—in the moment, in memory, in anticipating—and what it can do for you.

Feeling satisfaction or pride, and holding positive beliefs about your work or a hobby can be considered savoring. As can enjoying anything in the moment, and then remembering it later, or looking forward to being immersed in it again. Recent research examines the concept of savoring in terms of cognitive processes, and how different regions of the brain are activated depending on what sort of savoring we do, cultural influences, and other factors.[8] Rather than get into the complex and intricate details of positive neuropsychology as it applies to savoring, let's explore the concept in practice.

In Chapter Four, we saw Evelyn savoring her precious few moments with her grandsons when they visit for Christmas. In a Herculean feat of cognitive balance, she interacts with those boys while aware that her estranged son and his wife are watching and listening. Still, she immerses herself, purposely attending to her interactions with her grandsons. She takes mental snapshots she can call up later and enjoy. She memorizes the dimple in a grandson's chin or the spray of freckles across a nose. In the moment, she focuses on each grandson's unique tone of voice, the sayings and gestures they use, and then plays back the memories. Fully engaging in those precious moments, and later reliving them, helps her bounce back.

Savoring need not have to do with your estrangement situation though. To enhance your ability to savor, make a practice of taking notice of the simplest joys as they occur. Savor the taste of cinnamon on a graham cracker, notice the way the cream makes a pleasant swirl in your coffee, relish the feel of soft sheets as you slide into bed, or take childlike glee in the wind rushing in the car windows on a summer day. Make time for activities you enjoy. Attend to and savor the moments while immersed in them. Then enjoy them in memory and anticipate more to come.

As I do, our mother from the gardening example delights in her plantings: the smell of the rich earth as she tills the soil, the warmth of sunlight on her shoulders, the pride of seeing her plants flourish, and the anticipation of fragrant flowers and sweet fruits to come. In dreary winter, her ability to garden outdoors may be blocked, but rather than become frustrated, she reminisces, and anticipates next season's garden, thereby savoring.

Meg loves to cook, and she savors the meditative quality of stirring simmering pots while delicious aromas waft all around. She also feels pride for spearheading her cookbook-for-charity project. She anticipates the satisfaction of doing another cookbook, and helping even more kids.

Some mothers have fulfilling careers or vocations that interest them. When a project is completed, another successful event is over, or they punch in at the end of the day, they replay triumphs and look forward to the next. Other mothers quilt, write, paint, or sew, immersing themselves in the joy of creating, savoring the pleasure found in their work, and looking forward to doing more. They may also talk about the activities, as Lila does in her clubs. Some use the activities they enjoy for a higher good. They garner a sense of pride and community in doing so, like the mother whose quilt design will bring more attention to the plight of rejected parents. That's similar to Julia, whose estrangement lends empathy to her volunteer work with lonely seniors. These sorts of positive feelings and beliefs about one's activities, *savoring*, foster resilience, and lend meaning to life.

What do you find enchanting? What takes your breath away, makes time pass without awareness, and allows you to simply be? What can you look forward to, take pride in, and happily remember?

Right now, think of at least three pastimes that bring you joy. As you list them, take a moment to savor your positive experiences.

_____

_____

_____

Then write down three more things to try, that will bring you joy.

_____

_____

_____

Think about making more time for all of these things, and anticipate the possible feelings you'll derive: *elation, pride, connection, freedom, joy.* Come up with some positive feeling words of your own. Write them down, and say them aloud. Get used to using those feel-good words. Use them often to describe and savor your experiences.

_____

_____

_____

You may already practice more savoring than you realize. Do you ever hit the pillow at night, and find yourself smiling about something somebody said that day? That's savoring, and it feels great. Make a game of finding things to savor. After a shopping trip, think for a moment about any positive interactions, and enjoy them again. During almost any activity, if you're *looking* for things to later savor your whole outlook changes for the better.

If it feels helpful and positive, think about some of the good moments you once shared with your child too. While I didn't always savor memories of Dan, because they caused me such pain, recalling precious moments with Dan now can bring me joy.

I remember the accomplishment in his eyes at age four, when he showed me a colorful picture he'd created. In it, a fat bumble bee had hung a sign near its treehouse home that read: *Keyp out.* The memory of my clever little boy, using a word he knew (key) to make another sparks maternal pride, and a cascade of positive sensations that go with the feeling.

Other memories also make me smile. When Dan first visited us by himself after a year of estrangement, he mentioned a trip the two of us took to British Columbia when he was 18. We paddled a boat on the lake, saw intricate sand castles in a contest on the shore, and trudged through tangled brush after losing our way on a hiking trail. Despite the distance that gapes between us now, I can savor those memories. And because he mentioned them, I know he's also fond of those times. Someday, maybe I'll look at the pictures of that trip again. Dan once saved them for me on a CD that I have tucked away. For now, the mental snapshots are enough. In more than two decades with my son, some memories are happy, and some not so. Savoring the good ones is my privilege.

Look How Far You've Come

On any journey, discoveries are made. New territory and the people we meet along the way broaden perspective. Part of any trip is looking back. Savoring what we've seen, heard, and learned enlightens our ordinary lives. You've come this far. Now, let's unpack the journey, and sum up the ground we've covered.

We began with Chapter One: *The Early Daze*, the bewilderment and utter shock of estrangement. Your world tilted, your child moved on, and you were left standing in the storm. Smart, resilient mothers like Julia and Deanne helped you to *Give Voice To Your Feelings.* Verbalizing emotions reduces pain. Your descriptions provide clues to better care for yourself. Beyond the shock and confusion, a range of emotions and behaviors is normal. You're not crazy. There is science behind your responses. And as other mothers have done, you can cope mindfully, and practice peace in your everyday life.

You came to terms with the depth of your pain, released worry and speculation over the possibility of your child's later regrets, and uncovered strong beliefs and feelings that could hinder your progress. Time, energy, and courage are required as you commit to a satisfying future, step forward, and heal. *You're not running a race, but you are on your way.*

Though you decided that *Moving Ahead For Your Own Good* made sense, the question remains for Chapter Two: *Why?* Society, cultural shifts, individual circumstances, nonsensical and non-existent reasons, as well as difficult truths may play a part. You probably pored over memories, magnified the slightest errors, and self-blamed. But you turned your thinking to *The Good You Did.* You reclaimed your positive self-image, and settled on an answer that lets you stop asking *why?* Instead, you asked a question to propel you forward: *What now?* You delved deeper into coping mindfully, gained awareness, and shifted perspective to embrace your future. *You did your best for your children. Now, do your best for you.*

Pam advised you to avoid her mistakes in Chapter Three: *Get The Support You Need.* For years, Pam protected her estranged daughter's reputation at her own expense. But support is vital—from friends who remind you of your strengths, in positive groups, and in private settings with professionals who support your objectives. Laura, Meg, Daphne, Kathleen, Esther, and Ginny helped you avoid potential pitfalls. Trudy shared her system of ready answers to handle social situations, and Geneva helped you define goals.

By remembering who you are and how you act when you're *At Your Best,* you focused on your strengths and showed resourcefulness. To support yourself, you began to accept what you cannot control (your child's actions), and take charge of what you can. Hurt and loss provide an opportunity to step forward, and prove what I have witnessed in my own and others' lives: *The landscape of loss is fertile ground for growth.*

But the ambiguity of estrangement requires a plan: *Ready, Set, Prepare* (Chapter Four). Otherwise, you remain a victim to suffering that has no defined end. To move beyond your child's physical absence that nonetheless looms psychologically, you were encouraged to *Take Stock.* An honest look at your post-estrangement self provided insight into where you've lost touch and lost out. Use that knowledge. Begin to bounce back, and prepare for what's ahead.

Useful strategies aid decisions you make ahead to maintain your dignity and self-respect. In the unsettling accounts shared by Vicky, Evelyn, Ruby, and others, you recognized bits of your own predicament. Petra, Andrea, and Lauren helped you anticipate the *damned-if-you-do, damned-if-you-don't* situations, and cope in ways that honor your values and keep you feeling strong.

Even when emotional triggers crop up, you can quickly regain your composure, and get back on track. Whatever you do, don't get down on yourself. Acknowledge your feelings, so you can deal with them. Remember the utter shock you felt when your son or daughter first cut you off? Don't think of triggered emotions as setbacks. They're aftershocks—a normal occurrence that relieves pressure. Think to yourself: *Forward. I'm adapting. I'm healing. I'm moving on.*

Doing so, you *See Your Feelings In A New Light* (Chapter Five*).* You've adapted to other forms of loss throughout your life. Barb adapted to estrangement with a clever endeavor that brought new friends and fun into her life. You pinpointed specific gaps your son or daughter's absence created. Gaping holes require patching. In *Help Wanted? Help Yourself,* you gave yourself credit for ways you have already grown, devised new ways to fill the gaps, and began the *Wabi-sabi* acceptance of mending ragged holes with gold, and growing even stronger.

You also acknowledged what you *don't* miss. Seeing your child as an adult, separate and apart from the "child" you loved, shifted your perspective. Loads of specific strategies used by smart mothers like you helped you come to terms with uncomfortable feelings (anger, guilt, bitterness, and rage, to name a few). To move forward, Rowena, with her landslide of woes, demonstrated my *P, B, & J* method of digging out from beneath the pile: *P*rioritize, *b*reak into pieces, or *j*ust leave alone. Meg showed you how to use the **RA-RA** strategy. You *r*ecognized what needs attention, took time to *a*nalyze and *r*egroup, and then made a plan to *a*dapt. Give yourself a cheer—*Rah-Rah!* Letting go does not mean giving up. *You're not a quitter. You're a starter—in a new phase of life.*

The loss affects those closest to you. Chapter Six: *Managing Effects on the Family* covered couples suffering estrangement stress, and helped parents whose resulting self-doubt can influence their parenting of other children. Experiences from my own marriage, and those of Pauline, Diedre, Jennifer, Louisa, Candace, Marla, and Leilani, helped you recognize and work around trouble spots, anticipate potential pressures, and grow closer in a united front. Virgie shared her communication breakdown with her remaining son. And Char laid bare her fears, and also how she fulfilled her two daughters' unique needs as they dealt with the pain of their brother's estrangement. Talking about an estranged child all the time is not healthy, but neither is making the subject taboo. You *can* be honest about your feelings, while providing your children with a sense of security, and being a safe person to confide in. Don't let fear and pain get the better of you. Remember, "MOM," as an acronym to help you break free, live in the present, and do what you know is best: *M*ind *O*ver *M*emories.

A series of questions, and several mothers' admissions about their social media compulsions helped you analyze your feelings, manage conundrums, deal fairly with relatives, and help yourself. Detailed strategies and resources provided ways to break free, as well as protect yourself. Finally, by imagining *The Shape Of Your Family*, you embraced positive post-estrangement imagery.

Enduring estrangement's sometimes jagged points of contact, cliffhangers of hope, and disappointing descents requires reevaluating expectations. Parents must come to terms with reality, alter quixotic hopes, and accurately answer the question in Chapter Seven: *What Does It Mean To Reconcile?* My recounting of dashed hopes, despair, and failing health may mirror yours. Taking control and creating boundaries to support my family hopefully helped you recognize your right to set terms and do what's best for you. The ghosts of hope, love, and pain may come to visit, but you don't have to let them stay. By assigning your son or daughter, your *adult* child, the responsibility for his or her choices, you free yourself to accept the tiny hiccups of sadness or longing as part of being human. Pam, Marti, Sondra, Barb, and Jerri, helped you compassionately acknowledge your feelings, accept them, and then let them go.

With help from Elaine, Krista, and Camilla, you adopted new, self-supportive ways of thinking about estrangement. A series of questions helped you *Examine Your Relationship* with clear eyes rather than glasses tinted a rosy hue from past happiness or wishful thinking. Co-dependency, innate temperament, and self-esteem level may influence your thoughts about your future relationship, and what you're willing to put up with, excuse, or do—but with that knowledge, you can learn to change.

What counts as a reconciliation now, for reasons you believe in, may not be acceptable to you in the future. What seems insurmountable early on might later be more easily set aside. Through a recent study, you gained insight into estranged children's reasoning, and perhaps recognized your own son or daughter's view. Shared estrangements that included a variety of circumstances assisted you in analyzing your own. Exhausting all efforts means different things to different parents. In *Reconciling: What It Means, What It Takes*, you chose a definition that works for you.

Chapter Eight: *Life Goes On*, and for many parents, estrangements take place simultaneously with other disruptive transitions that can pile on stress. With a positive attitude, healthful strategies, and support from provided resources, you can prevail. Grandparents in the chapter helped you explore your rights in that capacity, and how you might assert them. Similarly, families shared their thinking on estate planning, so you could more fully consider your own. Although at first difficult to consider, end-of-life decisions can provide a sense of peace. With strategies and resources for these and other time-of-life topics, you were encouraged to *let loose the past you cannot change, unfold the future like a precious gift, and hold the present dear.*

Finally, we arrive at Chapter Nine: *Walk Forward.* There is wisdom in knowing when it's time to "fold," letting go of sorrows and expectations in favor of moving ahead and finding meaning in everyday life. We can lean on our own past patterns of strength, savor our positive experiences, and learn from others how to be resilient, resourceful, and strong. Hopefully, as we've looked back at the ground we've covered, you can see how each chapter has moved you forward.

Sunlight Ahead

My journey in writing this book has been an enlightening and life-changing experience for which I am deeply grateful. I have met amazing and intelligent people along the way. Some who have made me laugh, and some whose pain and confusion has torn at my heart yet strengthened my resolve to help.

As you contemplate how you'll move forward, keep in mind that perspective changes as we change. If you work at embracing change, and at creating a healthy, happy way forward, then how you feel today is not the same as how you'll feel in a year, five years, or even ten years from now. You're no longer stuck. Remember that. Don't tell yourself you'll never get over this. Don't count yourself among the broken. Step out from the shadow of heartbreak. Let the words of mother-of-four Kathleen's youngest daughter guide you: *Focus on the people who want you in their lives.*

For your health and well-being, play the cards you've been dealt. Set your mind on a positive outlook, smile at people, and make life meaningful as you go.

Right now, make a pledge to stop looking back and lamenting what you cannot change. *Be done with the crying.* Look forward. Continue weaving the artful tapestry of your life. Remember, you can't reach the good that's out in front of you until you let go of the bad, and leave it behind. *Reach for your life. Embrace it. There is sunlight ahead.*

✈ Practical Steps for Your Bright Future

Look back at your answers in the Chapter Four exercise, *Take Stock*. You took a hard look at how much you've changed since the estrangement began. Now, do something useful with that knowledge. Give it power.

What areas do you need most to improve in? Perhaps your sadness and preoccupation have taken a toll on family relationships, and you know you need to spend time and energy with the people you love. Or maybe like me you have a tendency to shop when you're feeling low, so recognize a need to better budget, and to get your financial life in order. Is your spiritual health calling for attention? Or does the *Take Stock* exercise show you that your mood crept into your leisure time, so that you no longer make room for recreation and fun. Maybe you've neglected important friendships. You've worked at restoring yourself. Now, expand the healing into all areas of your life.

Choose two areas where you can improve. You can use the S.M.A.R.T. goals method to devise plans to make progress. Or simply start by identifying two or three small things you can take action on within the next few days. Write your action items down. Then do them.

Let's look at a couple of examples.

If you chose to focus on your finances, you might begin with the following steps:

1. skip buying your morning Latte, and brew coffee at home instead

2. pay for everything with cash, and then save the change for a specific purpose

3. create a food budget and shop with a list

For better health, three action steps might be:

1. try a new vegetable

2. walk around the block on your lunch hour

3. swear off fast food for a month

You decide. Make your steps meaningful, but choose things you know you can accomplish. Give yourself a challenge, but don't make the tasks too daunting. Success builds confidence. When you feel better about the two areas in which you've chosen to work, reevaluate, and make more changes as needed. Then choose two more. Your goals can get bigger as you progress. Working on specific areas helps you move forward with purpose as you reclaim your happy, meaningful life.

Mark your calendar to do the *Take Stock* exercise again in two to three months, and see how you've improved. Celebrate your success. *You're not running a race. You're stepping forward—or even dancing through life.*

Postscript

No book can contain every question, answer or scenario. Trimming to hit the most common notes among thousands of estrangement stories was done with care. As was choosing the most helpful research among the stacks of clinical studies I waded through. On a subject as sad and important as this one, there is always more to say.

The truth is that I learn more about estrangement every day. Before this book went to print, I read and re-read the words to try and catch typos, and make every fact, story, or argument clear. And as I did, more ideas struck. So did concerns. Did I say enough? Tell each story right? Was I kind? Will the reader know I truly understand? But as every writer learns, there's a time stop mulling over ideas and fixing words. There's a time to stop worrying, to let go, and to send your thoughts out into the world. A book is never finished, but at some point, the writer must be done.

For mothers of estranged adults who are successful at moving forward in their own lives, the feelings are similar. The hope can remain. So can the love, attached to precious memories of a sweet boy or girl we once knew. But to cling to an adult who pushes us away, to remain stalled, and forever suffering, estranges us from ourselves. There comes a time when, although we may not be quite finished, we must be done.

While it's true that an enduring estrangement becomes a part of who we are, it doesn't have to be a crippling part. What's happened is. Forget the whys and what ifs. Move on to what's next.

I started this book as an extension of the work that began at my blog-site. Now, RejectedParents.NET can be an extension of this book and a source of continued support for you. There, I can expand on some of the ideas shared here, and present new ones. If there's an estrangement topic you'd like to learn more about, please email me via the contact form at the site. I'd love to hear from you.

If this book has helped you, I hope you'll tell others those thoughts in site comments and in reviews at online book stores—so more parents of estranged adult children can benefit.

Notes

CHAPTER ONE: The Early Daze

1. Eisenberger, N., Lieberman, M.D., & Williams, K.D. (2003). Does Rejection Hurt? A fMRI Study Of Social Exclusion. Science, 302(5643): 290-92.

2. Lieberman, M. D., Eisenberger, N. I., Crockett, M. J., Tom, S. M., Pfeifer, J. H., & Way, B. M. (2007). Putting Feelings Into Words: Affect Labeling Disrupts Amygdala Activity in Response to Affective Stimuli. Psychological Science (Wiley-Blackwell), 18(5), 421-428. doi:10.1111/j.1467-9280.2007.01916.x

3. Williams, A K. D., & Nida, S. A. (2011). Ostracism: Consequences And Coping. *Current Directions in Psychological Science*, 2011; 20 (2):71. doi:10.1177/0963721411402480

4. Taylor, S. E. (2006). Tend and Befriend: Biobehavioral Bases Of Affiliation Under Stress. *Current Directions In Psychological Science* (Wiley-Blackwell), 15(6), 273-277. doi:10.1111/j.1467-8721.2006.00451.x

5. Kross, E., Berman, M. G., Mischel, W., Smith, E. E., & Wager, T. D. (2011). Social Rejection Shares Somatosensory Representations With Physical Pain. Proceedings Of The National Academy Of Sciences Of The United States Of America, 108(15), 6270-6275. doi:10.1073/pnas.1102693108

6. Master, S., Eisenberger, N., Taylor, S., Naliboff, B., Shiranyan, D., & Lieberman, M. (2009). A Picture's Worth: Partner Photographs Reduce Experimentally Induced Pain. *Psychological Science*, 20(11), 1315-1318.

7. Oaten, M., Kipling, W.D., Jones, A., & Zadro, L. (2008). The Effects Of Ostracism On Self-Regulation In The Socially Anxious. *Journal of Social and Clinical Psychology*, 27(5), pp. 471-504.

8. Leary, Tate, Adams, Allen, & Hancock (2007). Self-Compassion And Reactions To Unpleasant Self-Relevant Events: The Implications Of Treating Oneself Kindly. *Journal of Personality and Social Psychology*, 92(5), 887-904). doi: 10.1037/0022-3514.92.5.887

CHAPTER TWO: Why?

1. Fass, P.S. (2012).The Child Centered Family? New Rules in Postwar America. In P.S. Fass & M. Grossberg (Eds.), *Reinventing Childhood After World War II* (pp. 1-18). Philadelphia, Pennsylvania: University of Pennsylvania Press.

2. Mintz, S. (2012). The Changing Face Of Children's Culture. In P.S. Fass & M. Grossberg (Eds.), *Reinventing Childhood After World War II* (pp. 38-50). Philadelphia, Pennsylvania: University of Pennsylvania Press.

3. Hulbert, A. (2004). *Raising America: Experts, Parents, and a Century of Advice About Children.* New York: Vintage Books.

4. Zelizer, V.A. (1994). *Pricing the Priceless Child: The Changing Social Value of Children.* Princeton, New Jersey: Princeton University Press.

5. Twenge, J.M., & Campbell, W.K. (2010). *The Narcissism Epidemic: Living in the Age of Entitlement.* New York: Atria Paperback.

6. Twenge, J.M. (2014). *Generation Me - Revised And Updated: Why Today's Young Americans Are More Confi•ent, Assertive, Entitle•—An• More Miserable Than Ever Before.* New York: Atria Books.

7. Opperman, J. (2004). What to do when your parents stops seeing you as mom or dad. *The Children's Voice Magazine,* July/August 2004.

8. Baker, A.J.L. (2007). *Adult Children of Parental Alienation Syndrome: Breaking the Ties that Bind.* New York: W.W. Norton & Co.

9. Suicide Data Report, 2012. Department of Veterans Affairs. Downloaded on February 15, 2015, from: http://www.va.gov/opa/docs/Suicide-Data-Report-2012-final.pdf

10. Motzkin, J.C., Newman, J.P., Kiehl, K.A., & Koenigs, M. (2011). Reduced Prefrontal Connectivity In Psychopathy. *Journal of Neuroscience,* 31(48): 17348-17357. doi:10.1523/JNEUROSCI.4215-11.2011

11. Raine, A. (2008). From Genes To Brain To Antisocial Behavior. *Current Directions In Psychological Science,* 17(5): 323-328. doi: 10.1111/j.1467-8721.2008.00599.x

12. Agllias, K. (2015). Difference, Choice, And Punishment: Parental Beliefs And Understandings About Adult Child Estrangement. *Australian Social Work,* 68:1, 115-129, doi:0.1080/0312407X.2014.927897

13. 2005, Jan. 25. Five for 2005: Five reasons to forgive. *Harvard Health Publications Newsletter.* 2(5), http://harvardhealth.staywell.com/viewNewsletter.aspx?NLID=30&INC=yes

CHAPTER THREE: Get The Support You Need

1. Sondergaard Christensen, A.M. (2013). The Role Of Guilt In Post-Conflict Work. *Journal of Applied Philosophy,* 30(4), 365-378.

2. Newberg, A., & Waldman, M.R. (2010). *How God Changes Your Brain: Breakthrough Findings From A Leading Neuroscientist.* New York: Ballantine Books.

3. Shih, M., Pittinsky, T.L., & Ambady, N. Stereotype Susceptibility: Identity Salience and Shifts in Quantitative Performance. *Psychological Science,* Volume 10, pp. 80-83.

4. Green S., Lambon Ralph, M.A., Moll, J., Deakin, J.F., & Zahn, R. (2012). Guilt-Selective Functional Disconnection Of Anterior Temporal And Subgenual Cortices In Major Depressive Disorder. *Archives Of General Psychiatry.* 69(10), 1014-1021.

5. Seligman, M. P., Steen, T. A., Park, N., & Peterson, C. (2005). Positive Psychology Progress. *American Psychologist,* 60(5), 410-421. doi:10.1037/0003-066X.60.5.410

CHAPTER FOUR: Ready, Set, Prepare

1. Sommer, K.L., Williams, K.D., Ciarocco, N.J., & Baumeister, R.F. (2001). When Silence Speaks Louder Than Words: Explorations Into The Intrapsychic And Interpersonal Consequences Of Social Ostracism. *Basic And Applied Social Psychology,* 23(4), 225-243.

2. Cohen, S., Alper, C.M., Doyle, W.J., Treanor, J.J., & Turner, R.B. (2006). Positive Emotional Style Predicts Resistance To Illness After Experimental Exposure To Rhinovirus Or Influenza A Virus. *Psychosomatic Medicine,* 68, 809-815.

3. Melnick, J., & Roos, S. (2007). The Myth Of Closure. Gestalt Review, 11(2), 90-107. http://www.gisc.org/gestaltreview/documents/TheMythofClosure.pdf

CHAPTER FIVE: See Your Feelings In A New Light.

1. Baskin, T. W., & Enright, R. D. (2004). Intervention Studies on Forgiveness: A Meta-Analysis. *Journal of Counseling & Development,* 82(1), 79-90.

2. Deiner, E., & Ng, W. (2013). Daily Use Of Reappraisal Decreases Negative Emotions Toward Daily Unpleasant Events. *Journal of Social and Clinical Psychology,* 32(5), 530-545.

3. Troy, A. S., Wilhelm, F. H., Shallcross, A. J., & Mauss, I. B. (2010). Seeing the Silver Lining: Cognitive Reappraisal Ability Moderates the Relationship Between Stress and Depressive Symptoms. *Emotion,* 10(6), 783–795. doi:10.1037/a0020262

CHAPTER SIX: Managing Effects On The Family

1. Graham, J.M., & Conoley, C.W. (2006). The Role Of Marital Attributions In The Relationship Between Life Stressors And Marital Quality. *Personal Relationships,* 13, 231-241.

2. Knudson-Martin, C. (2013). Why Power Matters: Creating A Foundation Of Mutual Support In Couple Relationships. *Family Process*, 52(1), 5-18. doi: 10.1111/famp.12011

3. Fox, J., & Moreland, J. J. (2015). The Dark Side Of Social Networking Sites: An Exploration Of The Relational And Psychological Stressors Associated With Facebook Use And Affordances. *Computers In Human Behavior*, 45, 168-176. doi:10.1016/j. chb.2014.11.083

4. Kramer, A.D.I., Guillory, J.E., & Hancock, J.T. (2014). Experimental Evidence Of Massive-Scale Emotional Contagion Through Social Networks. *PNAS*, 111(24), 8788-8790; *published ahead of print June 2, 2014*, doi:10.1073/pnas.1320040111

CHAPTER SEVEN: What Does It Mean To Reconcile?

1. Blake, L., Bland, B., & Golombok, S. (10 December, 2015). Hidden Voices: Family Estrangement in Adulthood, http://standalone.org.uk/wp-content/uploads/2015/12/HiddenVoices.FinalReport.pdf

2. Davis, L. (2002). *I Thought We'd Never Speak Again: The Road From Estrangement To Reconciliation*. New York: HarperCollinsPublishers.

3. Carr, K., Holman, A., Abetz, J. Koenig Kellas, J., & Vagnoni, E. (2015) Giving Voice to the Silence of Family Estrangement: Comparing Reasons Of Estranged ParentsAand Adult Children In A Nonmatched Sample, *Journal Of Family Communication*, 15:2, 130-140, doi: 10.1080/15267431.2015.1013106

CHAPTER EIGHT: Life Goes On.

1. Dewitt, G. J. (2006). The detritus of Troxel. *Family Law Quarterly*, 40(1), 133-147.

2. Richey, W. (2012, February 21). Do Grandparents Get Visitation rights? Supreme Court Declines Case. *Christian Science Monitor*.

3. Tate, J. (2007). Disinheritance Of Children And The Limits Of Testamentary Freedom. Conference Papers -- *Law & Society*, 1.

4. Brayne, S. (2011). *Sex, Meaning And The Menopause: A Book For Men And Women*. New York: NY: Continuum International Publishing Group.

5. Weed, Susan S. (2002). *New Menopausal Years: The Wise Woman Way, Alternative Approaches For Women 30 -90*. Woodstock, NY: Ash Tree Publishing.

6. Jahnke, R., Larkey, L., Rogers, C., Etnier, J., & Lin, F. (2010). A Comprehensive Review Of Health Benefits Of Qigong And Tai Chi. *American Journal of Health Promotion : AJHP*, 24(6), e1–e25. doi:10.4278/ajhp.081013-LIT-248

7. The Health Benefits Of Tai Chi. (2009, May). *Harvard Women's Health Watch,* http://www.health.harvard.edu/staying-healthy/the-health-benefits-of-tai-chi

8. Freedman, R. R. (2005). Hot flashes: Behavioral Treatments, Mechanisms, And Relation To Sleep. *American Journal Of Medicine,* 118(12), 1410. doi:10.1016/j.amjmed.2005.10.022

9. Sood, R. (n.d.). May Clinic, http://www.mayoclinic.org/diseases-conditions/hot-flashes/expert-answers/paced-breathing/faq-20119343

10. Freeman, E.W., Sammel, M.D., Lin, H., Gracia, C.R., Kapoo, S., & Ferdousi, T. (2005).The role Of Anxiety And Hormonal Changes In Menopausal Hot Flashes. *Menopause,* 12(3), 258-266.

11. Nelson, D. (2008). Effect Of Physical Activity On Menopausal Symptoms Among Urban Women. Medicine & Science In Sports & Exercise, 40, 50-58. http://www.simplyfit.com/RS.PhysicalActivityandMenopausalSymptoms.pdf

12. Alexander, A., & VanTine, J. (2015). *Sugar Smart Express: The 21-Day Quick Start Plan To Stop Cravings, Lose Weight, And Still Enjoy The Sweets You Love!* New York, NY: Rodale Books.

13. Reinhard, S.C., Levine, C., & Samis, S. (2012). *Home Alone: Family Caregivers Providing Complex Chronic Care.* Washington, DC: AARP Public Policy Institute. http://www.aarp.org/content/dam/aarp/research/public_policy_institute/health/2014/family-caregivers-providing-complex-chronic-care-spouses-AARP-ppi-health.pdf

14. Marriott, H. (2009). *The Selfish Pig's Guie To Caring.* London: Piatkus Books.

15. Robinson, L., Clare, L, & Evans, K. (2005). Making Sense Of Dementia And Adjusting To Loss: Psychological Reactions To A Diagnosis Of Dementia In Couples. *Aging and Mental Health,* 9(4), 337-47.

16. Barbee, A.P., Rowatt, T.L., & Cunningham, R.R. (1998). When A Friend Is In Need: Feelings About Seeking, Giving, And Receiving Social Support. In P.A. Anderson and L.K. Gierrero (Eds.), *Handbook Of Communication And Emotion* (pp. 281-301). San Diego, CA: Academic Press.

17. Cutrona, C.E., Suhr, J.A., & McFarlane, R. (1990). Interpersonal Transactions And The Psychological Sense Of Support. In S. Duck (Ed.), *Personal Relationships And Social Support* (pp. 30-45). Thousand Oaks, CA: Sage.

18. Cutrona, C.E. (1996). *Social Support In Couples.* Thousand Oaks, CA: Sage.

19. Jacobs, B.J. (2014, July 10). In Sickness, Health, And (Sometimes) anguish: Ways To Lower The Risks Of Physical And Mental Exhaustion For Spousal Caregivers. *AARP*, http://www.aarp.org/home-family/caregiving/info-2014/caregiving-spouses-marriage-stress-jacobs.html

CHAPTER NINE: Walk Forward

1. Segerstrom, S.C. & Miller, G.E. (2004). Psychological Stress And The Human Immune System: A Meta-Analytic Study Of 30 Years of Inquiry. *Psychological Bulletin*, 130(4), 601-630, http://dx.doi.org/10.1037/0033-2909.130.4.601

2. Miller, G.E. & Wrosch, C. (2007). You've Gotta Know When To Fold 'em. *Psychological Science*, 18(9), 773-777.

3. Wrosch, C., Miller, G.E., Scheier, M.F., & Brun de Pontet, S. (2007). Giving Up On Unattainable Goals: Benefits For Health? *Personality And Social Psychology Bulletin*, 33(2), 251-265.

4. Slayton, S.C., D'Archer, J., & Kaplan, F. (2010). Outcome Studies On The Efficacy Of Art Therapy: A Review Of Findings. *Journal Of The American Art Therapy Association*, 27(3), 108-118.

5. Gilgun, J. (1999) Mapping resilience as a process among adults with childhood adversities. In McCubbin, H.I., Thompson, E.A., Thompson, A.I. and Futrell, J.A. (Eds). *The Dynamics of Resilient Families.* Thousand Oaks, London, New Delhi: Sage.

6. Hildon, Z., Smith, G., Netuveli, G., & Blane, D. (2008), Understanding Adversity And Resilience At Older Ages. *Sociology Of Health & Illness*, 30: 726–740. doi: 10.1111/j.1467-9566.2008.01087.x

7. Smith, J.L., & Hollinger-Smith, L. (2015). Savoring, Resilience, and Psychological Well-Being In Older Adults. *Aging & Mental Health*, 19(3). doi: 10.1080/13607863.2014.986647

8. Bryant, F. B., Chadwick, E. D., & Kluwe, K. (2011). Understanding The Processes That Regulate Positive Emotional Experience: Unsolved Problems And Future Directions For Theory And Research On Savoring. *International Journal Of Wellbeing*, 1(1), 107-126. doi:10.5502/ijw.v1i1.18

Index

ABOUT THE AUTHOR

Sheri McGregor holds a bachelor's degree in psychology, a master's degree in human behavior, and is a certified life coach. She serves on the advisory board for National University's College of Letters and Sciences.

In her writing career of more than two decades, McGregor's articles on psychology, health, and a variety of other topics have appeared in dozens of national and international publications. She has also written for anthologies, websites, and organizations including the non-profit Families for Depression Awareness. In her three hiking guides, McGregor leads readers down the trails with descriptions that reveal her appreciation for nature and how it calms the mind.

Her work to help parents of estranged adult children began at RejectedParents.NET, which she founded in late 2013. You can sign up for her email newsletter at the site. She also maintains a Facebook page, located at facebook.com/rejectedparents. As a caring mother to whom the unthinkable happened, Sheri McGregor has become a powerful voice for the parents of estranged adult children.

Notes

38286473R00195

Made in the USA
Lexington, KY
06 May 2019